Introducing .NET 4.5

Alex Mackey
William Tulloch
Mahesh Krishnan

Apress®

Introducing .NET 4.5

ISBN-13 (pbk): 978-1-4302-4332-8

ISBN-13 (electronic): 978-1-4302-4333-5

President and Publisher: Paul Manning
Lead Editor: Ewan Buckingham
Development Editor: Matthew Moodie
Technical Reviewer: Stephen Godbold
Editorial Board: Steve Anglin, Ewan Buckingham, Gary Cornell, Louise Corrigan, Morgan Ertel, Jonathan Gennick, Jonathan Hassell, Robert Hutchinson, Michelle Lowman, James Markham, Matthew Moodie, Jeff Olson, Jeffrey Pepper, Douglas Pundick, Ben Renow-Clarke, Dominic Shakeshaft, Gwenan Spearing, Matt Wade, Tom Welsh
Coordinating Editors: Anita Castro, Christine Ricketts
Copy Editor: Ann Dickson
Compositor: Bytheway Publishing Services
Indexer: SPi Global
Artist: SPi Global
Cover Designer: Anna Ishchenko

Distributed to the book trade worldwide by Springer Science+Business Media New York, 233 Spring Street, 6th Floor, New York, NY 10013. Phone 1-800-SPRINGER, fax (201) 348-4505, e-mail orders-ny@springer-sbm.com, or web site www.springeronline.com.

For information on translations, please e-mail rights@apress.com, or visit www.apress.com.

Apress and friends of ED books may be purchased in bulk for academic, corporate, or promotional use. eBook versions and licenses are also available for most titles. For more information, reference our Special Bulk Sales–eBook Licensing web page at www.apress.com/bulk-sales.

Any source code or other supplementary materials referenced by the author in this text is available to readers at www.apress.com. For detailed information about how to locate your book's source code, go to www.apress.com/source-code.

For Belinda and Mum, a book neither of you will ever read. ☺

Alex Mackey

For my wife, Jacinta, whose patience and understanding while I worked on this book can't be measured, and to both my parents and my parents-in-law, whose faith and support in the dark days helped me get to where I am today.

William Tulloch

To my entire family—my loving parents, my sister Shoba, my brother Vish, my wife Lakshmi, and my daughters Riya and Samika. I've learnt a lot from every one of you (yes, even you, Samika, although you are not even a year old ☺). Now, if I could put all that learning to good use …

Mahesh Krishnan

Contents at a Glance

Contents

About the Authors

■ **Alex Mackey** is an experienced web consultant with over 12 years' experience in web development. He wrote the predecessor to this book, *Introducing .NET 4.0: With Visual Studio 2010* (Apress), and is a Microsoft MVP—Internet Explorer: Development.

Alex has just started a new position with the Australian-based consultancy Kiandra (http://kiandra.com.au/). He previously worked for another consultancy, Readify, in Melbourne, Australia.

Alex is very active in the development community and has spoken at a number of large conferences including TechEd, Remix, and Australian ALM. Alex also runs the annual community-development conference DDD Melbourne and user group DevEve.net.

■ **William Tulloch.** Originally an art school graduate, William has been professionally involved in software development for over 19 years and is currently working as a senior consultant for Readify (www.readify.net).

William is passionate about software development, and his interests range from database development to UX design. Though his origins are in web development, his focus over the last few years has been on WCF, security, and XAML in all its many and varied forms.

Active in the developer community, William has spoken at various user groups and conferences where he has been known to wax lyrical about Windows Identity Foundation and more recently .NET 4.5.

■ **Mahesh Krishnan** is fortunate enough to be paid for what he loves doing most—creating software. He has over 20 years of experience in the IT industry, having worked in India, the UK, the United States, and Australia on a number of projects ranging from shrink-wrapped products to large corporate applications. He currently works as a principal consultant at Readify, a company that specializes in consulting and training in Microsoft technologies. Prior to this, he was the technical director of The Thin Blue Line at Victoria Police, where he was responsible for delivering a number of key projects.

Mahesh is well-known in the .NET community and frequently speaks at community and industry events such as code camps, YOW!, Tech Ed, and REMIX. He organizes the DDD Melbourne Conference with Alex every year and runs Victoria .NET, which is one of the largest .NET user groups in Australia. He is also one of the founding members of Silverlight Developer and Designer Network as well as the Windows Azure Meetup in Melbourne.

He is married to Lakshmi and lives in Melbourne, Australia, with his two wonderful daughters—Riya and Samika.

About the Technical Reviewer

■ **Stephen Godbold** With a passion for development and application lifecycle management, Steve Godbold fills his days as a senior consultant with Readify and his nights working on projects that supplement the ALM capabilities of the Visual Studio offering. Having watched Visual Studio grow from its humble beginnings in 2002 to the current offering, Steve helps teams deliver software with a focus on quality through the world's premier development suite.

Acknowledgments

Writing a book takes a lot of time and effort. After my first book, I swore I would never write again. But it is like having another baby. After a few years, you start thinking, "That wasn't so bad, was it?" And you fall into the trap again! So, this year my wife and I ended up having another baby, and I agreed (foolishly?) to write another book.

Jokes aside, writing a book has its rewards—there is no better way to master a subject than to teach it or, better yet, write about it. And when people use your book to learn, it brings you immense satisfaction. So, first and foremost, I would like to ~~blame~~ thank Alex Mackey for inviting me to co-author the book with him. Thanks, Alex.

I would also like to thank William Tulloch for helping me out with some parts of the book when I was falling behind. Thanks heaps, Bill.

Thanks is also due to the editorial and support team at Apress—Mathew Moodie, Ann Dickson, Anita Castro, Christine Ricketts, and everyone else involved in the project. Thanks for your patience in working through the repeated changes we made as Visual Studio and Windows 8 moved from pre-release versions to its final release.

A big thanks also goes out to Stephen Godbold for being the technical reviewer and meticulously checking every line of the book for technical correctness.

Last but not least, a really big thanks to my wife, Lakshmi, who put up with me while I spent a lot of time writing the book (in spite of having a newborn in the house), and my daughter Riya, who had to sacrifice some of her playtime so that I could write. She probably thinks I will be reading the book to her at bedtime—sorry, sweetie, it's not that kind of book.

Mahesh Krishnan

When Alex Mackey asked me if I liked to write, I must admit I didn't know what I was letting myself in for. This is my first shot at being involved in writing a book or part thereof, and through it took a little longer than anticipated it has been a great experience.

First I would like to thank Alex for giving me the opportunity to be involved in this project. Writing a book is not something I considered doing before so to both Alex and Mahesh, thanks!

As Mahesh has already done, thanks to the Apress editorial and support team for their ongoing support throughout the process and Stephen Godbold for his input on all things technical. I would also like to give a special shout out to Nicholas Blumhardt who, at the time the book was being written, was part of the team that developed MEF 2.0. One of the first chapters I wrote was on MEF and his feedback early in the piece went some way to convincing me that I might actually be able to pull this off.

Finally I would like to thank my wife Jacinta for her patience, support and understanding over the past eight months while I was ensconced the fortress of solitude working on this book.

William Tulloch

Introduction

Who This Book Is For

This book is an overview of all the important features in .NET 4.5 and Visual Studio 2012. We believe that by providing introductory content and easy-to-read, hello-world-type examples, readers will be made aware of the opportunities available in this release and want to explore them in more detail.

How This Book Is Structured

We have split the book into a number of different chapters, each exploring a different area of .NET 4.5 and Visual Studio 2012:

- **Chapter 1 Introduction:** overview of NET 4.5 and Visual Studio 2012 including the dominant themes within this release

- **Chapter 2 IDE Improvements:** features that will benefit all users, such as Quick Launch, preview tabs, new search options, improved multi-monitor support, and test runners

- **Chapter 3 The BCL and the CLR:** covers what's new in the BCL and the CLR.

- **Chapter 4 MEF 2 in 4.5:** support for open generic types, defining parts through convention using the new RegistrationBuilder, changes to parts lifetime management, and MEF for Windows 8 and web apps.

- **Chapter 5 Language:** writing async code in .NET and tweaks made to VB.NET language

- **Chapter 6 ASP.NET 4.5:** model binding, better HTML5 support, validation and encoding tweaks, performance enhancements, and WebSockets support

- **Chapter 7 ASP.NET MVC 4:** new display mode API, improved default templates, and Razor syntax tweaks

- **Chapter 8 Windows Communication Foundation and Web API:** new features in WCF, primarily focused around Web API and WebSockets

- **Chapter 9 Data:** takes a quick look at LocalDb, what is in new in System.Data and finally what is new and improved in Entity Framework 5.0.

- **Chapter 10 Windows Azure:** introduction to Windows Azure

- **Chapter 11 Windows Workflow Foundation**: covers improvements to the designer experience, the introduction of C# expressions and how to version workflows using the new WorkflowIdentity class.

- **Chapter 12 WPF**: new features of WPF available with .NET 4.5

- **Chapter 13 Silverlight 5**: changes made from Silverlight 4 to Silverlight 5

- **Chapter 14 Windows 8 Applications**: introduction to Windows 8 including how to create Windows store applications in C# and XAML

Downloading the Code

We have made the longer code examples available online so that you don't have to type them in. These examples are available at Alex Mackey's web site: www.simpleisbest.co.uk/vs2012.

Contacting the Author

If you have any feedback or spot a mistake, the authors can be contacted at the following addresses:

- alexjmackey@gmail.com

- maheshs_2000@yahoo.com

- william.tulloch@readify.net

CHAPTER 1

■ ■ ■

Introduction

Welcome to *Introducing .NET 4.5*.

It is my pleasure to be your guide (along with my coauthors) as we take you through the best that Visual Studio 2012 and .NET 4.5 have to offer, covering everything from Async to WPF (er, well, OK, maybe not WPF so much).

Aims

About two years ago, I wrote a book (*Introducing .NET 4.0 with Visual Studio 2010*). This was an ambitious (and time-consuming!) project where I set out to provide a high-level overview of all the major changes across the framework from ASP.NET to WCF.

I had some specific ideas in mind when writing the previous book:

> *This book is about breadth rather than depth. It will get you up-to-speed quickly on new functionality in just enough depth to get you going but without getting bogged down with too much detail.*

> *When something big like Visual Studio 2010 is released, I believe developers need and want an overview of what's new. When they find an area of interest, they can then research it further.*

When writing it, I tried to keep in mind the following objectives:

- Give the reader an introduction to new technologies.

- Show how to perform the basics that any developer would want to know.

- Produce examples that are as simple as possible but still demonstrate the concept.

- Don't get too bogged down in detail so the book can still be easily read.

The book was well received (although not quite as well as one involving wizarding schoolchildren or lame-ass vampires) and enjoyed high sells, leading me to believe that there was a need for such a text (if not, don't buy it—it only encourages us!). Thus, despite promising myself that I wouldn't write another book in a hurry, I find myself writing about the changes in .NET 4.5 and Visual Studio 2012.

This book has the same aims as the previous book. However, I have also made a few changes to address what I felt were weaknesses of the first text.

Changes

Given the breadth of the subject matter, it was impossible to cover all the subject areas in as much detail as each topic deserved. Some chapters of the first book were much stronger and more in-depth than others. Sometimes the level of depth reflected the information available, but my own areas of interest and knowledge also influenced how thoroughly I covered any given topic. So, this time—with the added bonus of not having to do quite as much work!—I have taken some friends and colleagues along for the ride. It is my pleasure to introduce you to my fellow authors, Mahesh Krishnan and William Tulloch. I had the (dubious?) pleasure to work with Mahesh and William at the Australia-based consultancy Readify (www.readify.net). Mahesh specializes in the areas of Azure, WCF, and Silverlight, and he is the author of *Microsoft Silverlight 4 for Dummies*. William specializes in WCF and WIF.

Work in Progress!

As I write this, Visual Studio 2012 has yet to be released so it is very likely that there will be last-minute changes that won't make it into this book. As we become aware of these changes, we will release corrections and updates on the Apress web site.

Documentation and examples are also lacking in some areas, which has made researching them very difficult (particularly the core CLR changes), and some/most of the Microsoft teams were, er, not so chatty when asked for further information.

What We Will Cover

This book covers the core changes in .NET 4.5 and Visual Studio 2012. We have also included chapters on current and upcoming technologies included in this release, such as ASP.NET MVC 4, Windows Azure, and Silverlight 5, which we believe will be of interest to readers.

What We Won't Cover

We will not be covering some of the great new Team Foundation Server–related changes (these are huge and would require several books to discuss). We will only be covering the "core" IDE features. We have also had to make decisions as to which features and changes will be of most interest and/or importance to our readers so we have had to drop some of the minor changes. Additionally, to save space, examples are provided in C# only although we have covered changes to VB.NET.

Downloadable Examples

We have tried to keep examples as short as possible to avoid obscuring the concepts we are trying to demonstrate with plumbing code and also to keep typing to a minimum, but you can obtain a download of some of the longer sections and examples from my web site at simpleisbest.co.uk/vs2012.

.NET 4.5 Themes

Every release of .NET and Visual Studio tends to have a core set of themes or improvements. Visual Studio 2010's dominant themes, in my opinion, were parallel programming, dynamic types, extensibility, and bringing C# and VB.NET into line.

So, what are the big themes in .NET 4.5 and Visual Studio 2012?

Well, we have the rest of the book to answer that question, but if I had to pick the top five themes, they would include the following:

- Making async programming as easy as possible

- Promoting NuGet as the preferred distribution and update mechanism

- Making it easy to develop on different devices and platforms (Windows 8, Windows Phone, and Xbox)

- Supporting emerging standards and technologies

- Continuing the move toward openness

Making Async Programming as Easy as Possible

The biggest change in .NET 4.5 is a much-improved async programming model. Async programming techniques can keep our applications more responsive and help us make optimal use of available resources.

Traditionally, async programming has been rather tricky (and you'd probably be wearing sandals and own a rather good neck beard to *really* understand it); however, with .NET 4.5, we have an excellent and intuitive model with the new await and async keywords. The await and async model drastically reduces the amount of code you need to write, resulting in easier-to-maintain and more readable applications. A huge number of methods and classes in the base-class library has been upgraded to support this new model. The new WinRT framework (for developing Windows 8 applications) only supports Async APIs, illustrating just how important Microsoft believes this concept to be.

Promoting NuGet as the Preferred Distribution and Update Mechanism

Other development languages such as Ruby have long had an easy-to-use method for distributing, installing, and updating APIs (Gems in Ruby's case). Sometime in 2011, Microsoft released its own distribution framework called NuGet. NuGet enables you to easily include (or publish your own) libraries from either Microsoft's NuGet repository or a specified location.

With Visual Studio 2012, Microsoft will be using NuGet as the distribution and update method for a number of frameworks such as Entity Framework and ASP.NET MVC. When you first create certain types of projects, Microsoft's NuGet repository will automatically be contacted to obtain the latest version. This is great news as it means that Microsoft can push out updates much quicker and, I suspect, it will also encourage the uptake and distribution of open-source projects.

Supporting Emerging Standards and Technologies

Visual Studio 2012 provides improved support for HTML5, CSS3, and WebSockets (IIS 8 only) through IDE changes, additional APIs, and the updating of existing components.

Making It Easy to Develop on Different Devices and Other Platforms

Visual Studio 2012 is an excellent choice for developing applications for many different platforms including Windows Phone, Xbox, and Windows 8. Visual Studio 2012 has a number of new project templates, additional libraries, improved IDE components, and enhancements such as portable libraries.

Continuing the Move toward Openness

Microsoft has become much more open in the last few years. For example, ASP.NET MVC source code has been available since its earliest version, Microsoft teams have contributed to open-source projects such as jQuery, and we have seen the ASP.NET Web API and ASP.NET web pages (Razor) released under the Apache License.

Microsoft even says that for some of these projects, it will accept contributions and bug fixes from the community. (Don't worry—they will, of course, review them!) This should result in better products for everyone.

Visual Studio 2012 Editions

Visual Studio 2012 comes in the following flavors:

- Visual Studio 2012 Express (separate editions for Web, Desktop, Windows 8, and Windows Phone)

- Visual Studio 2012 Professional (no code clone detection, limited modeling and architecture tools, no collaboration features such as PowerPoint Storyboarding, limited testing tools)

- Visual Studio 2012 Premium (most features except IntelliTrace)

- Visual Studio 2012 Ultimate (everything including IntelliTrace)

- Visual Studio 2012 Test Professional (limited set of collaboration and testing tools)

Visual Studio Professional edition will be more than adequate for the majority of developers, but for a full breakdown of features please consult www.microsoft.com/visualstudio/11/en-us/products/compare.

What Others Think of Visual Studio 2012 /.NET 4.5

I have asked a number of different people in the development industry what their highlights and favorite features of .NET 4.5 and VS2012 are. Here are their responses:

Mitch Denny, Director at Unpedestrian

http://mitchdenny.com and http://mitchdenny.com/about/

Visual Studio 2012 and .NET 4.5 are each significant releases in Microsoft's developer platform. VS2012 will open up the ability for developers to target Microsoft's new WinRT platform using either C++, .NET, or JavaScript bindings all within the one unified IDE. For .NET developers, the .NET 4.5 runtime represents the continued drive to make .NET the most productive and powerful development environment available. The increased focus on asynchronous programming capabilities in the C# language, the framework, and the IDE mean that developers have what they need to produce high-performance solutions and responsive user interfaces.

Brendan Forster, ASP.NET MVP and Code52 Coordinator

brendanforster.com

I've limited myself to three things I like about the upcoming stuff:

- async/await: Baking asynchrony into the language has been a joy to work with—easy to get started with, hard to live without after a while.

- Test Explorer enhancements: Opening this up to third parties to write custom test adapters and being able to automatically run tests after build is a very underrated feature. Makes testing practices easier to introduce.

- Windows runtime: As someone who has experienced the "joys" of mixing Win32 and managed code, I am glad they finally revisited the abstraction and made it a first-class citizen.

And a shiny feature not specific to this release: Reactive Extensions—mind-warping fun to code with.

Richard Banks, MVP and Author of *Microsoft Visual Studio 2012 First Look Cookbook*

packtpub.com/microsoft-visual-studio-2012-first-look-cookbook/book

Visual Studio 2012 makes good on Microsoft's overarching goal of making developers "raving fans". This is now one very quick IDE! It's newfound speed and responsiveness belies the vastness of the functionality it offers and is by far the best version of Visual Studio that Redmond has produced so far. Visual Studio 2012 doesn't just enable you to develop new Windows 8 style apps or make it easier to take advantage of modern multi-core hardware, it will also greatly improve your overall productivity and enjoyment when working on existing applications and that's worth the price of admission alone!

And the book's authors and technical reviewer:

Phillip Laureano, Creator of Linfu framework

http://plaureano.blogspot.com.au/

My top favourite feature for .NET 4.5 is ReJITting:

http://chanel9.msdn.com/Shows/Going+Deep/CLR-45-David-Broman-Inside-Re-JIT

ReJITting is a step in the right direction for Microsoft, but it still falls short compared to the great IL rewriting tools that are out there, such as Cecil.

Steve Godbold (Technical Reviewer)

http://stevegodbold.com/

What am I most excited about with the upcoming changes to the .NET ecosystem? The changes to the asynchronous programming model provide a compelling and simple means for starting to build really responsive, dynamic, and interactive applications. Coupled with the design implications of Windows 8, it's a real push for software authors to start thinking more about how applications are consumed across multiple formats and needs.

There are number of developer-centric enhancements to the IDE that I think are exciting as a Visual Studio user. The interaction model Visual Studio is moving toward is making a big change to how I work—it's helping me focus on getting my current job done, allowing me to finish and deliver. A win for me and the clients I work with.

Outside of what I love, I think I'm looking forward to seeing how Web API evolves the mindset of the people I see working with .NET and the web. It's a great offering that I think will trigger a lot more semantic interaction with web-based resources.

Alex Mackey (Author); MVP Internet Explorer: Development

simpleIsBest.co.uk

.NET 4.5 and Visual Studio 2012 contain some real game changers such as Windows 8 applications and Async functionality. The new Windows 8 design is a really exciting and brave move by Microsoft and it will be interesting to see how it pans out. Windows 8 apps certainly have their issues and limitations at the moment (I am sitting opposite some developers working on a project and hearing various frustrations—Josh and Dan, I am talking about you here!) but there is no doubt its very innovative.

I am a little skeptical about developers wanting to create Windows 8 applications using JavaScript and HTML5 as feel developers skilled in these languages will probably stick to web sites. The web purists will also probably not like some of the proprietary APIs (although let's face it, this is becoming increasingly common with vendor prefixes) and that MS has tried to make JavaScript look a little like C# in places. Web sites are, of course, usable on pretty much any platform whereas the new design will be confined to use on Windows 8 and the next generation of Windows phones, which feels limited to me when I have limited time to invest in learning new skills.

I predict that XAML/C# will probably be the language and framework of choice for Windows 8 app development (and developers creating desktop applications will probably stick with what they know), but it is nice to see the flexibility to create applications using traditionally web-focused languages.

My top three changes in this release are:

- The IDE has been updated to include IntelliSense and code snippets for HTML 5 and CSS 3, which I can see myself making use of every day. Since Visual Studio 2010, Visual Studio is a really good IDE for all your web-development needs.

- I really like the new preview tabs and that navigating through code will open previously closed files so you can see their content—this is going to be a massive time saver and prevent the IDE from becoming really cluttered.

- The Web API framework is awesome. Perhaps unfairly I compare it to WCF and although they certainly have very different capabilities (and use cases), I have always felt that developing a simple web service with WCF seemed a little hard. For many scenarios, the Web API will be a great way to construct your services.

William Tulloch (Author)

Alex has asked me to nominate some of my favorite features in this release of the framework, and I must admit picking any particular thing is not easy but here goes:

- The move from role-based access control to a claims-based model and the incorporation of Windows Identity Foundation into mscorlib.

- MEF. Before this book, I hadn't looked at MEF for a while, but the changes in this version have enthused me, especially around the ability to use convention to manage part composition.

- TPL Dataflow. I haven't really thought about how I can use it, but something tells this going to be a player in future application development.

- Finally, it goes without saying that the introduction of async/await rates high on my list of favorite features—not just for what it offers us as developers but how it has impacted and changed some of the core functionality of the framework itself.

Mahesh Krishnan (Author)

Every time a new version of the framework, C#/VB.NET language or the IDE is released, .NET developers get excited. They try to learn what's been updated, what's new, and what feature doesn't exist anymore. They try and figure out the coolest additions and guess what the next big thing is. I am no different—looking at all the things Visual Studio 2012 and .NET 4.5 have to offer, I've come to the following conclusions:

- Programming in the new design for Windows 8 is going to be a pretty big change for developers. Even if you are familiar with WPF and Silverlight, you will still find that you need to change the way you think when you write an application for Windows 8. It will be a paradigm shift. You can write Windows 8 apps using XAML with C#/C++/VB.NET or HTML with JS and CSS, but I personally feel that it is a lot easier to write them using XAML—then again, I could be biased as I've written a fair bit of Silverlight applications in the past.

- If I were to pick out one stand-out feature in different versions of the C# language, the list would look something like this—generics in C# 2, LINQ and lambdas in C# 3, and dynamic types in C# 4. In C# 5, the stand-out feature has to be the introduction of async/await. (VB.NET follows a similar trend.)

- If you are web developer, you should also be reasonably excited about the support for HTML5 form types and the support for WebSockets. Web developers should also be fairly excited about Web API—Web API allows you to create RESTful services using ASP.NET MVC. This is in contrast to how in previous versions, you had to use WCF to create REST services. The new way of creating REST services is extremely easy and I think we will see a lot of REST services being written in the Microsoft platform.

- For developers writing rich client applications using WPF, there is nothing big to get excited about—maybe the support for Ribbon user interface component out of the box will give them something to look forward to.

- On the whole, the Visual Studio IDE is vastly improved, and don't let its new simplified look (which may throw some people off initially) fool you—it has lots and lots of nice features (which you could only get by installing third-party components in previous versions) that are easy to find and use.

On with the book and we await your feedback.

Alex Mackey, William Tulloch, and Mahesh Krishnan

CHAPTER 2

■ ■ ■

IDE Improvements

The last release of Visual Studio 2010 saw a radical overhaul of the internals of the IDE with much of the interface rewritten in WPF and a new MEF-based extension model introduced. With this release, the IDE has a fresh new look and the team has concentrated on making it easier than ever for developers to navigate around their code.

Compatibility with VS2010 SP1 Projects

Visual Studio 2012 allows the opening and modification of existing Visual Studio 2010 SP1 solutions without having to upgrade them to a new project format. This is fantastic news as it allows you to benefit from VS2012's many features without having to modify your projects in any way.

■ **Warning** This doesn't mean that you can use .NET 4.5 features in a .NET 4 project!

There are, however, some scenarios where VS2012 will need to update components if you open a Visual Studio 2010 project. For example, VS2012 only supports Silverlight 5. As a result, opening a Silverlight v3 or v4 project will not work without upgrade. For more information, please consult `http://blogs.msdn.com/b/visualstudio/archive/2012/03/28/round-tripping-with-visual-studio-11.aspx`. For a list of compatible projects, see `http://msdn.microsoft.com/enus/library/hh266747(v=VS.110).aspx`.

Toolbar Changes

One of the first changes you will notice when you run up VS2012 is that the toolbar is much less cluttered as shown in Figure 2-1. A number of buttons you probably never used have been removed. (Note: You can of course bring these back with the customization options.)

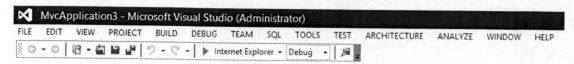

Figure 2-1. New, almost zenlike, VS2012 toolbar free from clutter

Quick Launch Box

New to VS2012 is a textbox in the top right-hand corner of the IDE that allows you to enter commands in order to quickly access various items of IDE functionality. By completing the following steps, you will be able to enjoy this new capability:

1. Press Ctrl+q to set the focus to the Quick Launch box.

2. Start typing the word *open*. A list of possible commands will appear containing the word *open* (see Figure 2-2).

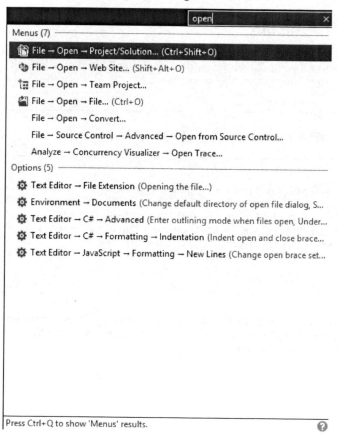

Figure 2-2. Quick Launch box

Note how the Quick Launch box has grouped commands into two groups in the example above: Menus and Options.

There are actually four different types of groups. You can filter commands by group as well; for example, I could restrict the search for the Open command in the menu group with the syntax @menu open.

The other types of groups and their corresponding shortcuts include the following:

- Most recently used (@mru)

- Menus (@menu)

- Options (@opt)

- Documents (@doc)

It is possible to page through results by category by using the keys Ctrl+q and Ctrl+Shift+q, which is useful if your results are spread across many pages.

Quick Launch Options

You can tell Visual Studio to restrict the type of results returned from Quick Launch (Tools ➤ Options ➤ Environment ➤ Quick Launch). There is also an option to show previous search results when Quick Launch is first activated as shown in Figure 2-3.

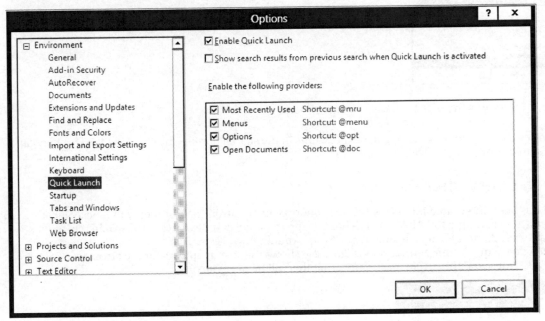

Figure 2-3. Quick Launch options

Search Improvements

Visual Studio 2012's search capabilities have been upgraded with new advanced search options. Let's take a look at these with the find/replace dialog box.

1. Open a code file in Visual Studio and press Ctrl+h to bring up the new find/replace screen (Figure 2-4).

Figure 2-4. *New find/replace screen*

2. In order to look at the advanced search option dialog box, click the down arrow at the end of either the find or replace box, and you should see something similar to Figure 2-5.

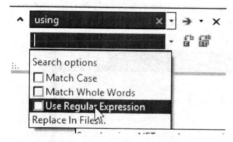

Figure 2-5. *Enabling regular Expression Search option*

Notice that we can now use regular expressions in the search options (by checking the Use Regular Expression option)—very nice!

Search Everywhere!

Search has been integrated into many VS2012 windows and controls making it easy to quickly locate items you are searching for. All the search boxes support camel case searches ("TS" would return files such as TestStub) and fuzzy searching (e.g., "Stub" would return TestStub class).

Let's take a quick tour of these now. Figure 2-6 shows the search options for the error view. (Hopefully, you won't have that many errors that this will be necessary!)

Figure 2-6. *Error list search integration*

Even the toolbox has its own search now (see Figure 2-7).

Figure 2-7. Toolbox search option

Solution Explorer also contains integrated search as shown in Figure 2-8.

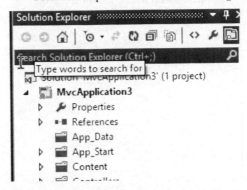

Figure 2-8. Solution Explorer search

Even the Threads window has search capabilities (see Figure 2-9).

Figure 2-9. Thread search window

Parallel Watch Supports Boolean Expressions

The parallel watch window (to see this, run your application in debug mode, right-click on a variable, and click Add parallel watch) has a new search option that allows you to enter a boolean filter expression. Figure 2-10 shows this in action where the thread will only be shown if the test value is greater than one.

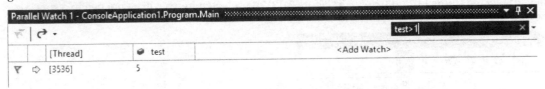

Figure 2-10. Parallel watch window

Solution Explorer Enhancements

The Solution Explorer has undergone a number of enhancements previously only available via Visual Studio extensions.

Collapse All

The Solution Explorer receives (a very overdue) Collapse All project option that is useful when navigating around very large projects. You will find this option toward the right-hand side of the Solution Explorer options pane (see Figure 2-11).

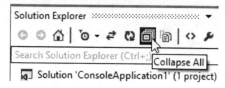

Figure 2-11. Collapse All button

Pending Changes and Open Files Filter

Often in large projects, you want to filter Solution Explorer to just show files that have pending changes or which are open. Visual Studio 2012 gives you this facility—to use, simply click the button to the right of the home icon. The drop-down next to it gives you the facility to switch the filter between open files and pending changes as shown in Figure 2-12.

Figure 2-12. Open files and pending changes filter

Preview Selected Items

In a large project, you might want to quickly jump back to a file selected in Solution Explorer. By clicking the Preview Selected Items button (shown in Figure 2-13) the selected items will be opened in a special new preview tab mode (more about this shortly!)

Figure 2-13. Preview selected files

Sync with Active Document

Sync with Active Document allows you to force Solution Explorer to show where a file is in the project structure when you are working on it (see Figure 2-14).

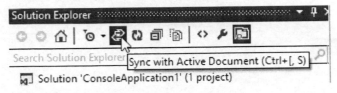

Figure 2-14. Sync with Active Document

Masked Renaming files

If you select an individual file to rename (either right-click/rename or F2), then only the file name will be selected to save you from accidently overwriting the file extension (see Figure 2-15).

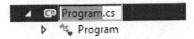

Figure 2-15. Rename file now only selects file name.

Image Preview

The Solution Explorer now contains the ability to preview images in your solution by hovering over them as shown in Figure 2-16.

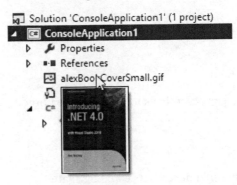

Figure 2-16. Solution Explorer allows you to preview images by hovering over them.

Scope to This

The Solution Explorer has a new option to filter the view relative to the selected item. To activate this feature, simply right-click on a file and select the Scope to This option on the context menu that appears as Figure 2-17 shows.

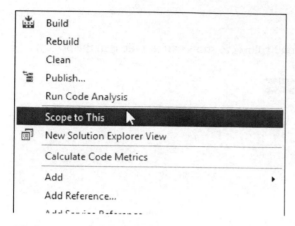

***Figure 2-17.** Scope to this context menu option*

The Solution Explorer will then filter the files displayed. In Figure 2-18, I selected the `HomeController` class to set the scope to.

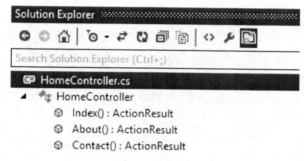

***Figure 2-18.** Results of scope to this context menu selection*

When you want to get back to the normal solution view, you can revert back by selecting the home or back button in Solution Explorer.

Hubs and Pivots

One of the issues the IDE team was keen to solve was to make sure that developers could navigate around their solutions as easily as possible, avoiding the need to switch to different windows to perform a task:

`http://blogs.msdn.com/b/visualstudio/archive/2012/02/24/introducing-the-new-developer-experience-part2.aspx`

In order to accomplish this, the team have added additional navigation and view options. Let's take a look at some of these.

If you explore various files, you will notice you can now expand them to view the classes and methods they contain. Right-clicking on a file will also bring up a new context menu showing the call hierarchy feature that was introduced in Visual Studio 2010. Figure 2-19 demonstrates this.

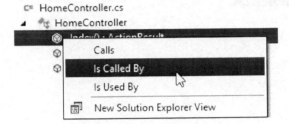

Figure 2-19. *New context menu in Solution Explorer*

A new context menu has also been added to the Class Explorer window that allows you to easily view a class or method's call hierarchy and usage. To see this, switch to the class view tab, search for a class or method, and then right-click on one of the results to see a context menu with further actions you can perform as shown in Figure 2-20.

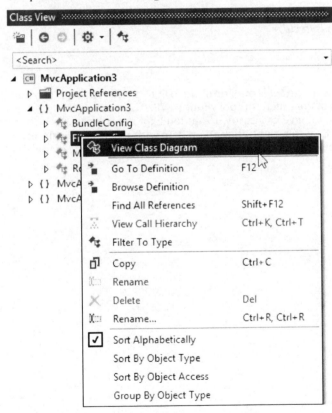

Figure 2-20. *New context menu on Class Explorer*

Note how in the Class Explorer that when selecting a class, the methods it contains are displayed in Figure 2-21, allowing you to quickly navigate around code.

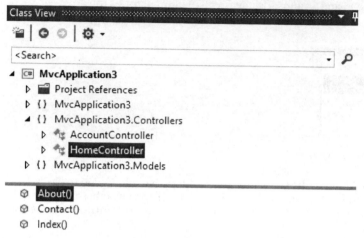

Figure 2-21. Solution Explorer showing methods in class

Improved Multi Monitor Support

Visual Studio 2010 introduced the ability to move windows outside of the IDE to a different monitor, but they were restricted to being of the same type of document or tool window. VS2012 removes this restriction and also allows each window group to have its very own Solution Explorer window.

To create a separate instance of Solution Explorer, right-click on an item within Solution Explorer window and then select the New Solution Explorer View context menu option to create a copy of the Solution Explorer window (see Figure 2-22).

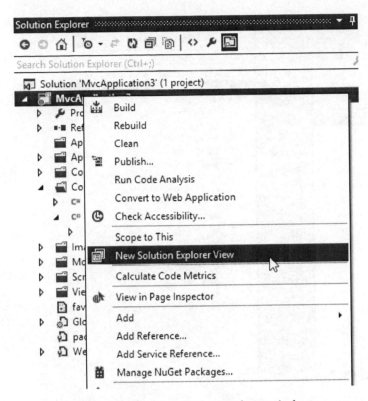

Figure 2-22. Creating a new Solution Explorer window

Now that you have a new Solution Explorer, you can drag it into another set of windows as demonstrated in Figure 2-23.

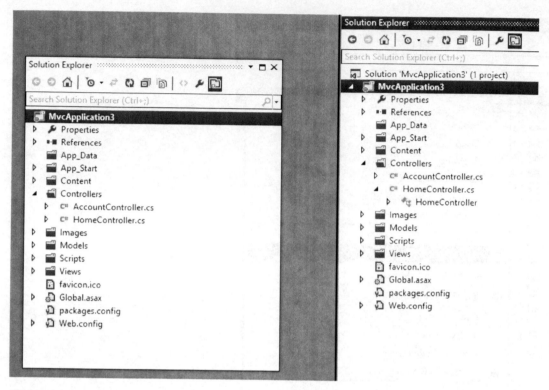

Figure 2-23. New solution window

Tabs and Preview Mode

Often when you are tracing a method through code, you can end up with many tabs open and leave you trapped in MDI hell (or, at the very least, with lots of tabs to close!). VS2012 resolves this issue by the introduction of a new preview tab mode. Files in preview mode can be modified the standard way, but if you then open up another file from within the preview window, it will replace the existing previewed file instead of opening up another tab.

So, how do you open a file in preview mode? Good question—glad you asked! To preview a file, simply click on a file once from Solution Explorer and it will appear separately to the right of the other files with a different icon to illustrate that it is in preview mode (see Figure 2-24).

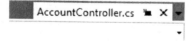

Figure 2-24. File opened in preview mode

You can promote a previewed tab to a normal tab by dragging it or clicking the small starred tab icon next to the file name. Preview mode also works when debugging, through the go-to definition option, and when viewing the results of a search.

If you find the preview files option kicking in accidently, you can temporarily disable it by holding down the alt button when you open a file. Alternatively, you can disable it in the Tools ➤ Options ➤ Environment ➤ Tabs and Windows screen by checking the Select allow new files to be opened in the preview tab checkbox.

Navigating Back and Forward Now Opens Closed Files

Previous versions of Visual Studio allowed you to navigate back and forward between files with the shortcut Ctrl– (back) or Ctrl+Shift+ (forward). VS2012 will now open any previously closed files in preview mode while doing this, saving you from having to open them again. I think this has to be Alex's number 1 VS2012 IDE improvement, and it will save you heaps of time!

Tabs Stay Put

In VS2012, tabs will not change their position as other files are opened.

Pinned Tabs Changes

VS2012 contains a new option to keep all pinned tabs in a separate row. To enable this, type Tabs in the Quick Launch window, select Environment ➤ Tabs and Windows, and then check the Show pinned tabs in a separate row option.

Add References

Previously, it was quite difficult to locate references in Visual Studio due to the way they were grouped and filtered. VS2012 simplifies this with one unified view of references with references that don't belong in the targeted framework version grayed out. If you should accidently select a previous framework's version, then VS2012 being up is an option to re-target the project. The screenshot in Figure 2-25 shows the new reference window.

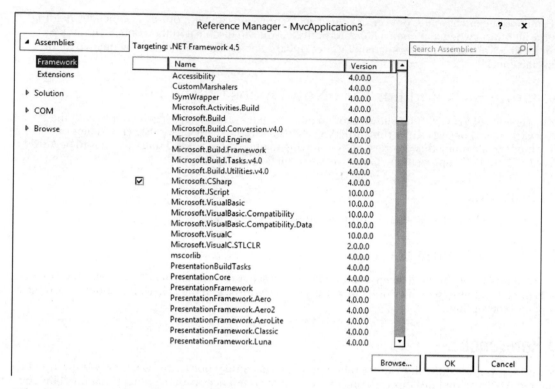

Figure 2-25. New add references window

Web IDE Improvements

The IDE experience for web developers within VS2012 has drastically improved over the last few versions (although design view still sucks!). VS2012 has some really good productivity enhancements for web developers and improved support for emerging standards and technologies such as HTML5, CSS3, and WS-ARIA.

New Debug in Different Browser Option

VS2012 has a new option to allow you to start debugging in different browsers that is activated by clicking the down arrow next to the browser name (see Figure 2-26).

Figure 2-26. New toolbar option to run in browser

Scott Hansleman has a nice post about customizing this to support different browser launch options (e.g., some browser support command line switches to avoid saving to the browsers history): www.hanselman.com/blog/CommentView.aspx?guid=ee1c533f-25f7-4c47-b85e-55097e29bebe

Page Inspector

Page Inspector is a marvelous new feature in VS2012 that allows you to easily identify the individual components that make up a page. At the time of writing, Page Inspector is limited to Web Pages 2 or ASP.NET 4.5 applications and pages displayed in IE standards mode, and it also requires Internet Explorer version 9 or above.

To view a page in Page Inspector, either right-click on it in Solution Explorer and select View in page inspector or select it from the main IDE menu and run the application (see Figure 2-27).

Figure 2-27. Running Page Inspector from browser menu

So, what we can we do with Page Inspector? I think one of the most useful aspects of Page Inspector is that by clicking on the Files tab, you can see the components that make up a page as shown in Figure 2-28.

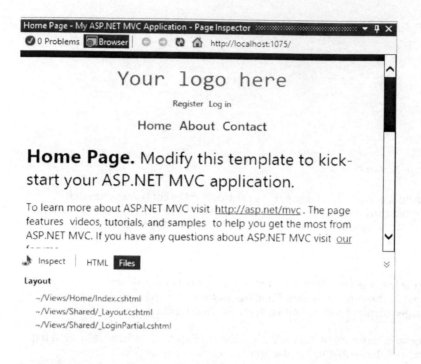

Figure 2-28. Page inspector allows you to see the files that make up a page

You can drill down into even more detail by activating the inspection feature (arrow with inspect located down at the bottom left-hand corner) and then hovering over an element as Figure 2-29 demonstrates.

Figure 2-29. Page Inspector element inspection features

There is also an HTML tab, as shown in Figure 2-30, that allows you to navigate and modify styling with an interface that looks very similar to IE's development tools (and given Internet Explorer is a requirement for the page inspector they could be the same tools).

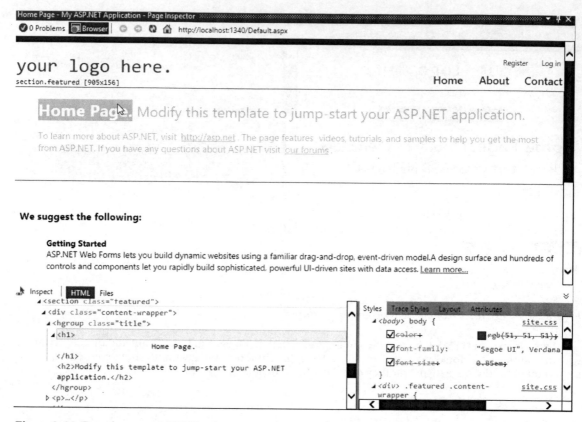

Figure 2-30. Page inspector, HTML tab

If you modify any files, then Page Inspector will alert you that you need to save and reload them with the message shown in Figure 2-31.

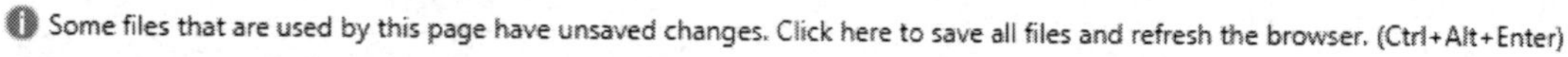

ⓘ Some files that are used by this page have unsaved changes. Click here to save all files and refresh the browser. (Ctrl+Alt+Enter)

Figure 2-31. Page inspector alert message due to unsaved changes

Rename Matched Tag

In VS2012, altering an opening tag element will also automatically update a closing tag. For example, if you had the following markup:

```
<div></div>
```

And modified it to something else such as

```
<myNewDiv>
```

Then the closing tag would also be updated at the same time as Figure 2-32 shows.

```
<myNewTa></myNewTa>
```

Figure 2-32. Match tag being renamed

IntelliSense Improvements

IntelliSense options can now be filtered by matching the start of a string and camel case searches. IntelliSense is now also provided when entering code inside attributes (see Figure 2-33).

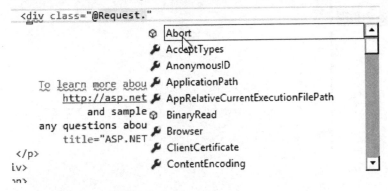

Figure 2-33. IntelliSense inside attributes

Quotation Tweak

One Visual Studio quirk I found very irritating was that when entering properties such as `runat="server"`, it was necessary to also enter the quotation marks. This is no longer necessary and VS2012 will automatically insert the quotation marks for you and move the cursor outside the quote block.

SQL Server Object Window

VS2012 contains an improved interface to SQL Server that is now very similar to SQL Management Studio interface and provides additional functionality over the integrated tools in previous versions. To access this window open, it from the main menu View ➤ SQL Server object window option as shown in Figure 2-34.

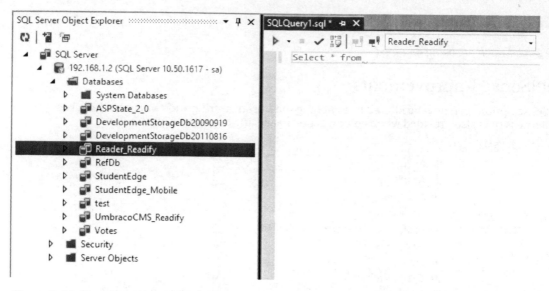

Figure 2-34. New SQL Server Object window

Additionally if you are accessing a SQL 2012 database, you will benefit from an enhanced table designer showing the SQL used to create the table alongside a graphical view.

Support for Different Test Frameworks

VS2012 supports the use of different testing frameworks through new adapters. The test adapters can be installed via Visual Studio's Extension Manager (Tools ➤ Extensions and Updates). Let's give this a try and run an xUnit test from within VS2012!

1. First of all, you need to install the xUnit runner extension. Go to Tools ➤ Extensions and Updates and search online extensions for xUnit. You should find xUnit.net runner. Now download and install this (note this will restart Visual Studio). See Figure 2-35.

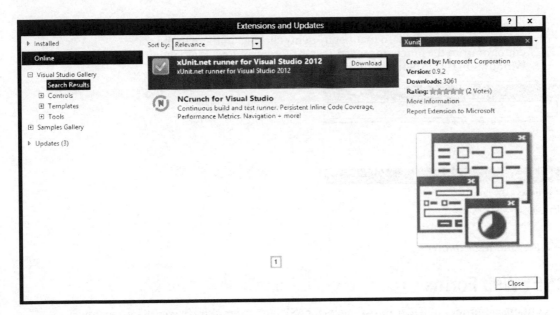

Figure 2-35. Installing xUnit.net runner

2. Now create a class project to contain our tests.

3. You now need to install xUnit from NuGet. Right-click on the project and select Manage NuGet Packages, search for xUnit (in the online section), and then hit the install button.

4. Create a new class file to contain the tests and add the following code:

```
using Xunit;

public class Class1
    {

        [Fact]
        public void The_Sky_Should_Be_Blue()
        {
            const string expected="Blue";
            string actual = "Blue";
            Assert.Equal(expected, actual);
        }

        [Fact]
        public void One_Plus_One_Should_Equal_Two_Or_Does_It()
        {
            Assert.Equal(1+1, 3);
        }
    }
```

5. Compile your project and you should be good to go. You can either run your xUnit tests in the standard manner by right- clicking on them in the code editor or from the much improved Test Explorer window (Main menu Test ➤ Windows ➤ Test Explorer), shown in Figure 2-36.

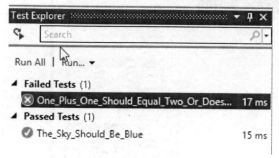

Figure 2-36. Unit test explorer

ASP.NET Web Forms

VS2012 contains a number of IDE improvements for ASP.NET users, which we will look at now.

Extract to User Control

Often when developing an ASP.NET application, developers will prototype a screen by adding a number of elements directly to an ASPX page. At some point, portions of the page are then extracted into a separate user control for readability or reuse. VS2012 has a new Extract to user control option to extract and register your new control with just a couple of clicks.

To use this with an ASP.NET web forms project, simply highlight a section of code you want to be extracted, right-click, and then from the context menu select the Extract to user control option. The extract to user control screen will then display allowing you to configure the file to extract (see Figure 2-37).

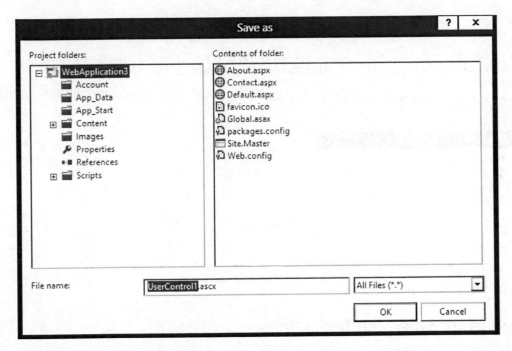

Figure 2-37. Extract to user control

Event Handler Creation

VS2012 makes it very easy to create and wire up event handlers. To see this, simply create a new button on an ASPX page:

```
<asp:button runat="Server">
```

Now type OnClick and from the smart task dialog box that appears, select the <Create New Event> option that pops up (see Figure 2-38).

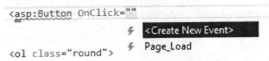

Figure 2-38. Event handler creation

Behind the scenes, VS2012 will now create and wire up a click handler for the button.

Smart Tasks Support in Code Editor

Previous versions of Visual Studio introduced smart tasks (kind of a wizard for certain tasks). VS2012 expands on these and allows you to use some of them directly from code view. Let's see this in action with the GridView smart task options.

Enter the following code on an ASPX page:

```
<asp:gridview runat="server">
</asp:gridview>
```

Now either click the small smart task arrow to the left of the element or position the cursor inside the element and click Ctrl+. to bring up the smart dialog box. You should see some new options as shown in Figure 2-39.

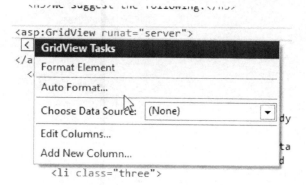

Figure 2-39. Smart tasks for GridView

Better Support for Emerging Technologies

The last few years have seen the development and increase in an astonishing number of technologies for web developers. VS2012 now contains IntelliSense support and snippets for the following technologies and standards:

- HTML5

- CSS3

- WS-ARIA (disability support)

HTML5

The IDE now supports new HTML5 input types such as e-mail, number, and so forth (see Figure 2-40).

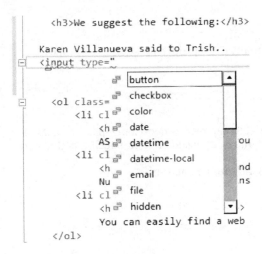

```
    <h3>We suggest the following:</h3>

    Karen Villanueva said to Trish..
    <input type="
                    button
                    checkbox
    <ol class=      color
        <li cl      date
            <h      datetime              ou
            AS      datetime-local
        <li cl      email                 nd
            <h      file                  ns
            Nu
        <li cl      hidden              >
            <h
            You can easily find a web
    </ol>
```

Figure 2-40. Input type snippet

In addition, the VS2012 IDE can now validate HTML 5 doctypes and HTML elements support ~/ syntax for referencing files.

■ **Note** HTML5 support has also been added in ASP.NET and ASP.NET MVC with enhanced versions of controls such as FileUpload, updating of existing controls such as UpdatePanel, and new HTML extension methods. Consult the ASP.NET and ASP.NET MVC chapters for more details.

Many HTML5 elements such as video and audio also have their own code snippets. Let's try the video snippet now.

Open up an ASPX page and type video. Press Tab. VS2012 will insert the video snippet and focus the cursor on the first element as shown in Figure 2-41.

```
<video controls="controls">
    <source src="file.mp4" type="video/mp4" />
    <source src="file.webm" type="video/webm" />
    <source src="file.ogv" type="video/ogg" />
</video>
```

Figure 2-41. Video snippet

■ **Note** VS2010 users can download a free IDE extension at http://visualstudiogallery.msdn. microsoft.com/d771cbc8-d60a-40b0-a1d8-f19fc393127d to benefit from some of these updates.

CSS Changes

VS2012 has improved IntelliSense and snippet support for many CSS3 properties such as rounded borders, animation, and media queries.

Smart indenting

Style sheets can quickly become unreadable and confusing. (I would recommend a pre-processor such as Less or SASS to minimize this.) VS2012 automatically indents rules based on their specificity that can alleviate this issue somewhat.

The below screenshot in Figure 2-42 demonstrates this indenting in action.

```
p {
}

    p.background {
    }

        p.background:hover {
        }
```

Figure 2-42. Style sheet indenting

If you would prefer not to use this automatic indenting feature, you can disable it by going to Tools ➤ Options ➤ Text Editor ➤ CSS ➤ Formatting and unchecking the Hierarchical Indentation checkbox.

CSS Hack Support

Sometimes it is necessary to use CSS hacks to target a specific browser. VS2012 now understands some of these hacks and will not mark them as invalid.

Comment/Uncomment CSS

VS2012 now allows you to comment out style sheet rules in a similar fashion to commenting out code (Ctrl+K+C and Ctrl+K+U).

CSS Color Picker

VS2012's new CSS editor contains a new color picker that is visible when setting color-based CSS properties such as background color. When you hover over a color property, the color picker will show colors already used within the style sheet allowing you to quickly select them as in Figure 2-43.

Figure 2-43. New CSS editor allows you to pick colors already used

It is also possible to select any color by clicking the + button to bring up a full pallet and eye dropper screen. Note that if you modify the opacity of a color, VS2012 shifts automatically between RGB and RGBA modes (see Figure 2-44).

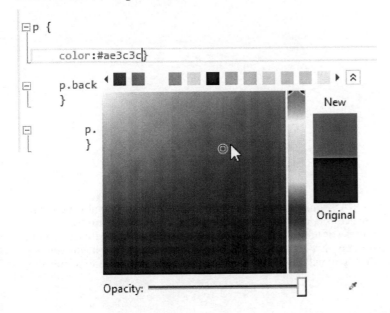

Figure 2-44. *New color picker*

WAI-ARIA (Accessible Rich Internet Applications)

VS2012 contains support for something called WAI-ARIA. Many developers probably haven't heard of WAI-ARIA, which "defines a way to make web content and web applications more accessible to people with disabilities," www.w3.org/WAI/intro/aria. This definition probably doesn't help clear up what exactly it is, so an example is in order.

Let's say that we have a fancy month slider control that allows users to search flights across different months. This slider control is probably made up of a number of div elements and transformed through the magic of curly braces and semicolons (yes, that's CSS & JavaScript) into something that resembles a slider control to users.

In HTML terms, our slider might look something like the following:

```
<div class="slider-container">
        <div class="slider">
        </div>
</div>
```

This is all well and good for our standard desktop browser users, but what if a user accessed a site on a screen reader device? It's very unlikely the screen reader will know how to interpret this and, thus, our site could be unusable for such users.

WAI-ARIA attempts to resolve this issue by adding metadata to elements to give devices a better chance of interpreting an element correctly. The markup below shows the above example but with some additional ARIA properties:

```
<div class="slider-container">

    <div
    class="slider"

    role="slider"
    aria-valuenow="1"
    aria-valuemin="1"
    aria-valuemax="12"
    aria-valuetext="January">

    </div>

</div>
```

As sites become more complex, WS-ARIA is going to become more important— especially if you are working on a government site where there is often legislation regarding this. It's probably not too farfetched either to think that search engines could begin (if they are not already) utilizing this metadata.

Anyway, back to how VS2012. VS2012 contains extensive ARIA IntelliSense support so if you add a div element to a page and start typing ARIA, you will find a list of all the available properties and roles (see Figure 2-45).

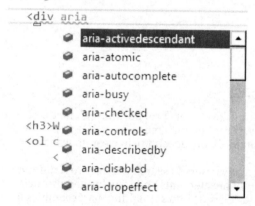

Figure 2-45. VS2012 ARIA IntelliSense support

Devices and applications that don't support WS-ARIA will just ignore these additional properties. So, with VS2012 IntelliSense now supporting WS-ARIA, it's a bit of a no-brainer as to whether to use it or not—do it!

JavaScript Improvements

The JavaScript editor has a number of great improvements:

- Automatic creation of collapsible regions for ease of navigation

- Automatically highlighted matching braces

- New go-to definition support for variables and functions to facilitate code transversal

- IntelliSense support for EcmaScript v5 and many new HTML 5 APIs such as DOM storage, query selector, canvas, and cross document messaging

- Ability to put a breakpoint on a single JavaScript statement, e.g.

```
var x="hello"; alert(x);
```

- Function signatures with auto completion

- Ability to delay the loaded of scripts for debugging purposes

JavaScript Console and DOM Explorer

VS2012 contains a new integrated JavaScript debug console and DOM explorer. These tools are similar to the integrated ones in Internet Explorer. At the time of writing this, only works with Internet Explorer version 10 (which also currently means Windows 8 only!) and only in debug mode.

As the tools can only be used when debugging, we will need to create a test application to play with these features.

1. Create an empty ASP.NET web application and add a new JavaScript file to the project called test.js and enter the following code:

```
var a = "test a";
var b = "test b";
var c = "test c";
```

2. Add an HTML file to the project called default.htm.

3. Drag the JavaScript file onto default.htm to create a reference to it in the HTML file:

```
<script type="text/javascript" src="test.js"></script>
```

4. Put a breakpoint on the second line of the JavaScript file (not strictly necessary but helpful for playing with this feature).

5. Check the selected debug browser is Internet Explorer and press F5 to run up the application.

6. Now bring up the JavaScript console from the Debug ➤ Windows ➤ JavaScript console (Ctrl+AltVC).

7. You should now see a screen similar to one in Figure 2-46 that can be used to run JavaScript and query object properties. In the example that follows, I have performed some simple math and used it to query an object's properties.

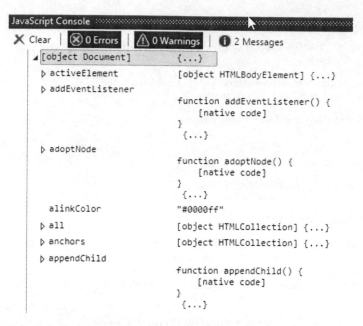

Figure 2-46. *JavaScript console window*

8. Now bring up the DOM explorer (again similar to IE's development tools) to examine the structure and styling of a page. This is again accessed from the Debug ➤ Windows ➤ DOM Explorer, shown in Figure 2-47.

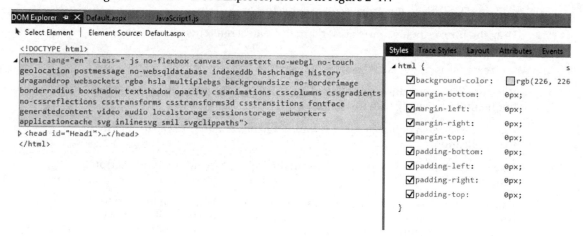

Figure 2-47. *DOM explorer window*

It's a bit of shame these features are only available with IE10 and other browsers arguably have better tools, but the integration into Visual Studio can only be a good thing.

Implicit References and Reference Groups

To obtain Visual Studio IntelliSense support when working inside a JavaScript file, previously you would add a special reference to it with the following syntax:

```
/// <reference path="common.js" />
```

In VS2010 if you dragged a file you wanted to reference into the file you were working on, the reference comment would be created. It would, however, be created where you dropped it. In VS2012, references will always be placed at the top of the page.

VS2012 allows you to create groups of JavaScript files that will always be in scope (and referenced for IntelliSense purposes) with the new reference group feature. Let's open this up now.

Go to Tools ➤ Options ➤ Text Editor ➤ JavaScript ➤ IntelliSense ➤ References, and you will see a dialog box that allows you to add files to be referenced as shown in Figure 2-48.

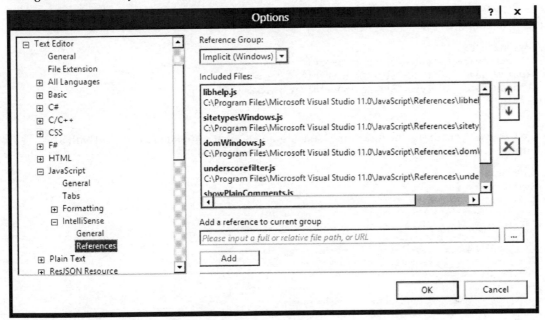

Figure 2-48. IntelliSense for "overloaded JavaScript functions"

VS2012 has three types of reference groups:

- Implicit: files that are in scope for all JS files
- Dedicated: in scope with an explicit reference to a worker reference group
- Worker: allows you to define groups of files to be referenced

Note how you can also configure the order of files and change the type of reference group.

IntelliSense for Overloaded JS Functions

JavaScript doesn't support function overloading in quite the same way as C#, but it is possible to create a function that accepts a different number of parameters. In JavaScript, if you only pass one value into a function (that accepts several), the function will be called but the other parameters set to null. You can then test for this to determine which version of the function is called and assign values accordingly.

VS2012 allows you to add IntelliSense support for "overloaded functions" by marking up functions with a special comment-based syntax. The following example shows how to use this to display two different overload options:

```
function doSomething(x, y, z) {

    /// <signature>
    ///     <summary>Gets the value</summary>
    ///     <param name="x" type="String">Something</param>
    /// </signature>

    /// <signature>
    ///     <summary>Gets the value</summary>
///     <param name="x" type="String">Something</param>
///     <param name="y" type="String">Something</param>
    /// </signature>
}
```

Now when we come to use the function, Visual Studio knows it's intended to be used with a different number of parameters and displays an option (see Figure 2-49).

```
function doSomething(x, y, z) {
    ///<signature>
    /// <summary>Gets the value</summary>
    /// <param name="x" type="String">something</param>
    ///</signature>(///<signature>
    /// <summary>Gets the value again</summary>
    /// <param name="x" type="String">something</param>
    /// <param name="y" type="String">something</param>
    ///</signature>
    ///<signature>
    /// <summary>Gets the value some more</summary>
    /// <param name="x" type="String">something</param>
    /// <param name="y" type="String">something</param>
    /// <param name="z" type="String">something</param>
    ///</signature>

}
```

```
doSomething(|
```

▲ 2 of 3 ▼ doSomething(**String x**, String y)
Gets the value again
x: *something*

Figure 2-49. IntelliSense for overloaded JavaScript functions

Miscellaneous Changes

There have also been a number of other important, miscellaneous improvements you should be aware of.

VSUpdate

VS2012 has a new automatic update option to alert you when new updates are available (different to the extension update notification in VS2010).

Performance Improvements

One of the biggest complaints of Visual Studio users was how long projects took to load ("#4 in our first performance survey to early VS2010 adopters" http://blogs.msdn.com/b/visualstudio/archive/2012/03/12/visual-studio-11-beta-performance-part-2.aspx).
Projects are now loaded in two phases:

1. Modal loading (this contains stuff you will need immediately and blocks the main UI thread)

2. Background loading (stuff you *might* need later on and occurs once modal loading has finished in the background)

If a user requests a project that hasn't been fully loaded yet, Visual Studio will immediately attempt to load it. So the final result of all this optimization is that you should be able to work on your projects right away instead of having to go and buy a cup of coffee while waiting for a large solution to load.
Other optimizations include the following:

- Building a project no longer occurs on UI thread, which means the IDE remains responsive.

- Toolbox components are loaded asynchronously.

- Massive reduction in memory requirements due to 300 less assemblies being loaded and a saving of 400mb of virtual memory due to optimizations made (http://blogs.msdn.com/b/visualstudio/archive/2012/03/05/visual-studio-11-beta-performance-part-1.aspx).

Simplified Remote Debugger Options

The remote debugger has been greatly simplified and avoids the need for any Windows firewall configuration on either debugger or "debugee". It also contains discovery options to enable you to easily connect to machines you may want to debug. For more information, please refer to http://msdn.microsoft.com/en-us/library/y7f5zaaa(v=vs.110).aspx.

Stand-Alone IntelliTrace Collector Utilities

VS2012 introduces new stand-alone utilities that allow you to collect IntelliTrace data from machines that don't have Visual Studio installed. These applications don't actually install anything and can be uninstalled by simply deleting a folder. For more information, please refer to http://msdn.microsoft.com/en-us/library/hh398365(v=vs.110).aspx.

Publish Profile Changes

Previous versions of Visual Studio introduced one-click publishing to easily enable the transfer of files to a remote server. Unfortunately, this feature didn't integrate so well with source control systems/multi users. In VS2012, publish profiles are now stored at the following locations as an MSBuild file:

- C#: Properties\PublishProfiles

- Visual Basic: My Project\PublishProfiles

The new publish profiles can be used from MSBuild with the following syntax:

```
msbuild.exe project.csproj /t:WebPublish /p:PublishProfile=ProfileName
```

Fakes Framework

VS2012 contains a new mocking framework (in more expensive versions that I believe to be Premium and Ultimate at the time of writing) based on work done by Microsoft Research (PEX and Moles) to assist with testing your applications. Many developers will probably wonder why Microsoft felt the need to introduce their own solution when so many good existing open source alternatives exist. According to Microsoft, this was done as the company received continual feedback that customers wanted an out-of-box solution, and some customers didn't want to use open source alternatives due to licensing issues.

The Fakes framework is divided into two main areas:

- Stubs: allow you to supply delegates or lambdas expressions to replace methods—similar in functionality and implementation to existing mocking frameworks such as Moq and NSubstitue (although currently lacking call verification abilities)

- Shims: allow the interception of method calls and even override core framework functionality

Let's take a look at stubs first.

Stubs

Stubs allow you to supply an alternative implementation of a method call via a delegate. They are often used when writing unit tests where methods don't yet exist or depend on a service call. You can even stub out private methods (only if all the types on the method signature are visible).

Let's look at an example now of how we can use a stub to replace an existing method call.

1. First, create a new Visual Studio Console project called TestFakeFramework.

2. Create a new interface called ICustomerRepository and add the following code to it:

```
public interface ICustomerRepository
    {
        Customer GetById(int id);
        bool Exists(string email);
        void Delete();
    }
```

3. Now create a new class called Customer:

```
public class Customer
{
    public string Firstname { get; set; }
    public string Lastname { get; set; }


}
```

4. Create a new class called CustomerService:

```
public class CustomerService
{
    private readonly ICustomerRepository _repository;

    public CustomerService(ICustomerRepository repository)
    {
        _repository = repository;
    }

    public bool DoesCustomerExist(string email)
    {
        return _repository.Exists(email);
    }

}
}
```
Listing x-x. Test classes

5. Now add a new unit test project to the solution called TestFakeFramework.Tests.

6. In the unit test project, add a project reference to TestFakeFramework.

7. Right-click on the project reference and select the Add Fakes Assembly option on the context menu as shown in Figure 2-50.

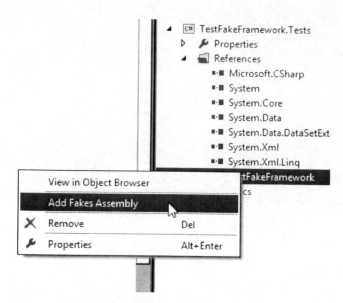

Figure 2-50.Adding Fakes assembly to project

When you select the Add Fakes Assembly option, Visual Studio does a number of things behind the scenes:

- A folder called fakes is created.

- The project's build file is modified.

- Visual Studio scans the target reference creating stubs and shims for all the methods.

- The fakes are added in an assembly created in a sub folder called fakeassemblies.

The Fakes framework will create alternative methods in the format stubxxx and shimxxx. If you want to regenerate the stub or fakes file, you just need to rebuild the solution.

As the generation of these classes can be computationally intensive on a large solution, Microsoft recommends creating a separate project containing the fakes. It is also possible to hide certain types from the fake build process by modifying the .fakes file. Please refer to the following link for more information:

http://msdn.microsoft.com/en-us/library/hh708916(v=vs.110).aspx

OK, back to the example ... let's use a stub for our Customer repository method:

```
using System;
using Microsoft.VisualStudio.TestTools.UnitTesting;
using TestFakeFramework.Fakes;

namespace TestFakeFramework.Tests
{
    [TestClass]
```

```
public class UnitTest1
{
    [TestMethod]
    public void Customer_Should_Not_Exist()
    {

        var stub = new StubICustomerRepository
        {
            ExistsString = (email) => { return true; }
        };

        var service = new CustomerService(stub);

        Assert.IsTrue(service.DoesCustomerExist("test@test.com"));

    }
}
}
```

Note how in our test above we were easily able to supply an alternative implementation of the exists method on the customer repository to always return true—nice!

If you want to test behavior within a stub, then you must use a closure as in the below example:

```
[TestMethod]
    public void Closure_Should_Set_Value_To_Expected()
    {
        //this will get set inside our stub
        string closureToTest="";

        var stub = new StubICustomerRepository
        {

        ExistsString = (email) => {
            closureToTest = "test"; //in reality set to some variable you want to test

            return true;
        }
        };

        var doesntMatter=stub.ExistsString("ignore@ignore.com");

        const string expected="test";
        Assert.IsTrue(closureToTest==expected);

    }
```

It's probably fair to say that this simple example could be arguably more easily developed using existing mocking frameworks such as Moq & NSubstitute that also contain additional functionality. It is nice however to have a mocking implementation out of the box and not to have to reference third party assemblies that may be forbidden in certain environments.

We are not done with the fakes framework, however; it also has an interesting feature called shims.

But what are Shims? Well it's important to note that you cannot stub sealed classes or static methods, as stubs rely on something called virtual method dispatch—in these scenarios, Shims to the rescue!

Shims

Stubs are great, but they can't be used in every scenario. What if, for example, you were working with third-party libraries where you couldn't modify the code to make it easily testable or with static methods? (Note that, generally, with static methods you can create a wrapper.) This type of situation is exactly what shims are for.

Shims can also be used with static methods and also internal methods that are decorated with the InternalsVisibleTo attribute. Under the hood, the framework injects callbacks at runtime into the method's MSIL, which is pretty awesome:

Let's see how shims can enable us to override .NET's DateTime.Now method call.

1. First, right-click on the System Reference and select the Add Fakes Framework option (yes, you can do this on System although it won't work on every type apparently).

2. Create a new test method with the following code:

```
[TestMethod]
public void Should_Override_DateTime_Now()
{
        using (ShimsContext.Create())
        {

        ShimDateTime.NowGet = () => new DateTime(2012, 1, 1, 12, 00, 00);
        Assert.IsTrue(DateTime.Now==new DateTime(2012, 1, 1, 12, 00, 00));
        }

}
```

Wow! We were able to override a system static method—how awesome is that!

Note the using statement around the ShimsContext create call. It's recommended you always use this pattern to ensure any shims you create are disposed. Otherwise, things could get a bit confusing!

Shims also have additional methods to allow you to specify how overridden behavior should be applied, saving some tedious typing. For example, to set all instances the same, use the following syntax:

```
ShimMyClass.AllInstances.MyMethod = () => 5;
```

Before you go ahead and create a shim, you might want to consider whether you would be better off creating a wrapper/anti-corruption layer around the item you want to test rather than creating a shim as this would have additional maintainability benefits.

Dotfuscator PreEmptive Analytics

Visual Studio has always included a cut-down version of an obfuscation tool produced by PreEmptive called Dotfuscator. VS2012 is no different. It contains an updated version that introduces the ability to automatically send exception information to TFS and create work items out of it (see Figure 2-51).

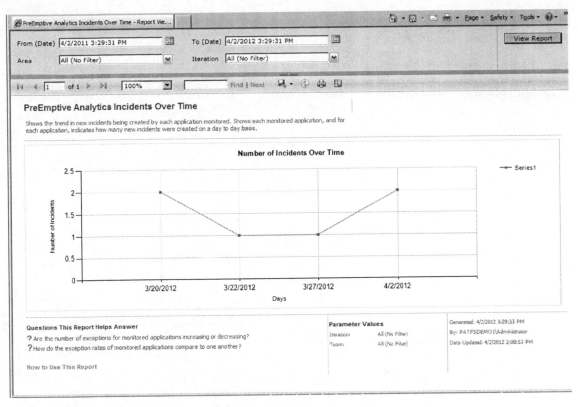

Figure 2-51. Pre-emptive analytics report showing incidents over time

Other Changes

The following changes have also been made that may interest some developers:

- New list designer for SharePoint devs
- Better support for building shaders and a new set of graphics debugging tools for C++ devs (Debug ➤ Graphics)

Conclusion

Visual Studio 2012 contains some fantastic IDE improvements that continue to facilitate development. Highlights include backwards compatibility, the new preview file functionality, re-opening of files when navigating back and forth, and the new Quick Launch box.

CHAPTER 3

■ ■ ■

The BCL and the CLR

Generics, LINQ, the Task Parallel Library (TPL) … these are some of the big-ticket items that have been introduced in previous versions of the .NET Framework. With this release of the framework, it is not so much about game changers or new features but rather about consolidation for the future.

Support for asynchrony has seen the biggest change in the Base Class Library (BCL) with more classes and interfaces, especially in the System.IO namespace, exposing new methods that utilize the TPL to facilitate a more robust asynchronous programming model. Improving performance has also been the focus of the BCL team, especially around the TPL and PLINQ, with a key goal that just by upgrading to .NET 4.5 will, without any other changes, improve code performance.

This chapter is going to be a bit of a mixed bag. In the first section, we will do a quick review of some of the changes that have been made to existing features in the BCL. Next, we will dive into the TPL to look at some of the changes there with a focus on the new dataflow feature. We will look at the portable class library feature, which has come in from the CTP cold to be a full-fledged member of the .NET 4.5 Framework. To finish off the chapter, we will review some of the changes in the Common Language Runtime (CLR).

Changes and Improvements in the BCL

In this section, we are going to review some of the changes and improvements that have been made to the BCL. This won't be a comprehensive review, but it will include a selection of features that we think are of particular interest.

Console Support for UTF-16

It is now possible to use UTF-16 encoding in console applications, but don't be fooled, as I was, into thinking I could now write console apps that display Japanese kanji. There are a number of caveats around implementing this, so if you are interested, my recommendation is to read the section on Unicode support for the console on MSDN (http://msdn.microsoft.com/en-us/library/system.console(v=vs.110).aspx).

Timeout Support for Regular Expressions

It is now possible to define a timeout interval for regular expression matches. This value can be set either via the Regex constructor or, if you are using the static methods, by using one of the matching overloads that has a matchTimeout parameter. If a match cannot be identified within the specified interval, then the matching operation throws a RegexMatchTimeoutException. The following code shows this in action:

```
using System;
using System.Text.RegularExpressions;

namespace TimeoutSupportForRegularExpressions
{
    class Program
    {
        static void Main(string[] args)
        {
            try
            {
                var regEx = new Regex("(a+)+$", RegexOptions.Singleline, TimeSpan.FromSeconds(2));
                var match = regEx.Match("aaaaaaaaaaaaaaaaaaaaaaaaaaaaaaaaaaaaaaaaaaaaa>");
                if (match.Success)
                    Console.WriteLine("Match found");
                else
                    Console.WriteLine("Not matched");
            }
            catch (RegexMatchTimeoutException ex)
            {
                Console.WriteLine("Failed to find a match for {0} after {1} seconds.",
                            ex.Pattern,ex.MatchTimeout.Seconds);
            }
            finally
            {
                Console.Read();
            }
        }
    }
}
```

System.IO.Compression

Within the System.IO.Compression namespace, there are a couple things of interest. The first one is that DeflateStream now uses the zlib library for compression, which provides an improved compression algorithm compared with previous versions. The second item of interest is support for zip archives through the introduction of two new assemblies:

- System.IO.Compression, which contains the classes ZipArchive and ZipArchiveEntry

- System.IO.Compression.FileSystem, which contains the class ZipFile and ZipFileExtensions (This class contains extension methods for the ZipArchive and ZipArchiveEntry classes.)

The ZipFile Class

The ZipFile is a static class that exposes four methods that allow you to create zip files from and extract them to a directory as well as two methods that allow you to open an archive. In the following code example, we will use the CreateFromDirectory() method to create a new zip file and then add another file using the Open() method. Finally, we will extract the zipped files into a new directory using the ExtractToDirectory() method. To run this example, you will need to add a reference to System.IO.Compression and System.IO.Compression.FileSystem as well as to add a using statement for the System.IO.Compression namespace.

```
static void Main(string[] args)
{
  var directoryToArchive = @"c:\temp\Presentations and materials";
  var archiveFileLocation = @"c:\temp\presentations.zip";
  var readMeFile = @"c:\temp\readme.txt";

  if (File.Exists(archiveFileLocation))
    File.Delete(archiveFileLocation);

  Console.WriteLine("starting zip");

  ZipFile.CreateFromDirectory(directoryToArchive, archiveFileLocation);

  Console.WriteLine("Zip completed");
  Console.WriteLine("Add readme file");

  using (var archive = ZipFile.Open(archiveFileLocation,ZipArchiveMode.Update))
  {
    archive.CreateEntryFromFile(readMeFile, "ReadMe.txt");
  }

  Console.WriteLine("Start Extraction");

  if (Directory.Exists(@"c:\temp\presentations"))
    Directory.Delete(@"c:\temp\presentations", true);

  ZipFile.ExtractToDirectory(archiveFileLocation, @"c:\temp\presentations");
  Console.WriteLine("Extraction completed");
  Console.Read();
}
```

As you can see, the ZipFile class provides a simple and succinct way for creating and extracting zip files.

▩ **Caution** It is worth noting at this point that the System.IO.Compression.FileSystem is not available in the .NET Framework subset provided for developing Windows 8-style applications. This is due to the fact that underneath the covers, it uses FileStream, which is not included in the framework subset. The ZipArchive class can be used in Windows 8 apps and an example is given in the next section.

The ZipArchive Class

If you want more control over your archiving process, then the ZipArchive class is what you are looking for. To use it, create an instance of the ZipArchive class and then for each file you wish to archive, create an instance of ZipArchiveEntry and add it to the ZipArchive instance.

For example, let's say that we just wanted to archive all of the PowerPoint slides in our source directory. The code would look something like this:

```
var filesToArchive = Directory.EnumerateFiles(directoryToArchive, "*.ppt*",
SearchOption.AllDirectories);

using (var fs = new FileStream(archiveFileLocation, FileMode.Create, FileAccess.ReadWrite))
{
  using (var archive = new ZipArchive(fs, ZipArchiveMode.Create))
  {
    foreach (var filename in filesToArchive)
    {
      //The following is for working explicitly with file streams.
      var archiveEntry = archive.CreateEntry(Path.GetFileName(filename));
      using (var filestream = new FileStream(filename,FileMode.Open,FileAccess.Read))
      {
        using (var archiveStream = archiveEntry.Open())
        {
          filestream.CopyTo(archiveStream);
        }
      }

      //Note: The following line of code does the same thing.
      //archive.CreateEntryFromFile(filename, Path.GetFileName(filename));
    }
  }
}
```

Not only can you create an archive file, but you can also update an existing one by changing the ZipArchiveMode value to Update in the ZipArchive constructor. Building on the previous example, if you wanted to add all the images associated with the presentations to the archive file, you could do the following:

```
var imagesToArchive = Directory.EnumerateFiles(directoryToArchive, "*.*",
SearchOption.AllDirectories)
                                .Where(fn => fn.EndsWith(".jpg", true, null) ||
fn.EndsWith(".png", true, null));

using (var fs = new FileStream(archiveLocation, FileMode.Open, FileAccess.ReadWrite))
{
  using (var archive = new ZipArchive(fs, ZipArchiveMode.Update))
  {
    foreach (var filename in imagesToArchive)
    {
      archive.CreateEntryFromFile(filename, Path.Combine(archiveSubDirectory,
Path.GetFileName(filename)));
    }
  }
```

```
}
```

It is worth noting that unlike `ZipFile.CreateFromDirectory()`, adding individual files does not automatically preserve the file's path in relation to the root directory. Therefore, if you want to preserve a file's relative path, you will need to add some code to extract or, as in the above example, append a folder name that suits your archiving requirements.

■ **Caution** Since `ZipArchive` uses streams, you need to ensure that when using file streams, the file mode and file access correspond to the action you are performing with the zip archive. For instance, if you created a new `FileStream` object with file mode set to `Create` and a new instance of `ZipArchive` with zip archive mode set to `Update`, your code would fail because updating an archive requires read, write, and seek capabilities.

You are not limited to archiving files in the file system. Zip archives can also be created on the fly. If, for example, you wanted to add a read me file to the archive, you can do the following:

```
using (var fs = new FileStream(archiveFileLocation, FileMode.Open, FileAccess.ReadWrite))
{
  using (var updateArchive = new ZipArchive(fs, ZipArchiveMode.Update))
  {
    var readmeEntry = updateArchive.CreateEntry("Readme.txt");
    using (var writer = new StreamWriter(readmeEntry.Open()))
    {
      writer.WriteLine("This zip file contains presentations and resources");
      writer.WriteLine("from 2011.");
    }
  }
}
```

Finally, the `ZipArchive` allows you to open an existing archive to query the individual zip archive entries and extract files:

```
using (var fs = File.OpenRead(archiveFileLocation))
{
  using (var archive = new ZipArchive(fs, ZipArchiveMode.Read))
  {
    foreach (var zipArchiveEntry in archive.Entries)
    {
      decimal originalSize = (decimal)zipArchiveEntry.Length;
      decimal compressedSize = (decimal)zipArchiveEntry.CompressedLength;
      decimal compressionRatio;
      if (originalSize == 0)
        compressionRatio = 0;
      else
        compressionRatio = Math.Round((1 - (compressedSize / originalSize)) * 100, 0);

      Console.WriteLine("Entry Name: {0}", zipArchiveEntry.Name);
      Console.WriteLine("Full Name: {0}", zipArchiveEntry.FullName);
      Console.WriteLine("Compression Ratio: {0}%", compressionRatio);
```

```
            Console.WriteLine();
        }

        archive.Entries.Where(zae => zae.Name.EndsWith(".pptx", true, null))
            .ToList()
            .ForEach(zae => zae.ExtractToFile(Path.Combine(@"d:\temp", zae.FullName), true));
    }
}
```

The ZipArchive class can be also be used in Windows 8 applications. The following example showing how to archive files should give you a good starting point for adding this functionality to your Windows 8 app:

```
private async Task ZipUpFiles(IProgress<Tuple<string, double>> progress)
{
    var files = await SelectFiletsoZip();
    var totalFiles = files.Count;

    var zipFile = await GetZipFile();

    using (var zipFileStream = await zipFile.OpenStreamForWriteAsync())
    {
        using (var zipArchive = new ZipArchive(zipFileStream, ZipArchiveMode.Create))
        {
            var counter = 0;
            foreach (StorageFile fileToCompress in files)
            {
                var entry = zipArchive.CreateEntry(fileToCompress.Name);
                using (var entryStream = entry.Open())
                {
                    using (var fileStream = await fileToCompress.OpenStreamForReadAsync())
                    {
                        await fileStream.CopyToAsync(entryStream);
                    }
                }
                counter++;
                double percentageDone = Math.Round(((double)counter / (double)totalFiles) * 100, 2);
                progress.Report(new Tuple<string, double>(fileToCompress.Name, percentageDone));
            }
        }
    }
}

private static async Task<IReadOnlyList<StorageFile>> SelectFiletsoZip()
{
    var openPicker = new FileOpenPicker();
    openPicker.CommitButtonText = "Archive";
    openPicker.ViewMode = PickerViewMode.List;
    openPicker.SuggestedStartLocation = PickerLocationId.ComputerFolder;
    openPicker.FileTypeFilter.Add("*");
```

```
   var files = await openPicker.PickMultipleFilesAsync();
   return files;
}
private async Task<StorageFile> GetZipFile()
{
   var fileSaver = new FileSavePicker();
   fileSaver.SuggestedStartLocation = PickerLocationId.ComputerFolder;
   fileSaver.FileTypeChoices.Add("Zip Files", new List<string> { ".zip" });
   return await fileSaver.PickSaveFileAsync();
}
```

So, whether you just use the static methods in the ZipFile or go for more fine-grained control with ZipArchive, though not earth-shattering, these classes are a nice addition to the BCL.

WeakReference<T>

A weak reference provides the means to reference an object while still allowing it to be reclaimed by garbage collection. This is particularly useful for managing large objects that can be easily regenerated. Prior to .NET 4.5, in order to use a weak reference you would code something like this:

```
public class AClassWithNoPurpose
{
  private WeakReference wr = new WeakReference(new StringBuilder("A weakly referenced string
builder"));

  public StringBuilder AStringBuilder
  {
     get
        {
            StringBuilder tempStringBuilder;
            if (wr.IsAlive)
            {
        tempStringBuilder = wr.Target as StringBuilder;
            }
            else
            {
                tempStringBuilder = new StringBuilder("String builder reserected");
        wr = new WeakReference(tempStringBuilder);
            }
            return tempStringBuilder;
        }
    }
}
```

The thing to notice about the previous code is that the WeakReference constructor only takes a type of Object, which means you need to cast the target to the expected type before you can use it.

With .NET 4.5, we can now define the type exposed by the weak reference by using WeakReference<T>. Let's modify the previous example to use this:

```
public class AClassWithNoPurpose
{
    private WeakReference<StringBuilder> wr = new WeakReference<StringBuilder>(
        new StringBuilder("A weakly referenced string builder"));
```

```
      public StringBuilder AStringBuilder
    {
      get
      {
          StringBuilder tempStringBuilder;
           if (!wr.TryGetTarget(out tempStringBuilder))
           {
               tempStringBuilder = new StringBuilder("String builder resurrected ");
               wr = new WeakReference<StringBuilder>(tempStringBuilder);
           }
           return tempStringBuilder;
        }
      }
    }
```

Aside from the fact that we now have a strongly typed weak reference, the key thing to note is that WeakReference<T> no longer exposes an IsAlive or Target properties. Instead you now use the TryGetTarget() method, which takes an uninitialized parameter of type T and returns true or false depending on whether the weak reference still holds a valid instance of T. This small change negates the potential where the target gets garbage collected after the IsAlive property is queried but before the Target is accessed. (As an aside, the recommended practice, when using WeakReference, is to just cast the target to the expected type and test for null.)

Changes in Streams

As mentioned above, improving the asynchronous story for developers has been a key driver in many of the changes made to .NET 4.5. To this end, four new methods (excluding overrides) have been added to base Stream class that takes advantage of the Task Parallel Library. These methods include the following:

- CopyToAsync()

- FlushAsync()

- ReadAsync()

- WriteAsync()

All of these methods return an instance of Task and can be called with the await keyword. So, for example, with FileStream you can now do the following:

```
private async static Task<string> GetFileAsync(string fileName)
{
  var unicodeEncoding = new UnicodeEncoding();
  byte[] result;

  using (var stream = new FileStream(fileName, FileMode.Open))
  {
    result = new Byte[stream.Length];
    var readTask = await stream.ReadAsync(result, 0, (int)stream.Length);
  }
  return unicodeEncoding.GetString(result);
}
```

Defining a Culture for an Application Domain

In previous versions of .NET, the culture of all threads was, by default, set to the Windows system culture. Using Thread.CurrentThread.CurrentCulture and Thread.CurrentThread.CurrentUICulture, you could change or set the culture on a thread, but any worker threads or tasks that you spun up would default to the current operating system's culture. Therefore, if you ran the following code, the output in Figure 3-1 would be the result:

```
class Program
{
  static void Main(string[] args)
  {
    Console.OutputEncoding = Encoding.UTF8;

    var culture = CultureInfo.CreateSpecificCulture("ja-JP");
    Thread.CurrentThread.CurrentCulture = culture;
    Thread.CurrentThread.CurrentUICulture = culture;

    Action randomCurrency = () =>
    {
      Console.WriteLine();
      Console.WriteLine("Current Culture:\t{0}",
        Thread.CurrentThread.CurrentCulture);
      Console.WriteLine("Current UI Culture:\t{0}",
        Thread.CurrentThread.CurrentUICulture);

      Console.Write("Random currency: ");
      var rand = new Random();

      for (int i = 0; i <= 2; i++)
        Console.Write("\t{0:C2}\t", rand.NextDouble());

      Console.WriteLine();
    };
    //Call the randomCurrency action on the current thread
    randomCurrency();

    //now run the same action on another thread
    Task.Run(randomCurrency);

    Console.Read();
  }
}
```

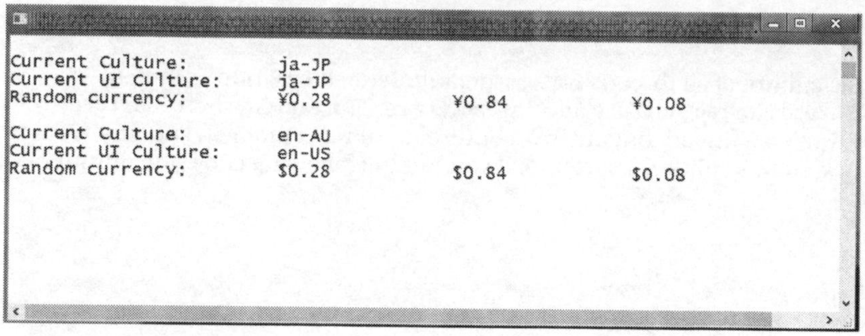

Figure 3-1. Output for current thread culture output

This behavior can be very frustrating. With .NET 4.5, though, the CultureInfo class now exposes two properties—DefaultThreadCurrentCulture and DefaultThreadCurrentUICulture—that allow you to define a culture to be applied to all threads within the app domain.

To do this, replace the lines:

```
Thread.CurrentThread.CurrentCulture = culture;
Thread.CurrentThread.CurrentUICulture = culture;
```

with:

```
CultureInfo.DefaultThreadCurrentCulture = culture;
CultureInfo.DefaultThreadCurrentUICulture = culture;
```

Running the code again, you would get the output as shown in Figure 3-2.

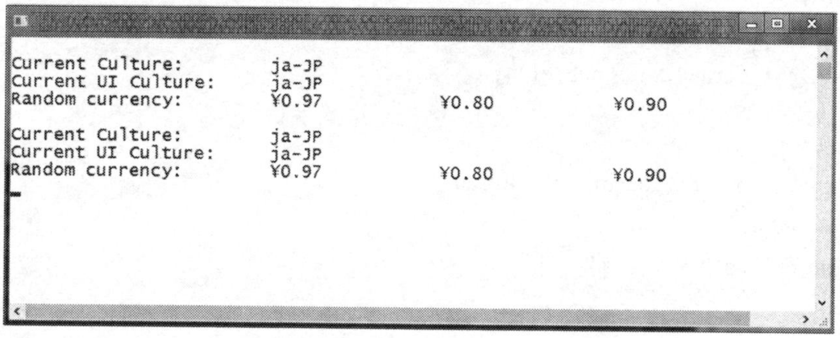

Figure 3-2. Output after setting a default culture

New Features in the Task Parallel Library

With the Task Parallel Library (TPL) becoming the primary player in parallelism, concurrency, and asynchrony, a lot of work has gone into this area to improve performance and functionality. In terms of performance, the BCL team asserts that just by updating to .NET 4.5 without making any other changes to your existing code, there is an immediate performance improvement.

With all of the improvements and additions to the TPL as well as the improved tooling in Visual Studio 11 to facilitate development of parallelized applications, there is no shortage of stuff to write about and explore. To keep things simple, we are going to limit the scope of this section to just a few of the new features. First, we will cover the new methods and functionality that are now part of the Task class as well as the new Progress<T> class. Next, we will look at the new TPL Dataflow (TDF) and, finally, we will finish with the new ConcurrentExclusiveScheduler.

New Task Methods

As part of the further development of the TPL, with .NET 4.5 the Task class exposes some new static methods. These methods are:

- Run()
- Delay()
- WhenAny()
- WhenAll()
- FromResult()
- Yield()
- ConfigureAwait()

All of these, except for ConfigureAwait(), return an instance of Task and can be used with the await keyword.

In the next few sections, we will have a quick look at each of these methods to give you a feel for how they work with the intention of giving you a starting point from which to explore these methods further.

Task.Run()

In .NET 4, a common way to create and start a new Task was to call Task.Factory.StartNew(). Now with 4.5, especially if you want to quickly schedule a task, there is also Task.Run(). In essence, this is equivalent to Task.Factory.StartNew(someAction, CancellationToken.None, TaskCreationOptions.DenyChildAttach, TaskScheduler.Default).

At its simplest, Run() can be called by passing in an Action:

```
var firstTask = Task.Run(() =>
  {
    Thread.Sleep(1500);
    Console.WriteLine("the first task has completed.");
  });
```

If you want to define a return type, you can use Run<TResult>() which takes a Func<TResult> as a parameter.

```
var secondTask = Task.Run<string>(() =>
  {
    Thread.Sleep(1000);
    return "The second task has completed.";
  });

secondTask.ContinueWith(task => Console.WriteLine(task.Result));
```

It is possible to call Run() without specifying a return type and still return a value. Therefore, the following code is also valid since it interprets the parameter we are passing in as being of the type Func<Task>:

```
var thirdTask = Task.Run(() =>
  {
    Thread.Sleep(1000);
    return "The third task has completed.";
  });
```

```
thirdTask.ContinueWith(task => Console.WriteLine(task.Result));
```

One of the features of Run() is that it will automatically unwrap an inner task. So, what does this mean? Let's say we were doing the following with the Task.Factory.StartNew() method:

```
var outerTask = Task.Factory.StartNew(async () =>
  {
    Thread.Sleep(1000);
    return await Task.Factory.StartNew(() =>"A result from an inner task");
  });
```

Though the result we want is the value being returned by the inner task, what we actually get, if we inspect the Result property of the outer task, is a type of Task<Task<TResult>>. To retrieve the inner task and ensure we handle any exceptions and cancellation requests, as well as the result we are expecting, we apply the extension method UnWrap() to the call:

```
var outerTask = Task.Factory.StartNew(async () =>
  {
    Thread.Sleep(1000);
    return await Task.Factory.StartNew(() =>"A result from an inner task");
  }).Unwrap();
```

With Run() this isn't necessary since it will automatically unwrap the inner task.

```
var outerTask = Task.Run( () =>
  {
    Thread.Sleep(1000);
    return Task.Run(() => "A result from the inner task.");
  });
outerTask.ContinueWith(t => Console.WriteLine(t.Result));
//Finally Run() provides overloads which allow you to pass in a CancellationToken.
var cancellationTokenSource = new CancellationTokenSource();

Task.Run(() => Thread.Sleep(5000), cancellationTokenSource.Token)
  .ContinueWith(task =>
    {
      if (task.IsCanceled)
        Console.WriteLine("The fourth task was cancelled.");
      else
        Console.WriteLine("The forth task has completed.");
    });

Console.WriteLine("Just hanging around, waiting");
cancellationTokenSource.Cancel();
```

```
Console.Read();
```

Task.Delay()

Delay() is a static method that can be called from the Task type. It has four overloads, which are as follows:

- Task.Delay(int millisecondsDelay)

- Task.Delay(int millisecondsDelay, CancellationToken cancellationToken)

- Task.Delay(TimeSpan delay)

- Task.Delay(TimeSpan delay, CancellationToken cancellationToken)

This method is analogous to Thread.Sleep(), but instead of blocking the thread, when coupled with the await keyword it releases the thread and then calls back into the method once the delay period has expired. To use it, you can code it as follows:

```
Task.Run( async () =>
  {
    var stopwatch = new Stopwatch();
    stopwatch.Start();
    await Task.Delay(3000);
    stopwatch.Stop();
    Console.WriteLine("Task  completed after {0} seconds", stopwatch.Elapsed.Seconds);
  });
```

Task.WhenAny()

The Task.WhenAny() method allows you to wait, asynchronously, on a set of Tasks for one of them to complete. An obvious case where this can be useful is when you want to query a number of services but only care about the first one to return completed:

```
class Program
{
  static void Main(string[] args)
  {
    ProcessSimpleTasks();
    Console.WriteLine("Waiting...");
    Console.Read();
  }

  private static async void ProcessSimpleTasks()
  {
    var tasks = new List<Task<string>>();

    tasks.Add(SimpleTask("Task 1", 2000));
    tasks.Add(SimpleTask("Task 2", 2000));
    var firstTaskBack  = await Task.WhenAny<string>(tasks);

    Console.WriteLine(t.Result);
```

```
    }

    private static async Task<string> SimpleTask(string identitifer, int millisecondsDelay)
    {
      await Task.Delay(millisecondsDelay);
      return string.Format("{0} has completed", identitifer);
    }
```

Another more interesting use of the WhenAny() method is in the case where you have a number of actions that you want to run, but rather than wait for all of them to complete, you want to process each one as it is completed:

```
class Program
{
  static void Main(string[] args)
  {
    ProcessSimpleTasks();

    Console.WriteLine("Waiting...");
    Console.Read();
  }

  private static async void ProcessSimpleTasks()
  {
    var tasks = new List<Task<string>>();

    tasks.Add(SimpleTask("Task 1", 2000));
    tasks.Add(SimpleTask("Task 2", 3000));
    tasks.Add(SimpleTask("Task 3", 4000));
    tasks.Add(SimpleTask("Task 4", 2000));

    while (tasks.Count > 0)
    {
      Task<string> task = await Task.WhenAny<string>(tasks);

      tasks.Remove(task);
      Console.WriteLine(task.Result);
    }
  }
  private static async Task<string> SimpleTask(string identitifer, int millisecondsDelay)
  {
    await Task.Delay(millisecondsDelay);
    return string.Format("{0} has completed", identitifer);
  }
}
```

It would be easy to underestimate the usefulness of this method. Stephen Toub, in his paper "The Task-based Asynchrous Pattern" (www.microsoft.com/download/en/details.aspx?id=19957), covers a few other scenarios where WhenAny() can be applied.

Task.WhenAll()

Task.WhenAll() allows you to wait on a set of tasks until all of them have completed. This differs from the WaitAll() method in that it creates a Task that will complete once all of the tasks within the set have completed. If the tasks in the set return a result, then WhenAll() will return a task of Task<TResult[]>. The following code example demonstrates this case:

```
class Program
{
  static void Main(string[] args)
  {
    var taskNames = new string[] { "Task 1", "Task 2", "Task 3", "Task 4" };
    ProcessSimpleTasks(taskNames);

    Console.WriteLine("Waiting...");
    Console.Read();
}

  private static async void ProcessSimpleTasks(IEnumerable<string> taskIdentifiers)
  {
    var randomSecond = new Random();
    IEnumerable<Task<string>> tasks = taskIdentifiers.Select(s => SimpleTask(s,
randomSecond.Next(1,5)));

    try
    {
      var completedTask = await Task.WhenAll<string>(tasks);
      Console.WriteLine("Tasks completed:");
      foreach (var taskName in completedTask)
      {
        Console.WriteLine("\t{0}", taskName);
      }
    }
    catch (AggregateException ex)
    {
      foreach (var exception in aggregateException.InnerExceptions)
      {
        Console.WriteLine(exception.Message);
      }
    }
  }

  private static async Task<string> SimpleTask(string identitifer, int secondsDelay)
  {
    await Task.Delay(TimeSpan.FromSeconds(secondsDelay));
    if (identitifer.Contains("5"))
    {
      throw new Exception("Task 5 throw an exception");
    }
    Console.WriteLine("{0} has completed", identitifer);
    return identitifer;
  }
```

```
}
```

If you run this code, you will notice that results returned are in the order that the tasks were added to the set and not in the order that the individual tasks completed.

If any of the tasks in the set complete in a faulted or canceled state, then the returned task will also complete in a faulted or canceled state. To see this, modify the first line in the Main() method of the previous code as follows:

```
var taskNames = new string[] { "Task 1", "Task 2", "Task 3", "Task 4", "Task 5" };
```

Task.FromResult<TResult>()

The FromResult() method allows you to create a finished Task object whose Result property is provided from a pre-existing value. This is particularly useful in cases where the value has already been pre-computed and/or is cached. Let's take an unrealistic example to see how this works:

```
class Program
{
  static void Main(string[] args)
  {
    var bookTitleToFind = "Ten Things I Forgot to Remember";
    Stopwatch stopwatch = new Stopwatch();

    Console.WriteLine("Looking for a book...");
    stopwatch.Start();

    BookStore.FindBookAsync(bookTitleToFind)
      .ContinueWith(t =>
      {
        stopwatch.Stop();
        Console.WriteLine("time taken to find \"{0}\": {1}", t.Result.Title,
stopwatch.Elapsed);
      })
      .Wait();
    stopwatch.Restart();

    //Try again. This time it should be much quicker
    BookStore.FindBookAsync(bookTitleToFind)
      .ContinueWith(t =>
      {
        stopwatch.Stop();
        Console.WriteLine("time taken to find \"{0}\": {1}", t.Result.Title,
stopwatch.Elapsed);
      })
      .Wait();

    Console.Read();
  }
}

public class Book
{
```

```
  public string Title { get; set; }
}

class BookStore
{
  static ConcurrentDictionary<string, Book> booksOnTheShelves =
       new ConcurrentDictionary<string, Book>();

  public static Task<Book> FindBookAsync(string bookTitle)
  {
    // First try to retrieve the content from cache.
    Book requestedBook;
    if (booksOnTheShelves.TryGetValue(bookTitle, out requestedBook))
    {
      return Task.FromResult<Book>(requestedBook);
    }

    return Task.Run<Book>(() =>
        {
          var newBook = Task.Run<Book>(async () =>
              {
                await Task.Delay(TimeSpan.FromSeconds(3));
                return new Book { Title = bookTitle };
              });
          booksOnTheShelves.TryAdd(bookTitle, newBook.Result);
          return newBook;
        });
  }
}
```

Task.Yield()

When you use the async/await keywords, you are telling the compiler to compile the method with a state machine so that the method can suspend and then resume at await points. By doing this, the TPL allows for single threaded aysnc. In cases where we have singled threaded aysnc, Task.Yield() provides you with the means to temporarily exit the current async method to permit other actions to be done on the current context. It is analogous to Application.DoEvents() though differs in that DoEvents() generates a new message loop and Yield() yields to the existing one. A common usage would be where a large amount of data is being processed in a foreach loop that could potentially block the UI thread for an unacceptable amount of time.

If you do a search on the web, you will more than likely stumble across this canonical example (or an approximation thereof):

```
private async void GetStuffButton_Click(object sender, RoutedEventArgs e)
{
  int counter = 0;
  for (int i = 0; i < 10000; i++)
  {
    var result = Process(i);
    ListOfThings.Items.Add(result);
    if ((++counter % 10) == 0) await Task.Yield();
```

```
  }
}
private  string Process(int i)
{
  Thread.Sleep(10);
  return string.Format("Thing {0}", i);
}
```

Regretfully, this doesn't actually work as you would expect. The UI is completely unresponsive for the duration of the for loop. This is because Task.Yield() targets the current SynchronizationContext's Post() method. In WPF, this is an instance of DispatcherSynchronizationContext, which implements Post() to use DispatcherPriority.Normal, a higher priority than the GUI events. The solution is to use the new method on the Dispatcher, InvokeAsync(), passing in the appropriate DispatchPriority. Therefore, the following example would provide the expected behavior (also the code has been modified to output the thread id to show that everything is running on the same thread):

```
private void GetStuffButton_Click(object sender, RoutedEventArgs e)
{
  Dispatcher.InvokeAsync(async () =>
  {
    for (int i = 0; i < 10000; i++)
    {
      Debug.WriteLine("Dispatcher Thread: {0}",
Dispatcher.CurrentDispatcher.Thread.ManagedThreadId);
      var result =  Process(i);
      ListOfThings.Items.Add(result);

    await Task.Yield();
    }
  }, DispatcherPriority.Background);
}

private string Process(int i)
{
  Debug.WriteLine("Process() Thread: {0}",Thread.CurrentThread.ManagedThreadId);
  Thread.Sleep(10);
  return string.Format("Thing {0}", i);
}
```

Task.ConfigureAwait()

By default, when an async method is suspended, the current context is captured and used to invoke the method's continuation upon resumption. There are cases where this isn't important and performance can be improved by not posting back to the original context. To achieve this, the ConfigureAwait() method can be used to prevent an await operation from capturing and resuming on the context.

```
await theTask.ConfigureAwait(continueOnCapturedContext:false);
```

By passing false as the parameter to this method, the awaited operation will continue execution wherever it completed.

The Progress<T> Class

This class implements the interface IProgress<T> and provides a means for asynchronous methods to report back a progress update. It exposes a ProgressChanged event that is raised on the SynchonizationContext, which is captured when the class is instantiated or, if none is available, a default context on the ThreadPool. It has a default constructor and one overload that takes an Action<T> as a handler. Updates are handled asynchronously so do not block the asynchronous operation. The following example uses an instance of Progress to report back on reading files from a directory:

```
class Program
{
  static void Main(string[] args)
  {
    var directoryToReadFrom = @"c:\temp";
    Console.WriteLine("Start");
    var progress = new Progress<Tuple<string, decimal>>();
    progress.ProgressChanged += Progress_ProgressChanged;
    var result = GetFilesAsync(directoryToReadFrom,progress);

    result.ContinueWith(t =>
      {
        Console.WriteLine("Done!");
        progress.ProgressChanged -= Progress_ProgressChanged;
      });
    Console.ReadKey();
  }

  private async static Task GetFilesAsync(string startDirectory, IProgress<Tuple<string,
decimal>> progress)
  {
    var files = Directory.GetFiles(startDirectory, "*.*", SearchOption.AllDirectories);
    var tasks = new List<Task<string>>();

    var counter = 0;
    foreach (var fileName in files)
    {
      var fileNameOnly = Path.GetFileName(fileName);
      await GetFileAsync(fileName);
      counter++;
      decimal percentageDone = Math.Round(((decimal)counter / (decimal)files.Length) * 100,
2);

      progress.Report(new Tuple<string, decimal>(fileNameOnly, percentageDone));
    }
  }

  private async static Task<string> GetFileAsync(string fileName)
  {
    var unicodeEncoding = new UnicodeEncoding();
    byte[] result;
    //Delay for demo purposes only
    await Task.Delay(50);
    using (var stream = new FileStream(fileName, FileMode.Open))
```

```
  {
    result = new Byte[stream.Length];
    var readTask = await stream.ReadAsync(result, O, (int)stream.Length);
  }
  return unicodeEncoding.GetString(result);
}

static void Progress_ProgressChanged(object sender, Tuple<string, decimal> e)
{
  Console.Clear();
  Console.WriteLine("percentage done: {0}%", e.Item2);
  Console.WriteLine(e.Item1);
}
}
```

TPL DataFlow

TPL Dataflow (TDF) is a new .NET library that provides a set of primitives for in-process message passing, dataflow, and pipelining. Building on the TPL, the goal of the TDF is to provide higher-level constructs that address parallel problems that are better framed in terms of agent-based or message-passing models.

Though originally included in the beta version of the .NET 4.5 Framework, this library is now being delivered in the NuGet package Microsoft.Tpl.Dataflow. The simplest way to install it is to open the Package Manager Console and at the prompt type the following:

```
Install-Package Microsoft.Tpl.Dataflow
```

The TDF library defines a set of data structures known as dataflow blocks (approximately 11 at the time of writing) that are designed to buffer and/or process data. There are essentially three kinds of blocks:

- Target blocks, which act as a data receiver and can be written to

- Source blocks, which act as a source of data and can be read from

- Propagator blocks, which can be both a source and target block and can be both read from and written to

In simple terms, what a block does is wait to receive a message and when it does, it spins up a Task to process that message. If a block has a number of messages queued, then it reuses the Task to process all of the messages until the queue is empty.

To give you a feel for TDF and what this library offers, we will look at some simple examples. All of the following examples just use a console application. If you want to try the code out, you will first need to install the NuGet package and then add a reference to the assembly System.Threading.Tasks.Dataflow.

Using an ActionBlock

The first block we will look at is the ActionBlock. This is a target block that can receive and queue messages that are then processed. The code is as follows:

```
static void Main(string[] args)
{
  var names = new string[] { "alice", "bob", "chris", "david", "elizabeth", "francis", "gary",
"harry", "ian" };

  SimpleActionBlockExample(names);

}

private static void SimpleActionBlockExample(IEnumerable<string> names)
{
  var actionBlock = new ActionBlock<string>(async s =>
    {
      await Task.Delay(500);
      Console.WriteLine(s.ToUpper());
    });

  foreach (var name in names)
  {
    actionBlock.Post(name);
  }

  Console.WriteLine("Data queued: {0}", actionBlock.InputCount);

  //meaningless loop so we can check the queue count
  while (actionBlock.InputCount > 0) { }

  Console.WriteLine("Data queued: {0}", actionBlock.InputCount);
 Console.Read();

}
```

In this example, we instantiate an instance of ActionBlock<T> where T is the type of the message that it will receive and pass it a delegate that will handle the message. Messages are then sent to the ActionBlock by calling the Post() method on the instance. If you run the code, the output should look something like Figure 3-3.

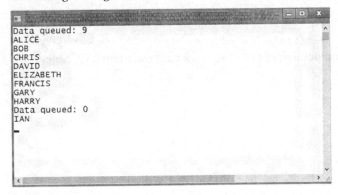

Figure 3-3. Output from simple ActionBlock example

Once all the messages have been processed, the action block simply waits until a new message is posted. So, for example, if we added the following lines of code just before the `Console.Read()` statement in the `SimpleActionBlockExample()` method, this message will also be processed:

```
Thread.Sleep(1000);
actionBlock.Post("Zac");
```

If you want to stop a block from processing any more messages, you can call its `Complete()` method, which in effect switches it off:

```
actionBlock.Complete();
actionBlock.Post("This message will never be processed");
```

By default, a block spins up only one Task and processes the messages one at a time. You can change this behavior by passing in an instance of `ExecutionDataflowBlockOptions` and setting its `MaxDegreeOfParallelism` property to define the maximum number of tasks it can run to process messages.

```
private static void SimpleActionBlockExampleWithIncreasedParallelism(IEnumerable<string>
names)
{
  var dataflowBlockOptions = new ExecutionDataflowBlockOptions
  {
    TaskScheduler = TaskScheduler.Default,
    MaxDegreeOfParallelism = 4
  };

  var actionBlock = new ActionBlock<string>(async s =>
    {
      await Task.Delay(1000);
      Console.WriteLine(s.ToUpper());
    }, dataflowBlockOptions);

  foreach (var name in names)
  {
    actionBlock.Post(name);
  }

  Console.WriteLine("Waiting...");
  Console.Read();
}
```

In this example, we have set the maximum number of tasks the block can spin up to four, which would result in the output shown in Figure 3-4.

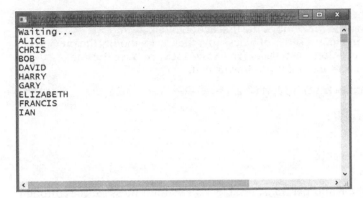

Figure 3-4. Output of action block using multiple tasks

Using a TransformBlock

Though the ActionBlock is interesting in itself, let's extend the previous examples and introduce the TransformBlock. The TransformBlock is an example of a propagator block that takes a message and processes it; the output of that process can then be relayed to another block. In the next example, we will introduce a transform block that will handle the conversion of the string to uppercase and then pass the resulting string to the action block:

```
private static void TransformAndActionBlock(IEnumerable<string> names)
{
  var actionBlock = new ActionBlock<string>(async s =>
    {
      await Task.Delay(500);
      Console.WriteLine(s);
    });

  var toUpperTransformBlock = new TransformBlock<string, string>(s =>
    {
      return s.ToUpper(); ;
    });

  toUpperTransformBlock.LinkTo(actionBlock);

  foreach (var name in names)
  {
    toUpperTransformBlock.Post(name);
  }

  Console.WriteLine("Waiting...");
  Console.Read();
}
```

In this example, along with the ActionBlock, we also create an instance of TransformBlock<TInput,TOutput>, which takes a parameter of Func<TInput, TOutput>. Once we have created the transform block, we specify the target block by passing it in as parameter of the LinkTo() method. If you run this code, the output will be the same as the first action block example.

By using the LinkTo() method, you can chain a series of blocks together. Let's modify the previous example to include another transform block. After the toUpperTransformBlock, remove the line toUpperTransformBlock.LinkTo(actionBlock); and add the following code:

```
var reverseStringBlock = new TransformBlock<string, string>(s =>
  {
    return new string(s.Reverse().ToArray());
  });

toUpperTransformBlock.LinkTo(reverseStringBlock);
reverseStringBlock.LinkTo(actionBlock);
```

With this additional code, we have added another transform block so that our message goes through two processes before being displayed on the screen. Again not a mind-blowing example, but it should give you a feel of how it is possible to build up a process flow using blocks.

Using a BufferBlock

The last example we are going to look at is the BufferBlock. This block is useful in scenarios where you have multiple processes running and want to queue messages through a central point so that each message is retrieved when a process is free:

```
private static void BufferBlockExample(IEnumerable<string> names)
{
  var ActionBlock1 = new ActionBlock<string>(s =>
    {
      Thread.Sleep(1000);
      Console.WriteLine("{0} from action block 1", s);
    }, new ExecutionDataflowBlockOptions { BoundedCapacity = 1 });

  var ActionBlock2 = new ActionBlock<string>(async s =>
    {
      await Task.Delay(800);
      Console.WriteLine("{0} from action block 2", s);
    }, new ExecutionDataflowBlockOptions { BoundedCapacity = 1 });

  var ActionBlock3 = new ActionBlock<string>(async s =>
    {
      await Task.Delay(500);
      Console.WriteLine("{0} from action block 3", s);
    }, new ExecutionDataflowBlockOptions { BoundedCapacity = 1 });

  var bufferblock = new BufferBlock<string>();
  bufferblock.LinkTo(ActionBlock1);
  bufferblock.LinkTo(ActionBlock2);
  bufferblock.LinkTo(ActionBlock3);

  foreach (var name in names)
  {
    bufferblock.Post(name);
```

```
  }

  Console.WriteLine("waiting...");
  Console.Read();
}
```

What we are doing in this example is first creating three action blocks that can accept one message at a time. We then create an instance of BufferBlock and link it to the three action blocks. As each action block completes processing, it retrieves another message from the buffer block. If you run the code, the output would be similar to Figure 3-5.

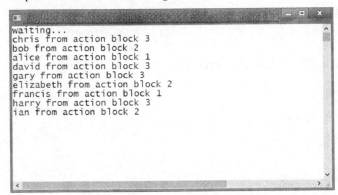

Figure 3-5. Output from BufferBlock example

In this section, we have really only dipped our toes into the TPL Dataflow water, but hopefully it has given you a sense of what it has to offer and inspires you to explore this new feature further.

The ConcurrentExclusiveSchedulerPair

The ConcurrentExclusiveSchedulerPair, in essence, provides the means to implement the equivalent of an asynchronous read/write lock. It provides two TaskScheduler instances through the properties ConcurrentScheduler and ExclusiveScheduler. Tasks assigned to the concurrent scheduler will run as long as there are no tasks assigned to the exclusive scheduler. Once a task has been assigned to the exclusive scheduler, no more concurrent tasks will be allowed to run until that task is completed. This functionality is useful when you have mutable data that can be shared among many tasks, but you also want to run tasks that can update that data.

In the following contrived example, we have two action blocks, one that can read a value and is assigned to the concurrent scheduler and another that can update the value and is assigned to the exclusive scheduler. If you run the example, anytime you post a message to the update action the concurrent scheduler will stop processing messages until the update is completed.

```
class Program
{
  static volatile int valueToChange;
  static void Main(string[] args)
  {
    var schedulerPair = new ConcurrentExclusiveSchedulerPair();
    var cts = new CancellationTokenSource();
```

```
    var readExecutionOptions = new ExecutionDataflowBlockOptions
    {
      TaskScheduler = schedulerPair.ConcurrentScheduler,
      CancellationToken = cts.Token,
      MaxDegreeOfParallelism = 3
    };

    var lockExecutionOptions = new ExecutionDataflowBlockOptions
    {
      TaskScheduler = schedulerPair.ExclusiveScheduler,
      CancellationToken = cts.Token
    };

    var readAction = new ActionBlock<string>(s => Console.WriteLine("{0}-{1}", s,
  valueToChange),
                      readExecutionOptions);

    var updateAction = new ActionBlock<int>(i =>
          {
            Console.WriteLine("Updating the value");
            Thread.Sleep(2000);
            valueToChange += i;
            Console.WriteLine("value has been changed");
          }, lockExecutionOptions);

    Console.WriteLine("Press any key to send an update message.\nPress Enter to end
  processing");

    Task.Run(() => SendMessagesToReadActionBlock(readAction, "Reader1", 50), cts.Token);

    var hasPressedEnterKey = false;

    while (!hasPressedEnterKey)
    {
      var keyPressed = Console.ReadKey();
      if (keyPressed.Key == ConsoleKey.Enter)
      {
        cts.Cancel();
        hasPressedEnterKey = true;
      }
      else
        updateAction.Post(3);
    }

    Console.WriteLine("Test finished. Press any key to quit");
    Console.ReadKey();
  }

private static async void SendMessagesToReadActionBlock(ITargetBlock<string> actionBlock,

string message, int counter)
```

```
  {
    for (int i = 0; i < counter; i++)
    {
      actionBlock.Post(string.Format("{0}:{1}", message,
Thread.CurrentThread.ManagedThreadId));
      await Task.Delay(500);
    }
  }
}
```

Portable Class Library

The Portal Class Library, originally development by the BCL team as an add-in, has now been integrated into the .NET 4.5/Visual Studio 2012 release. The underlying idea behind this feature is to provide the means to write managed assemblies that can be used on multiple .NET Framework platforms without the use of #defines or complicated build scripts to target the individual platforms. In essence, what the team has done is to provide a new project template that targets a subset of .NET assemblies that are valid for the platforms you are targeting. Under the covers, the team has modified the runtime so that the appropriate assemblies are referenced depending on the target platform.

To create a portable class assembly in a solution, open the Add New Project dialog box and select the Portable Class Library project, as shown in Figure 3-6.

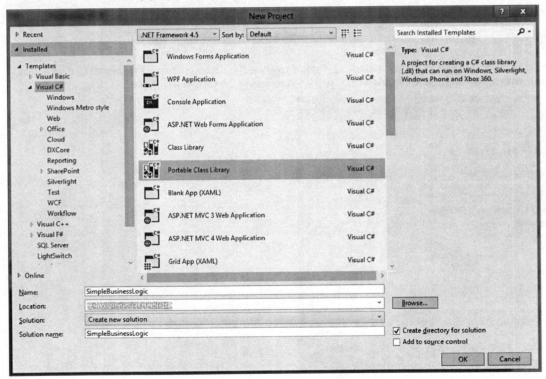

Figure 3-6. Add New Project dialog box

Once the project has been added, right-click on it and select Properties from the context menu. In the Target Frameworks section of the first page will be listed the default frameworks your new class can be used with, as shown in Figure 3-7.

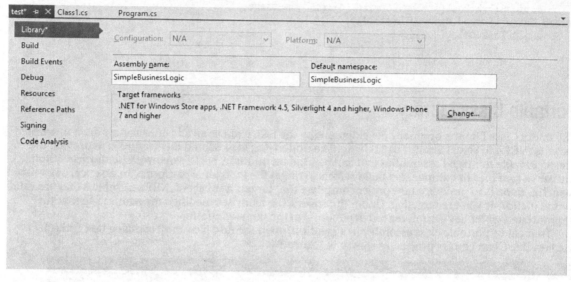

Figure 3-7. Project properties page with targeted frameworks listed

Clicking on the button labeled "Change..." will bring up the Change Target Frameworks dialog box. Here you can refine/change the frameworks you wish to target, as shown in Figure 3-8.

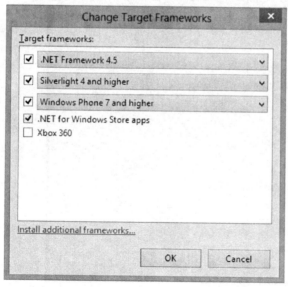

Figure 3-8. The Change Target Frameworks dialog box

Once you have set your target frameworks you are ready to go, but there are a couple of things you need to be aware of.

First, the subset of assemblies and functionality that can be accessed is determined by the frameworks that you target. For example, given the selection displayed in Figure 3-8, if you opened the solution in the Object Browser, you would see the list of available assemblies as shown in Figure 3-9.

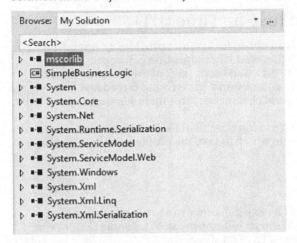

Figure 3-9. Available assemblies before adding Xbox 360

If you now modify your target frameworks to include Xbox 360, in the Object Browser you will see a reduced set of available assemblies as shown in Figure 3-10.

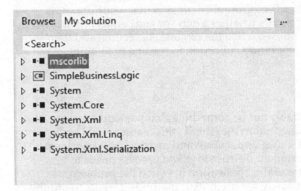

Figure 3-10. Available assemblies after adding Xbox 360 as a target

An aspect that is worth noting in this case is if you add a reference to an assembly that is not supported by one of your target platforms, the project will be retargeted to exclude that platform.

Another thing to keep in mind is that if you want to reference any other classes you have created, they will also need to be Portal Class Library projects.

And Then There Is the CLR Core

Unlike the BCL, there have been fewer changes in the CLR and these have mainly focused on internal improvements with a focus on performance.

ProfileOptimization and Multicore Just-in-Time (JIT)

Enabled by default in Silverlight 5 and ASP.NET, this is an opt-in feature that provides an optimized JIT that can use unused processing time to perform multi-threaded JIT compilation of frequently used methods. Multicore JIT works by first generating profile data that keeps track of the methods executed and then uses this data to determine which methods to compile on a background thread and on a multicore machine, on another core. By doing this in parallel, it means most methods are JIT compiled by the time they are needed.

To use this feature in your application, after adding a using statement for System.Runtime, you need to add only two lines of code—one to specify the folder in which to save the profile and another to start the process:

```
ProfileOptimization.SetProfileRoot(@"c:\profiles");
ProfileOptimization.StartProfile("profile");
```

The first time you run your application there won't be any difference in startup time since the profile needs to be generated, but after that, you should see an improvement. If, for some reason, your application is running a singe core machine, this code will have no affect.

Background Garbage Collection (GC) for the Server

Background GC, which was a feature that was introduced in CLR 4.0 for the workstation, is now supported on Server Garbage Collection. Basically what Background GC does is that while the GC is performing a full gen2 collection, it checks at specific points whether a gen0 or gen1 collection has been requested. If there is a request, the gen2 collection is paused while the request is executed and then resumes. This allows the code that initiated the low-generation collection to resume execution.

Re-JIT

On a day-to-day level, the new re-JIT feature will probably not be something that pops up on your radar, but if you are into writing profilers or injecting instrumentation into the IL, this feature could be for you. Currently, if you are running a profiler over, say, an ASP.Net application and an issue arises and you want to add additional instrumentation to track the problem down, the whole process needs to be restarted. The issue with doing this is you lose the state of the application in which the problem was occurring. What re-jitting allows is for the profiler to specify the method or methods it wants to modify and recompile at the IL level. The next time they are called they will be re-jitted and pushed back into the app domain without affecting the rest of the application.

If you are interested in this feature, David Broman from Microsoft has written a couple of blog posts on how to use it and some of its current limitations at http://blogs.msdn.com/b/davbr/. There is also a Channel 9 interview where he goes into depth on Re-JIT and this can be found at http://channel9.msdn.com/Shows/Going+Deep/CLR-45-David-Broman-Inside-Re-JIT.

Optimized Native Images

One of the options that has existed to improve application startup was to precompile code to a native image using the Native Image Generation (NGen) tool. Especially with large desktop applications, this provided a significant improvement in startup times compared with JIT compilation. With .NET 4.5, an additional tool has been added called Managed Profile Guided Optimization (MPGO), which is designed to optimize the layout of native images to further improve performance. Using optimization technology similar to that used for multi-core JIT, the MPGO tool creates profile data for an IL DLL and then adds the profile as a resource to the IL DLL. The NGEN tool can then use this data to perform additional optimization.

Large Object Heap (LOH)

In .NET 4.5, work has been done to make more efficient use of memory fragments in the LOH, in particular with how the free list is managed. With these changes being implemented in both workstation and server garbage collection, the lack of application responsiveness and out-of-memory exceptions that can occur with memory fragmentation in the LOH should be addressed.

Conclusion

Clearly the big story in this release is parallelization and asynchrony and the changes made within the BCL in this area that will echo through the rest of the .NET Framework. In this chapter, we have tried to cover some of the key features, but there is still much more both within the TPL and the rest of the BCL that will be worth getting your hands on. But that is not the only story in this release. Under the covers, core assemblies have been rethought and refactored to provide a solid base for future development and improved code portability. And, finally, there has been general performance tuning, such as improved resource loading, to ensure your applications run better.

CHAPTER 4

MEF 2 in 4.5

The first version of the Managed Extensibility Framework (MEF) was released as part of .NET 4 and with .NET 4.5 we see the release of MEF 2.0. The MEF team has added a number of new features that will be the focus of this chapter. These features include, but are not limited to, improved lifetime management, convention-based parts registration and, via NuGet, a new lightweight composition engine for web and Windows 8 apps.

In this chapter, we are going focus on providing an overview of each of the key new features in MEF with some simple examples of how they can be implemented. Before we discuss the new features, we will provide a quick recap of what MEF is.

What Is MEF?

The concept of extensibility is not new. At some point, you have probably rolled your own, but a custom solution becomes limited especially if you want to open your application to third parties to provide extensions. What MEF offers is a standardized way to provide application extensibility that is readily available by being part of the .NET Framework.

With MEF 1, the focus was solely on extensibility and there was clear delineation between it and IOC containers. On the other hand MEF 2, with the introduction of the `RegistrationBuilder`, support for open generics, and more granular lifetime management, the distinction has become less clear. The focus is still on extensibility, but in version 2 basic IOC is now also possible.

To provide this extensibility, MEF uses attributes to declare what a class consumes and what it offers. For example, in the following code snippet, the class `ProjectView` is decorated with the `Export` attribute that identifies it as a dependency. The `SomeViews` class imports `ProjectView`, and this is done simply by decorating the appropriate property with the `Import` attribute:

```
[Export]
public class ProjectView : UserControl
{
}

[Export]
public class SomeViews
{
    [Import]
    public ProjectView AProjectView{get; set;}
}
```

To pull all of this together, we write some bootstrapping code for MEF, commonly in the application's entry point, to kick off the composition:

```
public partial class App : Application
{
  [Import]
  public SomeViews ViewsWeNeed {get; set;}
  public App()
  {
      this.Startup += new StartupEventHandler(App_Startup);
  }

  void App_Startup(object sender, StartupEventArgs e)
  {
    var catalog = new DirectoryCatalog(@".\");
    var container = new CompositionContainer(catalog);
    container.ComposeParts(this);
  }
}
```

Though a simple example, what we have done with MEF is create an object graph based on declarative information rather than using imperative code to do the assembly.

SOME KEY TERMINOLOGY

MEF, like most technologies, has its own terminology:

- Composition Container: This is the core of MEF. The composition container contains all of the parts that are available and matches up imports and exports. The most commonly used container is the CompositionContainer.

- Catalog: A catalog is used by a container to discover what parts are available. MEF has a number of catalog types and each provides a different means for discovering export parts.

- Part: A part is any class that is defined as being available for export or specifies dependencies (imports).

Note that you are not limited to exporting classes. The Export attribute can also be applied to properties and methods.

What Is New in .NET 4.5

A number of new features have been added to MEF in .NET 4.5 that include the following:

- Support for open generic parts
- Convention-based part registration
- Composition scoping enhancements
- Diagnostic improvements

Many of these changes have been in response to user feedback and have been aimed at increasing the flexibility of MEF and addressing use cases that weren't covered by the first version.

From here on in, we are going to look at these features. To keep things simple, we have chosen to use a console project for the sample code to avoid distraction by any unnecessary coding. For all of the examples that follow you will need, at a minimum, to add a reference to `System.ComponentModel.Composition`.

In addition, please remember any code here is sample code and more than likely will not adhere to best practice.

Support for Open Generic Parts

With the first version of MEF, you could only export closed generic types. For example, take the following interface:

```
public interface IRepository<T> where T : class
{
    T FindById( int id);
    void Save (T item);
}
```

And then add the following classes:

```
[Export]
public class ProjectsWindow :Window
{
    [ImportingConstructor]
    Public ProjectsWindow (IRepository<Project> projects)
    {
        // use projects;
    }
}

[Export]
public class ClientsWindow :Window
{
    [ImportingConstructor]
    public ProjectsWindow (IRepository<Client> clients)
    {
        // use clients;
    }
}
```

With this interface, you would need to create a specific implementation for the project and client repositories as well as any others that were needed.

With MEF in .NET 4.5, you can negate the need for individual concrete implementations by defining an open generic class type that implements the IRepository interface:

```
[Export(typeof(IRepository<>))]
public class EntityFrameworkRepository<T> : IRepository<T> where T :class
{
    // implement generic repository
}
```

What this means is that for any property or constructer where you have defined an Import that uses IRepository, MEF will instantiate an instance of a closed generic type of EntityFrameworkRepository for the specified class.

Using Open Generic Types

Let's look at an example of a repository factory that exposes two repositories whose actual concrete implementations are resolved at runtime using MEF:

1. Create a new Console project.

2. Add references for the required MEF assemblies.

3. Add a new interface to the project and name it IData. Then add the following code:

```
public interface IData<T>
{
int Id { get; set; }
void Update(T source);
}
```

4. Add another interface name IRepository and update it as follows:

```
public interface IRepository<T>
{
T FindById(int id);
void Save(T item);
}
```

5. Now add two classes, one called Client and the other Project. Both of these implement IData<T> and should look something like this:

```
public class Client : IData<Client>
{
  public int Id { get; set; }
  public string CompanyName { get; set; }
  public string ContactName { get; set; }


  public void Update(Client source)
  {
    CompanyName = source.CompanyName;
    ContactName = source.ContactName;
  }
}

public class Project : IData<Project>
{
  public int Id { get; set; }
  public string ProjectName { get; set; }


  public void Update(Project source)
```

```
  {
    ProjectName = source.ProjectName;
  }
}
```

6. Next, add a class called FakeRepository. This will be an open generic type class that implements the interface IRepository. For this class, you will need to add a using statement referencing System.ComponentModel.Composition. Notice that this class is decorated with Export attribute that specifies IRepository as its contract:

```
[Export(typeof(IRepository<>))]
public class FakeRepository<T> : IRepository<T> where T : class, IData<T>
{
  IList<T> items;
  public int Count { get { return items.Count; } }
  public T FindById(int id)
  {
    return items.FirstOrDefault(i => i.Id == id);
  }

public void Save(T item)
{
  var existingItem = FindById(item.Id);
  if (existingItem == null)
  {
    items.Add(item);
  }
  else
  {
    existingItem.Update(item);
  }

}

  public FakeRepository()
  {
    items = new List<T>();
  }
}
```

7. Add one more class called RepositoriesFactory. This class will expose your Client and Project repositories and in this instance handle the bootstrapping of MEF:

```
public class RepositoriesFactory
{
  [Import(typeof(IRepository<>))]
  public IRepository<Client> Clients { get; set; }

  [Import(typeof(IRepository<>))]
  public IRepository<Project> Projects { get; set; }
```

```
    public RepositoriesFactory()
    {
      var assemblyCatalog = new        AssemblyCatalog(Assembly.GetExecutingAssembly());
      var container = new CompositionContainer(assemblyCatalog);
      container.ComposeParts(this);
    }
}
```

In the RepositoriesFactory class, we have decorated the Clients and Projects properties with the Import attribute specifying the contract we expect for each. Then in the class's constructor, the code to get MEF to resolve the imports has been added.

■ **Note** This would normally be done at a higher level in the application.

---

8. Finally, add some code to see this working. Open the Program.cs file and add the following code:

```
static void Main(string[] args)
{
  var repositories = new RepositoriesFactory();
  Console.WriteLine(GetTypeName(repositories.Clients.GetType()));
  Console.WriteLine(GetTypeName(repositories.Projects.GetType()));
  Console.ReadKey();
}

private static string GetTypeName(Type type)
{
  return string.Format("{0}<{1}>", type.Name.Replace("'1",""),
      type.GetGenericArguments()[0]);
}
```

9. Press F5 and you should see something similar to Figure 4-1.

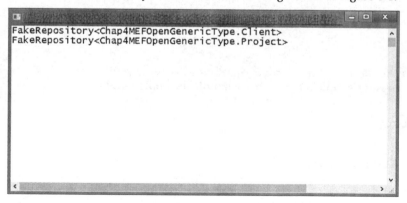

```
FakeRepository<Chap4MEFOpenGenericType.Client>
FakeRepository<Chap4MEFOpenGenericType.Project>
```

Figure 4-1. Closed generic types from open type definition

As you can see, even though you only defined IRepository<T> for the Clients and Projects properties, MEF has instantiated them as closed types of FakeRepository.

Let's extend this example to actually return some data.

1. Add a new class with the name DummyData, add a using statement for System.ComponentModel.Composition, and code it as follows:

```
public class DummyData
{
  [Export]
  public IList<Client> FakeClientData
  {
    get {return GetFakeClientData();}
  }

  [Export]
  public IList<Project> FakeProjectData
  {
    get { return GetFakeProjectData();}
  }

private IList<Client> GetFakeClientData()
  {
    return new List<Client> {
      new Client { Id = 1,
        CompanyName = "The Factory",
        ContactName = "Andy Warhol"} };
}

 private IList<Project> GetFakeProjectData()
  {
    return new List<Project>{
      new Project{Id = 1,
        ProjectName="Campbell Soup Cans"}};
 }
}
```

2. Next, modify the FakeRepository class to include a new constructor that will allow you to pass in a list of items. This constructor is decorated with the ImportingConstructor attribute, which declares to the container what the part needs when instantiating it:

```
[ImportingConstructor]
public FakeRepository(IList<T> preLoadedItems)
{
  if (preLoadedItems != null)
  {
    items = preLoadedItems;
  }
  else
  {
    items = new List<T>();
  }
```

87

```
}
```

3.   Reopen Program.cs and modify it with the following:

```
static void Main(string[] args)
{
  var repositories = new RepositoriesFactory();
  var client = repositories.Clients.FindById(1);
  Console.WriteLine("Company Name:{0}", client.CompanyName);
  var project = repositories.Projects.FindById(1);
  Console.WriteLine("Project Name: {0}", project.ProjectName);
  Console.ReadKey();
}
```

4.   Press F5 to see the output, which should be similar to Figure 4-2.

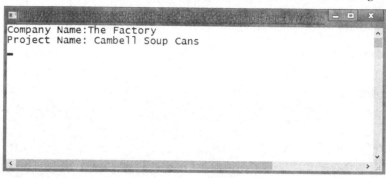

Figure 4-2. Example with data

Convention-based Part Registration

In MEF 1.0, the only way to identify an export part was for it to be decorated with the Export attribute. With MEF 2.0, an alternative way of identifying export parts has been provided with the addition of the RegistrationBuilder. What the RegistrationBuilder provides is the means to define a set of rules for Identifying export parts without them having to be explicitly defined. Where this is particularly useful is in a scenario where MEF is used to compose the internal structure of an application rather than manage external dependencies. In this case, it is easier to define a convention for how parts should be written and to communicate that to the team rather than having to specify every detail of every part.

■ **Note** To use the RegistrationBuilder in your project, you will need to also include references to System.ComponentModel.Composition.Registration and System.Reflection.Context.

Creating Rules

To create a rule, you first need to define how to identify a part by using one of the three For*() methods. These three methods return a PartBuilder and are as follows:

- **ForType<T>()**: This selects a single type of T.

- **ForTypesDerivedFrom<T>()**: This will select any type derived from a contract type T, which may be a base class or interface.

- **ForTypesMatching(Predicate<Type> predicate)**: This method gives you the ability to define a Boolean selector to select types. For example, this can be used to select types based on a naming convention.

So, for example, within your company all view models are inherited from the base class ViewModelBase. Rather than having every view model decorated with the Export attribute, you can do the following in the MEF bootstrap code:

```
var registrationBuilder = new RegistrationBuilder();
registrationBuilder.ForTypesDerivedFrom<ViewModelBase>().Export<ViewModelBase>();
var catalog = new AssemblyCatalog(Assembly.GetExecutingAssembly(),registrationBuilder);
```

Or as an alternative, if within your company the convention is that all view model class names must end with ViewModel, you could do the following:

```
registrationBuilder.ForTypesMatching(x => x.Name.EndsWith("ViewModel") && x.IsPublic)
.Export<ViewModelBase>();
```

And, finally, if it is a specific type and you just want to make sure that it is exported:

```
registrationBuilder.ForType<Logger>().Export();
```

Once you have defined a part or parts, you can then configure all aspects of a MEF part such as export interface, importing constructors, part creation policy, and part metadata. Say, for example, you wanted to set the creation policy for the view models. You could do the following:

```
registrationBuilder.ForTypesDerivedFrom<ViewModel>()
                    .SetCreationPolicy(CreationPolicy.NotShared)
                    .Export<ViewModelBase>();
```

With imports being defined at either the constructor or property level, the RegistrationBuilder provides the means for managing a selection of the appropriate constructor and properties for a given class. Let's look at four examples.

- By default, RegistrationBuilder will select the public constructor with the largest number of parameters. In this example, we are instead specifying that for any type of IRepository, RegistrationBuilder should use the constructor with the least number of parameters:

```
registrationBuilder.ForTypesDerivedFrom(typeof(IRepository))
  .SelectConstructor(ctrs =>
    {
      var minParameters = ctrs.Min(ctr => ctr.GetParameters().Length);
      return ctrs.First(ctr => ctr.GetParameters().Length == minParameters);
    });
```

- Given a case where we know what the concrete type is, the constructor can be selected using a strongly typed syntax:

```
registrationBuilder.ForType<Logger>()
    .SelectConstructor(pb => new Logger(pb.Import<IConnection>()));
```

- In this example, again we know the explicit type we are using so we use ImportProperty() to explicitly identify the property we want to apply the import to:

```
registrationBuilder.ForType<FakeFactory>()
    .ImportProperty(ff => ff.Tiles);
```

- Finally, in this example, we use ImportProperties() to declare that for all public properties on the class we want MEF to manage the import:

```
registrationBuilder.ForType<FakeFactory>()
.ImportProperties(pi => pi.PropertyType.IsPublic);
```

Convention + Attributes

Choosing to use a convention-based programming model with MEF doesn't automatically rule out the use of attributes. Instead, they become the means by which you can override registration conventions. This really comes in handy when you want to handle exceptions to a rule. Rather than creating overly verbose rules to handle all exceptions to the rule or having to create numerous single component rules, attributes can be applied to specific parts, methods, or properties to modify how a rule is applied. In other words, as Nick Blumhardt says, any "MEF attribute applied to a part will override any rules that affect the same aspect of the same member."

If you are interested in learning more about the interaction of rules with attributes in MEF, I recommend you read Nick Blumhardt's post on the topic, which can be found at http://blogs.msdn.com/b/bclteam/archive/2011/11/03/overriding-part-registration-conventions-with-the-mef-attributes-nick.aspx.

The End View

Personally, I like the explicit nature of attributes and believe it should be your first choice if you are developing an application that is going to be extended by third parties. On the other hand, if MEF is being used to manage internal development or you have an aversion to attributes, the RegistrationBuilder is a very powerful addition to the MEF armory.

Composition Scoping Enhancements

In MEF 1.0, there were only two types of lifetime that could be applied to an object:

- A shared global lifetime

- A per instance lifetime

Taking the conservative path, MEF by default assumes all parts to be shared unless the creation policy on a part was set to NonShared. Though functional, the application of the creation policy was limited in the scenarios it could address in terms of managing the lifetime of objects. To give finer-grained control of object lifetimes, MEF 2.0 now includes the ExportFactory (originally part of the Silverlight 4 SDK) and the CompositionScopeDefinition.

ExportFactory<T>

Simply put, the export factory allows us to more finely control the lifetime of dependencies by creating an ExportLifetimeContext<T>, which implements IDisposable.

The best way to see how this works is to code it up. So, let's take the canonical example of a request listener that has a dependency on a request handler.

Before Implementing the Export Factory

1.   First, create a new Console project, add a reference to System.ComponentModel.Composition, and then create the following classes:

     •   FakeDatabaseConnection

     •   HandlerNameCreator

     •   RequestHandler

     •   RequestListener

2.   Open FakeDatabaseConnection.cs and add the following code. This class represents a database connection that will be shared by all of the request handlers:

```
[Export]
[PartCreationPolicy(CreationPolicy.Shared)]
public class FakeDatabaseConnection
{
  private readonly DateTime dateTimeCreated;
  public FakeDatabaseConnection()
  {
    dateTimeCreated = DateTime.Now;
  }

  public string DatabaseName
  {
    get
    {
      return string.Format("Database {0}",
        dateTimeCreated.Millisecond);
    }
  }
}
```

3.   Next, open the HandlerNameCreator.cs file and add the following code. This class allows you to assign a unique name to each instance of a request handler:

```
[Export]
public class HandlerNameCreator
{
  int counter = 0;
  string prefix = "Handler";

  public string GetAHandlerName()
  {
   counter += 1;
   return string.Format("{0} {1}", prefix, counter);
  }
}
```

4. Next, open RequestHandler.cs. This class is used by the request listener to process requests. It has a dependency on FakeDatabaseConnection and HandlerNameCreator:

```
[Export]
[PartCreationPolicy(CreationPolicy.NonShared)]
public class RequestHandler
{
  FakeDatabaseConnection dbConnection;
  public string HandlerName { get; private set; }

 [ImportingConstructor]
 public RequestHandler(FakeDatabaseConnection dbConnection,
   HandlerNameCreator nameCreator)
 {
   HandlerName = nameCreator.GetAHandlerName();
   this.dbConnection = dbConnection;
 }

 public string GetDatabaseName()
 {
   return this.dbConnection.DatabaseName;
 }
}
```

5. Now open the file RequestListener.cs and add the following code. This class exposes a single method that is called to handle a request and for this exercise will write out the names of the handler and the database:

```
[Export]
[PartCreationPolicy(CreationPolicy.NonShared)]
 public class RequestListener
{
   private readonly RequestHandler handler;
   [ImportingConstructor]
   public RequestListener(RequestHandler handler)
   {
     this.handler = handler;
   }
```

```
  public void HandleRequest()
  {
      Console.WriteLine("{0}: {1}", handler.HandlerName,
      handler.GetDatabaseName());
  }
}
```

6. Finally, to glue this all together, open Program.cs and add the following code:

```
class Program
{
  public CompositionContainer Container { get; set; }
  static void Main(string[] args)
  {
      var p = new Program();
      var listener = p.Container.GetExportedValue<RequestListener>();
      for (int i = 0; i < 3; i++)
      {
        listener.HandleRequest();
        Console.WriteLine();
        Thread.Sleep(1000);
      }

      Console.ReadKey();
  }

  public Program()
  {
      var global = new TypeCatalog(
      typeof(RequestHandler),
      typeof(FakeDatabaseConnection),
      typeof(HandlerNameCreator),
      typeof(RequestListener));

      Container = new CompositionContainer(global);
  }
}
```

In this code, we use the Program constructor to create a new CompositionContainer using a TypeCatalog. In the Main() method, we use the container to get an instance of RequestListener and then call the method HandleRequest() three times.

By pressing F5, you should see something similar to Figure 4-3.

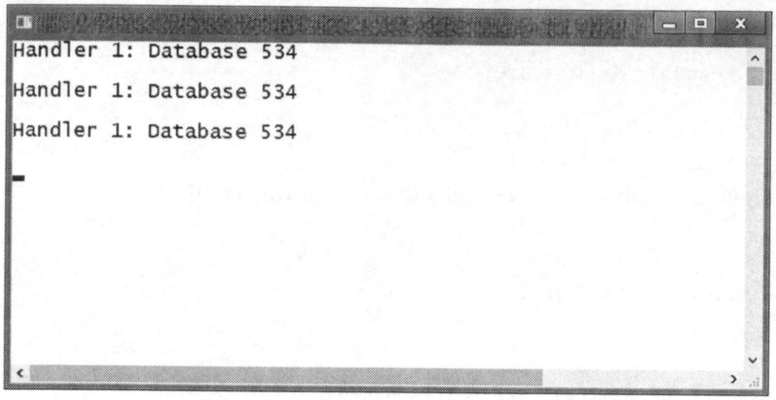

Figure 4-3. *Result pre-ExportFactory*

The thing to note here is that even though we set the creation policy on the RequestHandler to NonShared, the RequestListener used only one instance of it. So, what if you wanted to use a single instance of the RequestListener but with multiple instances of the RequestHandler? This is where ExportFactory<T> comes into play.

Implementing Export Factory

1. First, open RequestHandler.cs and remove the PartCreationPolicy attribute.

2. Next, open RequestListener.cs and modify the code so that it looks like the following:

```
[Export]
public class RequestListener
{
    private readonly ExportFactory<RequestHandler> factory;
    [ImportingConstructor]
    public RequestListener(ExportFactory<RequestHandler> factory)
    {
      this.factory = factory;
    }

    public void HandleRequest()
    {
      using (var instance = factory.CreateExport())
      {
        var handler = instance.Value;
        Console.WriteLine("{0}: {1}", handler.HandlerName,
    handler.GetDatabaseName());
      }
    }
}
```

Now if you run the program, what you should see is that a unique instance of RequestHandler has been created for each call to HandleRequest(). (See Figure 4-4.)

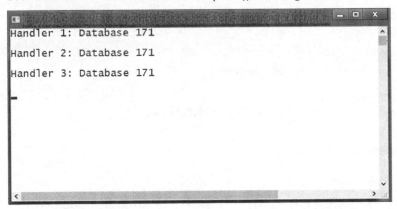

Figure 4-4. Unique handler instances

As you can see, it doesn't take much to implement the export factory to extend part lifetime management.

Using CompositionScopeDefinition

Along with the ExportFactory class, with this version of MEF we also see the introduction of another class called CompositionScopeDefinition, which provides even more fine-grained control over the lifetime of parts by grouping them into parent–child relationships.

In the previous example, each request handler shared the same database connection object, but what if we had a slightly more complex scenario? Here's the scenario breakdown:

- The request handler now accesses the database connection via a data access layer.

- The request handler now also includes a logger.

- The logger has a direct dependency on the database connection object.

- For each call to the request handler, you want a new database connection that will be shared by both the logger and the data access layer.

Essentially, what we want to do in this scenario is have the instantiation and lifetimes of the logger, data access layer, and database connection "scoped" within the lifetime of the request handler.

Before CompositionScopeDefinition

Let's try this without CompositionScopeDefinition to demonstrate the problem we are trying to solve:

1. First, open up the project from the previous exercise if it isn't open already and add two new classes: DataAccessLayer and Logger.

2. Open DataAccessLayer.cs and add the following code:

```
[Export]
public class DataAccessLayer
{
  private string dabId;
  FakeDatabaseConnection dbConnection;

  [ImportingConstructor]
  public DataAccessLayer(FakeDatabaseConnection dbConnection)
  {
    this.dbConnection = dbConnection;
    dabId = string.Format("Data Access Layer {0}", DateTime.Now.Millisecond);
  }

  public string DataAccessLayerInfo(string handlerName)
  {
    return string.Format("{0} using {1}",
                              dabId,
                              dbConnection.DatabaseName);
  }
 }
```

3. Next, open Logger.cs and add the following:

```
[Export]
public class Logger
{
  FakeDatabaseConnection dbConnection;
  private string loggerId;

  [ImportingConstructor]
  public Logger(FakeDatabaseConnection dbConnection)
  {
    this.dbConnection = dbConnection;
    loggerId = string.Format("Logger {0}",DateTime.Now.Millisecond);
  }

  public string LoggerInfo(string handlerName)
  {
    return string.Format("{0} using {1}",
                              loggerId,
                              dbConnection.DatabaseName);
  }
}
```

4. Next, modify the RequestHandler by opening the file and making the following changes:

```
[Export]
public class RequestHandler
{
  private DataAccessLayer dataAccessLayer;
  private Logger logger;
  public string HandlerName { get; private set; }
```

```
[ImportingConstructor]
public RequestHandler(DataAccessLayer dataAccessLayer,
    Logger logger, HandlerNameCreator nameCreator)
{
  HandlerName = nameCreator.GetAHandlerName();
  this.dataAccessLayer = dataAccessLayer;
  this.logger = logger;
}

public string GetRequestHandlerInfo()
{
  var sb = new StringBuilder();
  sb.AppendLine(HandlerName);
  sb.AppendLine(dataAccessLayer.DataAccessLayerInfo(HandlerName));
  sb.AppendLine(logger.LoggerInfo(HandlerName));
  return sb.ToString();
}
}
```

5. Next, make a minor change to the RequestListener's HandleRequest() method to output a new message:

```
public void HandleRequest()
{
  using(var instance = factory.CreateExport())
  {
    var handler = instance.Value;
    Console.WriteLine(handler.GetRequestHandlerInfo());
  }
}
```

6. Finally, modify the Program constructor to include the two new classes:

```
public Program()
{
  var global = new TypeCatalog(
  typeof(RequestHandler),
  typeof(FakeDatabaseConnection),
  typeof(RequestListener),
  typeof(HandlerNameCreator),
  typeof(Logger),
  typeof(DataAccessLayer));

  Container = new CompositionContainer(global);
}
```

7. Press F5 to run the application and you should see something similar to Figure 4-5.

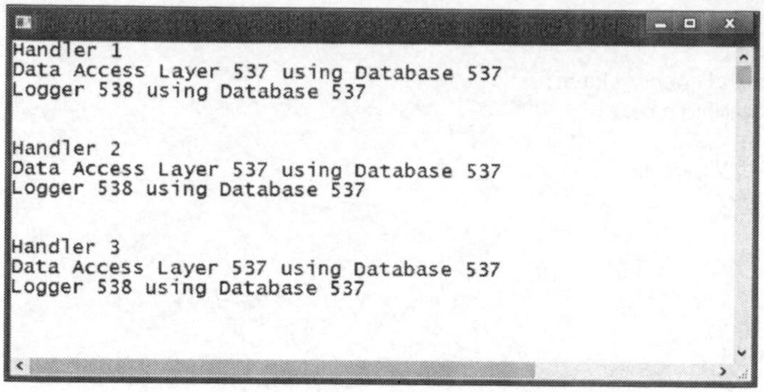

Figure 4-5. Before implementing CompositionScopeDefinition

This result isn't quite what we were after. Each instance of request handler is using the one instance of the data access layer and logger and they, in turn, are using the same database connection. You could try modifying the part creation policy of any of the child parts, but you still wouldn't achieve the original aim. The solution is to use CompositionScopeDefinition class.

In essence, what the CompositionScopeDefinition class allows you to do is define a parent–child relationship of scoped catalogs. What this means is that given an underlying catalog of composable parts, the lifetime of these parts will determine the lifetime of any child catalog/parts associated with it. To go back to our current example, what we want is that for each instance of the request listener, the system creates a single unique instance of the logger, data access layer, and database connection.

Implementing the ComponentScopeDefinition

1. First, open the FakeDatabaseConnection.cs file and remove the PartCreationPolicy attribute. By default, MEF treats all parts as shared.

2. Next, open Program.cs and update the constructor as follows:

```
public Program()
{
  var requestLevel = new TypeCatalog(
      typeof(RequestHandler),
      typeof(FakeDatabaseConnection),
      typeof(Logger),
      typeof(DataAccessLayer));

  var listenerLevel = new TypeCatalog(
      typeof(RequestListener),
      typeof(HandlerNameCreator));

  Container = new CompositionContainer(
      new CompositionScopeDefinition(listenerLevel,
          new[] {
              new CompositionScopeDefinition(requestLevel, null)
      }));
}
```

With the previous code, you have now created two catalogs to group the objects by scope. In the constructor for the CompositionContainer, we pass in a new instance of CompositionScopeDefinition, which in turn takes a "parent" catalog and an array of CompositionScopeDefinitions (only one in the case) that contain the "child" catalog(s).

Press F5 and check the result of these changes. You should see something similar to Figure 4-6.

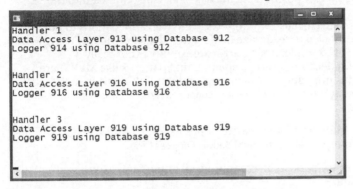

Figure 4-6. Result after using CompositionScopeDefinition

Composition Scoping in Summary

With the addition of both the ExportFactory and CompositionScopeDefinition, MEF 2.0 provides much greater flexibility in terms of managing the scope and creation of parts. It should be noted that the MEF team considers that CompositionScopeDefinition is orientated more toward advanced desktop application solutions.

Diagnostic Improvements

The last thing you want in an application that provides third-party extensibility is for it to go down in flames because of composition problems. To ensure this doesn't happen, the approach MEF takes is to silently reject the failed part. This makes sense for third-party extensibility, but if MEF is being used purely for internal development, it can be an issue when trying to debug an issue. To expose composition exceptions in the new version of MEF, you can now define a CompositionOptions.DisableSilentRejection flag in the CompositionContainer's constructor that raises an exception when composition errors occur:

```
var container = new CompositionContainer(catalog,
CompositionOptions.DisableSilentRejection);
```

The current recommendation from the MEF team is that this flag should be set for non-third-party-extensible applications.

The other improvement in terms of diagnostics is with the actual exception message text. In the previous version of MEF, the exception messages were less than self-evident. With this version of MEF, the exceptions have been formatted so that the most important information is up front.

The Microsoft.Composition Package

In November 2011, the MEF team developed and released an experimental NuGet package for integrating MEF with MVC. Though the MVC integration has been dropped from this release (see the section Missing in Action), the web-optimized composition engine has been consolidated into the Microsoft.Composition package.

This NuGet package has been designed specifically for Windows 8 and web applications to not only provide a lightweight composition engine but also to recognize the fact that the scenarios for using MEF differ from those of desktop applications. For example, third-party extensibility is not really a requirement for Metro apps, but application decoupling and implementing patterns like MVVM are.

There are some differences between this implementation of MEF and the "full" version in the .NET Framework. A full list of these can be found at found at http://mef.codeplex.com/documentation, but some of the key ones include the following:

- A different namespace is used. MEF for Windows 8/web apps uses the namespace System.Composition as opposed to System.ComponentModel.Composition.

- Import/export visibility. In order for parts to be composed, all import and export members must be publicly visible.

- Field exports and imports are not supported.

- Parts are nonshared by default. If a part needs to be shared, it needs to be decorated with the [Shared] attribute.

- The Shared() attribute accepts a simple scope name parameter to control sharing, for example, Shared("HttpRequest"). This works in conjunction with ExportFactory<T> and the SharingBoundary attribute.

- Catalogs are not used. Instead, assemblies and part types are added to a ContainerConfiguration from which a container is created and exports can be requested or imports satisfied.

- There is no RegistrationBuilder. For Windows 8 apps, the equivalent functionality is provided with the ConventionBuilder class.

Most of these points are self-explanatory, but let's have a look at the last two to see what this means in terms of coding. (Note that the following explanation will be in terms of Windows 8 applications but should be equally applicable to web apps.)

Using the ContainerConfiguration

Rather than using catalogs, assemblies and part types are added to a ContainerConfiguration from which a container can be created to resolve imports and exports. The reasoning behind this is that support for open, extensible applications is not required for Windows 8 apps so the process has been simplified. The following code should give you a rough idea of how this works:

```
public interface IDatabaseConnection{}
interface IMessageHandler
{
    IDatabaseConnection DbConnection { get; }
}
```

```
[Export(typeof(IDatabaseConnection))]
public class FakeDbConnection: IDatabaseConnection{}

[Export(typeof(IMessageHandler))]
public class SimpleMessageHandler : IMessageHandler
{
  public IDatabaseConnection DbConnection { get; private set; }
  [ImportingConstructor]
  public SimpleMessageHandler(IDatabaseConnection dbConnection)
  {
    this.DbConnection = dbConnection;
  }
}

class MessageFactory
{
  [Import]
  public IMessageHandler MessageHandler { get; private set; }
  public MessageFactory()
  {
    var configuration = new ContainerConfiguration()
    .WithAssembly(typeof(App).GetTypeInfo().Assembly);

    using (var container = configuration.CreateContainer())
    {
        container.SatisfyImports(this);
      //alternatively could call GetExport
      // MessageHandler = container.GetExport<IMessageHandler>();
    }
  }
}
```

Using the ConventionBuilder

As mentioned earlier in this chapter, one of the new features in MEF for .NET 4.5 is the
RegistrationBuilder, which provides the means of defining exports and imports using convention
rather than attributes. This same functionality is available for Windows 8 apps but is provided through
the ConventionBuilder class. If we take the previous code for the MessageFactory, we can rewrite it to use
the ConventionBuilder:

```
class MessageFactory
{
  [Import]
  public IMessageHandler MessageHandler { get; private set; }
  public MessageFactory()
  {
    var conventionBuilder = new ConventionBuilder();
    conventionBuilder.ForType< FakeDbConnection>()
                    .Export<IDatabaseConnection>();
    conventionBuilder.ForTypesDerivedFrom<IMessageHandler>()
                    .Export<IMessageHandler>();
    var configuration = new ContainerConfiguration()
```

```
            .WithAssembly(typeof(App).GetTypeInfo().Assembly)
            .WithDefaultConventions(conventionBuilder);
    using (var container = configuration.CreateContainer())
    {
     try
     {
      MessageHandler = container.GetExport<IMessageHandler>();
     }
     catch (Exception ex)
     {
      //Handle the exception
     }
    }
  }
}
```

Though it may seem a little odd to use different names for classes that basically provide the same functionality, the MEF team foresees the ConventionBuilder class evolving along its own path and retaining the RegristationBuilder name would lead to confusion down the track.

To add the NuGet package to your solution, open the NuGet console window and enter the following command.

```
Install-Package Microsoft.Composition
```

Missing in Action

Though initially released as an experimental package via NuGet, as mentioned earlier, MEF integration for ASP.NET MVC won't be released on the same time line as the core package. The MEF team is actively working on straightening out the MVC story, but at this point there is no indication what final shape it will take. The source code for this has been migrated to use the new Microsoft.Composition package and is available on the Codeplex site (http://mef.codeplex.com) if you are interested in having a look at it (in the source code, look for oob\demo\Microsoft.Composition.Demos.Web.Mvc).

Conclusion

With this version of MEF, the team has extended the scenarios that can be covered by the framework without losing sight of its primary function. The inclusion of a convention-based programming model and finer control over composition scope has introduced a degree of flexibility that, for some developers, was a stumbling block with the previous version. Finally, the targeting of different application models such as Windows 8 and web apps should see some interesting developments in the future.

CHAPTER 5

■ ■ ■

Language

One of the dominant themes throughout this release of .NET is the ability to perform work in an asynchronous manner. Each release of .NET has given us new (and easier) ways to write async code such as the Asynchronous Programming Model (APM) and the Task Asynchronous Pattern (TAP) in C# 4.0. In the latest release, a new model using the new keywords `async` and `await` is introduced. Although this book is C# focused we will also briefly cover the new changes in VB.NET.

What Does It Mean to Do Something Asynchronously?

Let's take a real-world example that illustrates some of the advantages and disadvantages of performing work asynchronously. A real-world frustration we all face occasionally is calling a company that leaves us on hold for a very long time—tax departments and telecom organizations are, of course, notorious for doing this. Let's imagine we have a query about our taxes and need to call up the taxation department. We call up the department and we are automatically put on hold. You could think of this situation as being similar to a program operating synchronously so that until our call is answered, we are prevented from doing anything else.

Of course, in this scenario what most of us tend to do is then put the call on speaker phone and do something else, like find cat videos on YouTube. This could be compared to implementing multithreading in an application as it involves a context switch to see if the call has been answered yet.

Let's imagine, however, that instead of making you wait, these companies have a new system that will automatically call you back if they are busy at the time of your call (some organizations already do this). With this facility, you are free to go and do other tasks without having to monitor the phone call with the knowledge that a representative from the company will call you as soon as one is available. This could be seen as similar to performing a task asynchronously.

Why Do Something Asynchronously?

There are a few main reasons why you would want to run code asynchronously in your applications:

- To keep your application responsive while waiting for something that is likely to take a long time to complete

- To make your application as scalable as possible (particularly important for services and ASP.NET that have limited threads/resources to service requests)

- To ensure growth in cloud applications/storage and latency, which makes performing actions asynchronously more important

However, not all problems are suited to be run asynchronously through. As a rough guide, consider using async functionality in the following situations:

- You are waiting for a response from a remote service.

- The task you want to perform is computationally expensive and doesn't complete very quickly (otherwise the overhead may exceed any benefits).

Can't We Currently Do This Kind of Thing?

.NET already contains functionality to run code in an asynchronous manner, but the 4.5 features have the following advantages:

- Less complicated code—it's all wrapped up in one method

- Much tidier because the callee method is responsible for handling its work rather than the method calling it

- Easier exception handling

- More defined methods (via interfaces) of handling cancellation and reporting on progress

Handling complications regarding thread synchronization contexts. OK, enough theory—let's take a look at how this is done.

Async and Await

C# 5.0 introduces two new keywords—async and await—for running a method asynchronously. Let's look at a simple example of using these now. Open up Visual Studio 2012, create a new Console application, and enter the following code:

```
public class Program
{
  static void Main(string[] args)
  {
    DoWorkAsync();
    //I get called immediately & before PretendToDoSomething is completed
    Console.WriteLine("Main method is all done");
    Console.ReadKey();
  }

  static async void DoWorkAsync()
  {
    await Task.Run(() => PretendToDoSomethingAsync());
    Console.WriteLine("Once PretendToDoSomething is run I will be printed");
  }

  static void PretendToDoSomethingAsync()
  {
    System.Threading.Thread.Sleep(2000);
    Console.WriteLine("I have finished pretending to do something");
  }
```

}

The screenshot in Figure 5-1 shows the output of running this program.

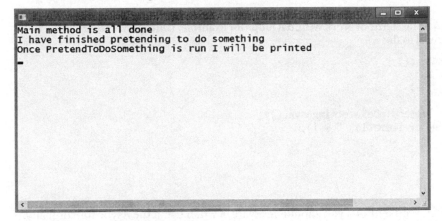

Figure 5-1. Output of listing above

Let's summarize what happened:

1. The DoWorkAsync method was called.

2. DoWorkAsync created a new task called PretendToDoSomethingAsync. As this is marked with the await keyword, control flow returned immediately to the main thread until this method was completed.

3. "Main method is all done" was output.

4. Once the Thread.Sleep was completed, then PretendToDoSomethingAsync output "I have finished pretending to do something".

5. Control then resumed to DoWork method that could print out "Once PretendToDoSomething is run I will also be printed".

We could actually do something very similar in C# 4.0 as follows:

```
static void Main(string[] args)
{
  Task.Run(() =>
  {
    System.Threading.Thread.Sleep(2000);
    Console.WriteLine("I have finished pretending to do something");
  }).ContinueWith((result) =>
    {
      Console.WriteLine("Once PretendToDoSomething is run I will be printed");
    });
  //I get called immediatly & before PretendToDoSomething is completed
  Console.WriteLine("Main method is all done");
  Console.ReadKey();
}
```

So, what is the await keyword doing? The await keyword stops the async method that was called until the awaited method is completed. In the meantime, the control flow goes back to the code that first called the method.

This example isn't too useful and could be easily accomplished with current functionality, but let's say we wanted to perform several items of work within a loop (for example, calling several services); the new keywords make this trivial to do:

```
static async void DoWorkAsync()
{
  for (int i = 0; i < 5; i++)
  {
    await Task.Run(() => PretendToDoSomethingAsync());
    Console.WriteLine("End of iteration " + i);
  }
}
```

Async Rules

There are a couple of rules and conventions you should be aware of when using the Async functionality:

- The compiler will give you a warning for methods that contain async modifier but no await operator.

- A method that isn't using the await operator will be run synchronously.

- Microsoft suggests a convention of post-fixing an Async method with the words Async e.g. DoSomethingAsync, which seems sensible.

Async methods can return any of the following:

- void (note an Async method that returns void cannot itself be awaited)

- Task

- Task<T>

Changes to BCL Methods

A number of BCL methods now have an Async version for you to use with the await keyword (see Chapter 3 for more information). The following example demonstrates the WebClient downloading the content of a web page using one of these new async methods:

```
class Program
{
 static void Main(string[] args)
 {
 DoWork();
 }

 static async void DoWork()
 {
 string url = "http://www.microsoft.com";
 string content = await new WebClient().DownloadStringTaskAsync(url);
```

```
  }
}
```

Handling Errors

One of the language team's goals when developing the async functionality was to make it easy to integrate into existing code. One of the aspects of this is, of course, exception handling. In the next piece of code, we have two synchronous methods: PrintMessage, which in turn calls ProcessMessage. ProcessMessage will throw an exception if the value passed to it is null or empty, so in PrintMessage the call is wrapped in a try/catch block.

```
class Program
{
  static void Main(string[] args)
  {
    PrintMessage("");
    Console.WriteLine("Waiting...");
    Console.ReadKey();
  }

  private static void PrintMessage(string name)
  {
    try
    {
      var result = ProcessMessage(name);
      Console.WriteLine(result);
    }
    catch (ArgumentNullException ane)
    {
      Console.WriteLine(ane.Message);
    }
  }

  private static string ProcessMessage(string name)
  {
    Thread.Sleep(1000);
    if (string.IsNullOrEmpty(name))
    {
      throw new ArgumentNullException("name", "name must have a valid value.");
    }

    return string.Format("Hi there {0}", name);
  }
}
```

If you run this code, the exception, as would be expected, gets caught and handled.

Now let's change these two methods to be asynchronous (if you are trying this out, don't forget to change the method being called in Main to PrintMessageAsync).

```
private static async Task PrintMessageAsync(string name)
{
  try
  {
    var result = await ProcessMessageAsync(name);
    Console.WriteLine(result);
  }
  catch (Exception ex)
  {
    Console.WriteLine(ex.Message);
  }
}

private static async Task<string> ProcessMessageAsync(string name)
{
  await Task.Delay(1000);
  if (string.IsNullOrEmpty(name))
  {
    throw new ArgumentNullException("name", "name must have a valid value.");
  }

  return string.Format("Hi there {0}", name);
}
```

As you can see, with the exception of adding the async and await keywords, we haven't had to change anything in the PrintMessage method. If you run the code, the exception is caught and handled exactly as it was in the synchronous version.

Under the covers, what is actually happening to facilitate changing methods from synchronous to asynchronous is that the first exception in the Task's AggregateException is thrown. In most cases, this behavior is acceptable, but there are instances where another approach will be necessary.

Take, for example, the following code where in the DoSomething method we await another two methods, both of which will throw exceptions (if you want to try this, just create a WPF project and add a button to the form):

```
private async void Button_Click_1(object sender, RoutedEventArgs e)
{
  try
  {
    var result = await DoSomething();
    MessageBox.Show(result);
  }
  catch (Exception ex)
  {
    MessageBox.Show(ex.Message);
  }
}

private async Task<string> DoSomething()
{
  var task1 = Action1Async(true);
  var task2 = Action2Async(true);
  var result = await Task<string[]>.WhenAll(task1, task2);
```

```csharp
  return string.Join("\n", result);
}

private async Task<string> Action1Async(bool throwException = false)
{
  await Task.Delay(2000);
  if (throwException)
  throw new IOException();
  return "action 1 completed";
}

private async Task<string> Action2Async(bool throwException = false)
{
  await Task.Delay(2000);
  if (throwException)
  throw new ArgumentNullException();
  return "Action 2 completed";
}
```

Even though both Action1Async and Action2Async threw exceptions, the only one that gets reported is the IOException thrown by the first method. As you can imagine, this could result in some interesting side effects in your code and become problematic when debugging. One solution is to modify the DoSomething method to use ContinueWith and an instance of TaskCompletionSource to pass back the AggregationException to the calling method.

```csharp
private Task<string> DoSomething()
{
  var task1 = Action1Async(true);
  var task2 = Action2Async(true);
  var tcs = new TaskCompletionSource<string>();
  Task<string[]>.WhenAll(task1, task2)
    .ContinueWith(tsk =>
    {
      if (tsk.IsFaulted)
      {
        tcs.SetException(tsk.Exception);
      }
      else
      {
        tcs.SetResult(string.Join("\n", tsk.Result));
      }
    });

  return tcs.Task;
}
```

Cancelling Async Methods

Something you need to consider when writing async methods, especially long-running ones, is providing a way to cancel and bail out of the process. This is easily done by modifying or providing an overload of your method to take a CancellationToken as a parameter. Within your method, you would then query the token's IsCancellationRequested property to see if a cancellation has been requested and if it has do any clean up that is necessary and either exit the method or call the token's ThrowIfCancellationRequested method.

The following trivial example illustrates a possible implementation:

```
class UsingCancellationTokens
{
  public async static void Run()
  {
    var cts = new CancellationTokenSource(3000);
    await LongRunningProcess(1000, cts.Token).ContinueWith(tsk =>
      {
        if (tsk.IsCanceled)
          Console.WriteLine("Process cancelled");
        else
          Console.WriteLine("Process completed");
      });
  }

  private async static Task LongRunningProcess(int counter, CancellationToken token)
  {
    for (int i = 0; i < counter; i++)
    {
      await Task.Delay(100);
      if (token.IsCancellationRequested)
      {
        token.ThrowIfCancellationRequested();
      }
      Console.WriteLine(i);
    }
  }
}
```

Async/Await under the Hood

Given the relative simplicity of implementing asynchronous methods using the async/await keywords, clearly there is more going on than meets the eye. Before we look at what is happening under the covers, let's first review what is actually happening when we use the async and await keywords.

When you call an async method, it runs until it encounters an awaitable method (that is, a method marked with await). At that point, it returns to the calling code and then happily continues running. Once the awaited method completes, however, any other code in the async method is then processed.

But how is the compiler achieving this magic?

Behind the scenes, the compiler is generating code for managing the state of your method and intercepting calls to it. When a method is tagged with the async keyword, the compiler creates a helper state machine for the method. A stub method is created with a signature corresponding to the original method but with a shiny new implementation containing code for setting up the state machine and initiating it with a call to its MoveNext method.

The state machine then maintains what's going on across asynchronous await points. Within it, if required, it will contain the method's original code but segmented to allow results and exceptions to pass into the returned Task and facilitate continuation after an await.

Phew, that is a lot to take in!

■ **Note** Stephen Toub, in his MSDN article on Async performance (http://msdn.microsoft.com/en-us/magazine/hh456402.aspx), said that when you start working with asynchronous methods, "a new mental model is needed."

Implementing async/await By Hand

At this point, we would crack open our preferred IL decompiler and look at how the compiler rewrites an async method. Instead, taking inspiration from Mads Torgersen's article "Pause and Play with Await" (http://msdn.microsoft.com/en-us/magazine/hh456403.aspx), we are going to hand roll our own state machine to mimic async/await functionality and understand what's really going on here.

First, here is the method we are going to make asynchronous:

```
public void GetHtml(string url)
{
  var webClient = new WebClient();
  try
  {
    var result = webClient.DownloadString(url);
    Console.WriteLine(result);
  }
  catch (WebException webEx)
  {
    Console.WriteLine(webEx.Message);
  }
  finally
  {
    webClient.Dispose();
  }
}
```

1. To get started, create a new console application project.

2. Once you have that up, add a new class and call it `Example`, open it, and add using statements for the following namespaces:

   - `System.Diagnostics`

   - `System.Net`

   - `System.Runtime.CompilerServices`

   - `System.Threading`

   - `System.Threading.Tasks`

3. Within the `Example` class, you are going to add a nested type to act as our state machine. The following code defines your state machine:

```
private struct GetHtmlAsyncStateMachine
{
  public int state;
  public AsyncTaskMethodBuilder builder;
  public string result;
  private WebClient webClient;
  public string url;
  private TaskAwaiter<string> awaiter;

  public void MoveNext()
  {
    try
    {
      if (state == 1)
      goto doStuff;

      webClient = new WebClient();
      doStuff:
      try
      {
        if (state == 1)
          goto completed;
        awaiter = webClient.DownloadStringTaskAsync(url).GetAwaiter();
        if (!awaiter.IsCompleted)
        {
        state = 1;
        //Specify this method as the continuation action
        //for when the await action completes
        awaiter.OnCompleted(this.MoveNext);
        return;
        }
        completed:
        result = awaiter.GetResult();
        //continue processing at this point
        Console.WriteLine(result);

      }
      catch (WebException webEx)
      {
        Console.WriteLine(webEx.Message);
      }
    }
    catch (Exception ex)
    {
      state = 2;
      builder.SetException(ex);
      return;
    }
    finally
    {
      webClient.Dispose();
    }
```

```
  state = 2;
  builder.SetResult();
  }
}
```

4. Next, you will modify your original method to function in an async manner by instantiating the state machine and then kick it off by calling its MoveNext method. Add the next piece of code to the Example class:

```
public Task GetHtmlAsync(string url)
{
  var stateMachine = new GetHtmlAsyncStateMachine();
  stateMachine.builder = AsyncTaskMethodBuilder.Create();
  stateMachine.url = url;
  stateMachine.MoveNext();
  return stateMachine.builder.Task;
}
```

5. Finally, to see this all working, open Program.cs and in the Main method add the following:

```
var example = new Example();
example.GetHtmlAsync("http://www.microsoft.com");
Console.WriteLine("Waiting ...");
Console.ReadKey();
```

With this example what we have done, in a simplified form, is essentially what the compiler does when you use the async/await keywords on a method. So, for example, if we take our original synchronous and modify it to be asynchronous like so:

```
public async Task GetHtmlAsync(string url)
{
var webClient = new WebClient();
  try
  {
    var result = await webClient.DownloadStringTaskAsync(url);
    Console.WriteLine(result);
  }
  catch (WebException webEx)
  {
    Console.WriteLine(webEx.Message);
  }
  finally
  {
    webClient.Dispose();
  }
}
```

Here is how it would look when viewed in an IL decompiler:

```
public class Example
{
  [DebuggerStepThrough, AsyncStateMachine(typeof(<GetHtmlAsync>d__0))]
  public Task GetHtmlAsync(string url)
  {
```

```
      <GetHtmlAsync>d__0 d__;
      d__.<>4__this = this;
      d__.url = url;
      d__.<>t__builder = AsyncTaskMethodBuilder.Create();
      d__.<>1__state = -1;
      d__.<>t__builder.Start<<GetHtmlAsync>d__0>(ref d__);
      return d__.<>t__builder.Task;
    }

    // Nested Types
    [CompilerGenerated]
    private struct <GetHtmlAsync>d__0 : IAsyncStateMachine
    {
      // Fields
      public int <>1__state;
      public Example <>4__this;
      public AsyncTaskMethodBuilder <>t__builder;
      private object <>t__stack;
      private TaskAwaiter<string> <>u__$awaiter3;
      public string <result>5__2;
      public WebClient <webClient>5__1;
      public string url;

      // Methods
      private void MoveNext()
      {
        try
        {
        bool <>t__doFinallyBodies = true;
        switch (this.<>1__state)
        {
          case -3:
            goto Label_0121;
          case 0:
            break;
          default:
            this.<webClient>5__1 = new WebClient();
            break;
        }
        try
        {
          int CS$4$0000 = this.<>1__state;
          if (CS$4$0000 == 0)
          {
          }
          try
          {
            TaskAwaiter<string> CS$0$0001;
            CS$4$0000 = this.<>1__state;
            if (CS$4$0000 != 0)
            {
              CS$0$0001 = this.<webClient>5__1.DownloadStringTaskAsync(this.url).GetAwaiter();
```

```
                if (!CS$0$0001.IsCompleted)
                {
                    this.<>1__state = 0;
                    this.<>u__$awaiter3 = CS$0$0001;
                    this.<>t__builder.AwaitUnsafeOnCompleted<TaskAwaiter<string>,
Example.<GetHtmlAsync>d__0>(ref CS$0$0001, ref this);
                    <>t__doFinallyBodies = false;
                    return;
                }
            }
            else
            {
                CS$0$0001 = this.<>u__$awaiter3;
                this.<>u__$awaiter3 = new TaskAwaiter<string>();
                this.<>1__state = -1;
            }
            string result = CS$0$0001.GetResult();
            CS$0$0001 = new TaskAwaiter<string>();
            string CS$0$0003 = result;
            this.<result>5__2 = CS$0$0003;
            Console.WriteLine(this.<result>5__2);
        }
        catch (WebException webEx)
        {
            Console.WriteLine(webEx.Message);
        }
        }
        finally
        {
            if (<>t__doFinallyBodies)
            {
            this.<webClient>5__1.Dispose();
            }
        }
    }
    catch (Exception <>t__ex)
    {
        this.<>1__state = -2;
        this.<>t__builder.SetException(<>t__ex);
        return;
    }
    Label_0121:
    this.<>1__state = -2;
    this.<>t__builder.SetResult();
}

[DebuggerHidden]
private void SetStateMachine(IAsyncStateMachine param0)
{
    this.<>t__builder.SetStateMachine(param0);
}
}
```

```
}
```

True, there is a lot more going on here, but in essence it is the same as our hand-rolled version. However, instead of us having to write it, the IL compiler is doing all the heavy lifting for us.

Some Things To Think About

The ease with which the async/await keywords allows us to create asynchronous methods is beguiling, but as you can see from the previous example, there is more to it than meets the eye. This, in turn, can lead to performance issues. Stephen Toub covers these issues in depth in his article mentioned earlier, but here some key points to consider:

- Methods should be chunky, not chatty. When working synchronously, using small, discreet methods incurs little cost when compiled. It is a different story when we switch to an asynchronous approach. For any given async method, the compiler has to, as we have seen, generate a fair amount of extra scaffolding to make a method asynchronous and that is an extra cost. So, where possible, it is worthwhile consolidating a logical piece of functionality into a single method.

- Beware that any variables within an async method will be lifted into the state machine and this can impact on garbage collection.

- Consolidate multiple awaits. If you have multiple awaits, consider rationalizing them into a single await by using the Task.WhenAll method.

- Know when not to async.

Caller Information

Another new feature that has been added to both C# and VB.NET is caller information attributes. Defined in the System.Runtime.CompilerServices namespace, there are three attributes:

- CallerFilePathAttribute, which returns the full path to the source file of the caller as of compile time

- CallerLineNumberAttribute, which identifies the line number in the source file where the method was called

- CallerMemberNameAttribute, which holds the name of the method or property of the caller

To use these attributes, you need to apply them to optional parameters on a method with a default value. For example:

```
SomeMethod(string message, [CallerFilePath] string sourceFile = "",
        [CallerLineNumber] int sourceLineNo = 0, [CallerMemberName] string memberName = "")
```

The attributes don't make the parameters optional but determine the default value when the argument is omitted. Unlike the StackTrace property of an exception, they are not affected by obfuscation since they are injected as literals into the IL.

Essentially, the idea behind these attributes is to facilitate debugging, tracing, and the creation of diagnostic tools. The following example shows how this could be used:

```
class Program
{
 static void Main(string[] args)
  {
    Trace.Listeners.Clear();
    Trace.Listeners.Add(new ConsoleTraceListener());
    var repository = new ProjectRepository();
    repository.AddProject(new ProjectModel { ProjectName = "Test Project" });
    Console.ReadKey();
  }
}

public class ProjectModel
{
  public string ProjectName { get; set; }
}

public class ProjectRepository
{
  public void AddProject(ProjectModel project,
        [CallerFilePath]string srcFilePath = "",
        [CallerLineNumber] int srcLineNo = 0,
        [CallerMemberName] string memberName = "")
  {
    Trace.WriteLine("Project Added");
    Trace.WriteLine("Member name: " + memberName);
    Trace.WriteLine("Source file path: " + srcFilePath);
    Trace.WriteLine("source line number: " + srcLineNo);
  }
}
```

Running this example would generate something similar to Figure 5-2.

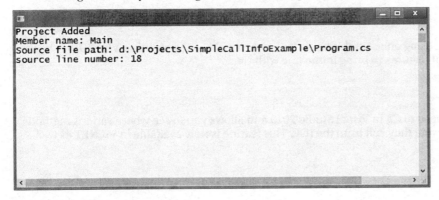

Figure 5-2. The trace output

Though useful for diagnostic purposes, using these attributes adds clutter to your method signatures, which you do need to consider if you are going to use them. Outside of the diagnostics realm, the `CallerMemberNameAttribute` comes into its own when implementing the `INotifyPropertyChanged` interface.

When implementing this interface on, say, a view model, a common practice is to create a method that takes a property name as a string literal to then raise the `PropertyChanged` event—for example, `OnPropertyChanged("PropertyName")`. This can introduce subtle bugs if the property name is changed, but the value in the method call isn't. An alternative to this was to create a method that took an expression, `OnPropertyChanged<T>(Expression<Func<T>> e)`, that could then be called as follows: `OnPropertyChanged(() => this.PropertyName)`. By using the `CallerMemberNameAttribute` the whole thing can be simplified as seen in this code example:

```
public class ProjectVM : INotifyPropertyChanged
{
  public event PropertyChangedEventHandler PropertyChanged;
  private ProjectModel model;
  public string ProjectName
  {
    get { return model.ProjectName;}
    set
    {
      model.ProjectName = value;
      OnPropertyChanged();
    }
  }

  private void onPropertyChanged([CallerMemberName] string memberName = "")
  {
    if (PropertyChanged == null)
          return;
    PropertyChanged(this, new PropertyChangedEventArgs(memberName));
  }
}
```

VB.NET

Although we are mainly focusing on C# in this book, we want to make you aware that VB.NET has been enhanced with a number of features to bring it into line with C#.

Call Hierarchy

Call Hierarchy was introduced to C# in Visual Studio 2010 and allows you to see where various methods are being called from and what they call from the IDE. This feature is now available in VB.NET as well. (See Figure 5-3.)

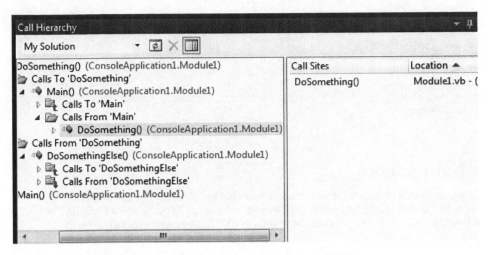

Figure 5-3. Call Hierarchy has now been introduced to VB.NET.

Iterators

An iterator is a type of collection object that allows a client to iterate through each object in the collection. Microsoft defines it as the following:

> *An iterator is a method, get accessor or operator that enables you to support foreach iteration in a class or struct without having to implement the entire IEnumerable interface. Instead, you provide just an iterator, which simply traverses the data structures in your class. When the compiler detects your iterator, it will automatically generate the Current, MoveNext and Dispose methods of the IEnumerable or IEnumerable<T> interface.*

```
http://msdn.microsoft.com/en-us/library/dscyy5s0(v=vs.80).aspx
```

Iterators are particularly useful for wrapping up complex logic to transverse complex structures, for example, a hierarchical tree. When you use an iterator behind the scenes, the compiler generates a state machine (for more information, see www.abhisheksur.com/2011/01/internals-to-c-iterators.html) that tracks the current item and provides get next methods each time it is called.

Iterators were first introduced in the first release of C# and have now been introduced into VB.NET. The following example shows how to create an iterator that will return a name from a predefined list each time it is called:

```vb
Sub Main()
 For Each name As String In NamesIterator()
 Console.WriteLine(name)
 Next

 Console.ReadKey()
End Sub
```

```
Private Iterator Function NamesIterator() As System.Collections.Generic.IEnumerable(Of String)
Dim ListOfNames As New List(Of String)
ListOfNames.Add("Karen")
ListOfNames.Add("Trish")
ListOfNames.Add("Billy")

For Each name In ListOfNames
Yield name
Next
```

End FunctionNamespaces

By constructing your namespaces in a specific manor, it is possible to block access to certain namespaces. For example, the following will not compile (when the error Type 'System.Guid' is not defined) as the use of MyNamespace.System prevents access to .NET's System namespace:

```
Namespace MyNamespace
  Namespace System
    Public Class SomeClass
          Function DoSomething()
              Dim myGuid = New System.Guid
          End Function
    End Class
  End Namespace
End Namespace
```

If you find yourself in this situation, you probably want to refactor your namespaces. However, if you can't for some reason or you are using third-party libraries, you can use the Global keyword to tell .NET to start at the outermost namespace (for more on Global see the next section):

```
Dim myGuid = New Global.System.Guid
```

Global and Namespace

In Visual Basic, all namespaces are based on the project's root namespace (often the project's name, for example, ConsoleApplication1—you can override this in project properties). The Global keyword allows you define a namespace outside of this:

```
Namespace Global.OutsideTheProjectNamespace
End Namespace
```

Or the more verbose:

```
Namespace Global
    Namespace OutsideTheProjectNamespace

    End Namespace
End Namespace
```

The Global keyword also allows you to specify namespaces that would clash with .NET'S namespace—note that this will only work if you prefix them:

```
Namespace MyNamespace
    Namespace System
        Public Class SomeClass
            Sub DoSomething()
                Dim obj As New Global.System.IO.AlexClass
                Dim wouldntWorkWithoutGlobal As Global.System.IO.StreamReader
            End Sub
        End Class
    End Namespace
End Namespace
Namespace Global.System.IO
    Class AlexClass
    End Class
End Namespace
```

This seems like a bad idea to me and would likely cause you more hassle than it's worth, so I would avoid it.

Real-World Async

Jake Ginnivan, MVP VSTO http://jake.ginnivan.net/

In January 2012, we decided that we would upgrade a large WPF application (from a two-year-old project) to use the async CTP. We put a lot of effort into making sure that the application never blocked the UI thread and gave the user visual feedback when the application was busy. The application also had a suite of UI automation tests that understood when the application is doing background work so the test doesn't continue.

This meant that our code suffered from a fair amount of lambda tax. As an example, a WCF call looked something like this:

```
_uiService.CallWithBusy(
    _someService,
    service => service.ServiceCall(arg1, arg2),
    complete =>
    {
        if (DoDefaultErrorHandling(complete))
            return;
        // Update UI etc
    }
```

So, our main motivation for adopting the async CTP was to make our code cleaner and easier to write. Now a service call looks like the following:

```
Try
{
    var result = await _someServiceAsync.ServiceCall(arg1, arg2);
    // Update UI etc
}
Catch (Exception ex)
{
    ex.DoDefaultErrorHandling(_uiService);
}
```

These examples are simple, but often we had multiple service calls or other async tasks. It is a very common occurrence in rich clients that you need to use the result of one call to pass to another. This makes it very hard to follow the logic and flow of the code. There were places in the code base where we reduced 100 lines of code to about 30 just by using the async/await keywords. After using these language features, it makes it very hard to go back!

For us, async/await is like LINQ—we really struggle to go back and do it the old way. We are also now adopting ASP.NET Web API and making use of the support for Asynchronous Controller actions, allowing us to get much greater throughput on our central server. This is what makes the async stuff so great—it can help you write fast asynchronous code, but even if you don't need the additional throughput, the async language features in .NET 4.5 can help you write cleaner code as well.

Conclusion

The async and await keywords will make it much easier and intuitive to integrate Asynchronous functionality into your applications. It is probably a sign of the maturity of both C# and VB.NET that the only other new feature in this release has been the introduction of Caller Info attributes.

CHAPTER 6

■ ■ ■

ASP.NET 4.5

Although ASP.NET MVC continues to grow in popularity, Microsoft estimates that between 80% and 90% of their customer base is still using ASP.NET Web Forms as their development platform of choice (Damian Edwards, ASP.NET program manager, Build Conference 2012).

It should thus come as no surprise that Microsoft continues to invest in the improvement of the ASP.NET Web Forms framework. ASP.NET MVC is, of course, built on top of ASP.NET Web Forms. As a result, many of these enhancements will also affect ASP.NET MVC developers—so please don't skip this chapter!

ASP.NET 4.5 Web Forms has been influenced by its newer MVC brother, and it introduces support for strongly typed data controls and model binding. Other shiny new features include better async support, built-in minification and bundling of JavaScript and CSS files, and a new WebSockets API.

Strongly Typed Data Controls and Model Binding

Previously when working with template controls such as GridView, you would declare the item you wanted to bind to with a syntax similar to the following:

```
<%# DataBinder.Eval (Container.DataItem, "Price") %>
```

With this type of syntax, it's very easy to make a mistake, such as a typo, since the IDE doesn't know the type you are binding to until runtime. Additionally, if any properties in the bound class are renamed or changed, you must remember to update the binding code. Otherwise, the error will only appear at runtime.

ASP.NET 4.5 solves these issues by allowing you to specify the type that is bound to a control with the new ItemType property. Let's see this in action:

1. Create a new ASP.NET 4.5 Web Forms project.

2. Add a reference to System.ComponentModel.DataAnnotations assembly. (We will need this later to demonstrate cool declarative validation features.)

3. Create a new class called Person:

```
using System.ComponentModel.DataAnnotations;

public class Person
{
    public int ID { get; set; }
    [Required(ErrorMessage="First name is required")]
    public string FirstName { get; set; }
```

```
    public string LastName { get; set; }
    public int Age { get; set; }
}
```

4. Create something to display the data, so open default.aspx and add the
   following:

```
<asp:FormView ID="FormView1" ItemType="WebApplication7.Person" UpdateMethod="UpdatePeople"
AllowPaging="true" runat="server" SelectMethod="GetPeople" DataKeyNames="ID"
DefaultMode="Edit">
        <EditItemTemplate>
        <ol>
            <li>
            <%#Item.ID%>
            </li>

            <li>
             <asp:TextBox ID="textFirstName" runat="server" Text='<%# BindItem.FirstName
%>' />
            </li>
            <li>
             <asp:TextBox ID="txtLastName" runat="server" Text='<%# BindItem.LastName%>'/>
            </li>
        </ol>


            <asp:linkbutton id="UpdateButton"
            text="Update"
            commandname="Update"
            runat="server"/>


            <asp:ValidationSummary ID="ValidationSummary1" runat="server"/>
            </EditItemTemplate>
    </asp:FormView>
```

5. Note the use of the new ItemType property. You might also have noticed we set
   two new properties: SelectMethod and UpdateMethod. SelectMethod and
   UpdateMethod are new methods that unsurprisingly allow us to specify the
   methods to bind and update data. We will complete our binding example by
   creating these select and update methods.

6. We will return an IQueryable list of our person class (you can think of
   IQueryable as a query that hasn't been run yet and can be modified on the
   fly—this is needed to enable the FormView control's paging functionality). To
   do this, open default.aspx.cs and add the following code:

```
public IQueryable<Person> GetPeople()
    {

        IQueryable<Person> people = new List<Person>(){
        new Person()
        {
```

```
        ID=0,
        Age=33,
        FirstName="Belinda",
        LastName="Lord"
        },

        new Person()
        {
        ID=1,
        Age=62,
        FirstName="Rhonda",
        LastName="Lord"
        },

        new Person()
        {
        ID=2,
        Age=64,
        FirstName="Gary",
        LastName="Lord"
        },


        new Person()
        {
        ID=4,
        Age=1,
        FirstName="Darcy",
        LastName="Lord"
        },


        }.AsQueryable();
        return people;
    }

public void UpdatePeople(Person model)
{
    var success = TryUpdateModel<Person>(model);
    if (success)
    {
        //TODOwritebackupdate
    };
}
```

7. Run the application and you should see a highly exciting form view control bound to the list of people we created.

BindItem

BindItem is similar to Item but should be used if you want to persist changes that the user has made. To see the difference between Item and BindItem, follow these steps:

1. Modify the textboxes in the example above to the following:

```
<asp:TextBox ID="textFirstName" runat="server" Text='<%# Item.FirstName %>' /></asp:TextBox>
<asp:TextBox ID="txtLastName" runat="server" Text='<%# BindItem.LastName %>' /></asp:TextBox>
```

2. Put a breakpoint on UpdatePeople method and run the application.

3. Make a change in both textboxes.

4. Click the Update button and the breakpoint should be hit.

You will see only the LastName property in the submitted model has been populated with changes.

Validation

In the example above, we added a special validation attribute to our Person class:

```
[Required(ErrorMessage="First name is required")]
public string FirstName { get; set; }
```

This attribute, of course, specifies that the FirstName field is required. To see the effect of this attribute, run the example, remove any entry in the first name textbox, and click the Update button. ASP.NET validation will then kick in and you should then see the error message "First name is required." This feature should look familiar to MVC users.

There is a number of different validation attributes that you can apply to your classes; ASP.NET 4.5 introduces some new ones such as e-mail address, telephone number, and credit card number. Refer to the source at http://msdn.microsoft.com/en-us/library/system.componentmodel.dataannotations(v=vs.110).aspx for more detail.

These simple binding improvements bring us a number of advantages:

- Since the control is strongly typed, we get "intellisense"—yea!

- Our presentation and logic is cleanly separated, which is great for a number of reasons:

  - It's easy to unit test the save and load methods.

  - It makes the code easier to maintain.

  - Work flow between designers and developers is simplified.

- We can easily specify validation rules with attributes.

- The markup in the page clearly describes what's going on (so simple even your average project manager could work it out).

These new binding features give you some of the benefits ASP.NET MVC users have been enjoying. They could be a good starting point for upgrading existing applications to a cleaner, happier way of doing things.

HTML Encoded Databinding

While we are on the subject of databinding, I want to mention two new databinding-related features in ASP.NET 4.5:

- HTML encoding databind expressions
- DataGrid's AllowCustomPaging and VirtualItemCount

HTML Encoding Databind Expressions

New to ASP.NET 4.5 is the ability to HTML encode databinding expressions by appending ":" to the end of the <%# block. For example:

`<%#: BindItem.LastName %>`

DataGrid's AllowCustomPaging and VirtualItemCount

Normally when you page data with a control such as DataGrid, a data source containing every row of the data set is loaded, which can take time with large data sets.

ASP.NET 4.5 introduces a new mode that is enabled by setting AllowCustomPaging to "true". Once this is set, it tells ASP.NET that the currently bound data source doesn't contain every row of data, and it should instead refer to the VirtualItemCount to determine the number of items to display. The user would then use the OnPageIndexChanged event to set the current page index and calculate the block of data to display.

Microsoft has an example of this at http://msdn.microsoft.com/en-us/library/system.web.ui.webcontrols.datagrid.allowcustompaging.aspx.

Value Providers

It is common in web applications to need to read from a QueryString or other posted value. ASP.NET 4.5 introduces new attributes to do this declaratively.

Let's modify our GetPeople method to filter the list of people based on a value from the QueryString using this new approach.

1. Open up default.aspx.cs.

2. Add the following directive:

```
using System.Web.ModelBinding;
```

3. Modify the GetPeople method to the following code. Note the use of the new [QueryString] attribute on the method signature:

```
public IQueryable<Person> GetPeople([QueryString] string firstName)
    {
        var people = new List<Person>(){
            new Person(){
                ID=1,
                Age=31,
```

```
                    FirstName="Alex",
                    LastName="Mackey"
                },
                new Person(){
                    ID=2,
                    Age=33,
                    FirstName="Belinda",
                    LastName="Lord"
                }

            }.AsQueryable();

            if (!String.IsNullOrWhiteSpace(firstName))
            {
                return people.Where(person => person.FirstName == firstName);
            }
            else
            {
                return people;
            }
}
```

4. Run the application.

5. Append a parameter called firstname to the URL e.g. ?firstName=Belinda.

6. Results should then be filtered to people who have the first name *Belinda*.

When applying the value type attribute, ASP.NET will match values to parameters based on name (in this case firstName from QueryString is matched to firstName in the method parameters). If this isn't what you want, you can of course specify the value to bind to as below:

```
GetPeople([QueryString("nameIWantToFilterOn")] string firstName)
```

Binding to Other Types of Items

As well as binding to QueryString values, you can bind the variable to a number of other types of variables:

- Control properties

- Cookies

- Form values

- Profile values

- RouteData

- Session data

- UserProfile data

- ViewState (Ewww!)

… and if none of these serve your purposes, you can even create your own value providers.

Creating Your Own Value Providers

The example below demonstrates how to create your own binder. Our binder won't do much apart from append the string echo to the requested value. (Note: This is very similar to how you would do this in ASP.NET MVC with the IValueProvider interface.)

```csharp
using System.Globalization;
using System.Web.ModelBinding;

public class TestBinderAttribute : ValueProviderSourceAttribute
    {
        private readonly string _key;
        public TestBinderAttribute()
        {
        }

        public TestBinderAttribute(string key)
        {
            _key = key;
        }

        public string Key
        {
            get
            {
                return _key;
            }
        }
        public bool ValidateInput { get; set; }

        public override string GetModelName()
        {
            return "";
        }

        public override IValueProvider GetValueProvider(ModelBindingExecutionContext
modelBindingExecutionContext)
        {
            return new TestBinderAttributeProvider();

        }

    }

    public class TestBinderAttributeProvider : IValueProvider
    {
        public bool ContainsPrefix(string prefix)
        {
            return false;
        }
```

```
        public ValueProviderResult GetValue(string key)
        {
            var result = new ValueProviderResult("Echo " + key ,key ,
CultureInfo.InvariantCulture);
            return result;

        }
    }
```

That's it! You can then simply apply the new value provider with the attribute [TestBinder]:

```
public IQueryable<Person> GetPeople([TestBinder] string firstName)
{
...
}
```

HTML5 Changes

HTML5 introduces a huge number of changes, some of which have necessitated ASP.NET server controls being updated (please see the IDE chapter for a number of changes):

- The ASP.NET textbox control has been updated to include new input types such as Email, DateTime, and so forth.

- Validator and UpdatePanel controls work with these new element types.

File Upload Control Supports Multiple File Uploads

The file upload control now supports the multiple file upload feature (for browsers that support this).
    To enable, simply set the AllowMultiple property to "true". For example,

```
<asp:FileUpload ID="uploadFile" runat="server" AllowMultiple="true" />
```

You can then iterate through the files uploaded with the PostedFiles property:

```
foreach (var file in uploadFile.PostedFiles) {
    file.SaveAs("");
}
```

Bundling and Minification

During development, it is common to separate JavaScript and CSS files for maintainability and ease of development. Unfortunately, this division isn't the best way to deliver the files to your users, which is where bundling and minification come in.
    Bundling is the combining of files to reduce the number of requests a browser has to make. Minification is the removal of unnecessary characters (e.g., comments and spaces) to produce as tiny a file as possible.
    Bundling and minification give you the following advantages:

- The site should load quicker as there is less content to load.

- Some browsers limit the number of HTTP requests that can be made at one time to an individual domain. Thus, reducing the number of requests means that your site should load more quickly. (You may also be interested in the concept of domain sharding, which attempts to get around this restriction by serving content from different domains.)

- Bandwidth bills are reduced as less data is transmitted.

- They obscure CSS and JavaScript from casual peeking. (Warning: It's pretty trivial to unscramble a minified file—many browsers now have this functionality built in to their development tools)

Prior to VS2012, bundling and minification would have to be implemented using one of many third-party tools and libraries such as ClientDependency and JSMin.

Bundling and Minification for VS2010 Users

VS2010 users can enjoy these new features by downloading and applying the NuGet package ASP.NET Optimization (see Figure 6-1).

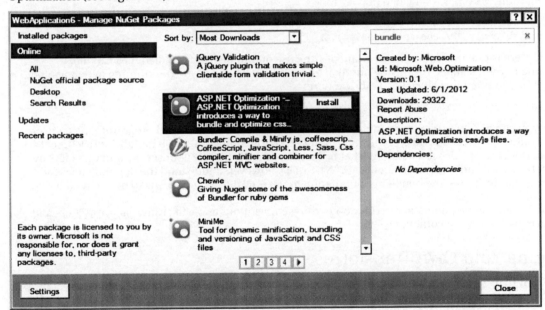

Figure 6-1. NuGet package ASP.NET Optimization

App_Start and Bundling/Minification Configuration

So, how do we configure the files to bundled and minified? This configuration is done in BundleConfig.cs, which is located in a new directory called App_Start. App_Start is used to contain programmatic configuration for ASP.NET applications (by default bundles/minification in ASP.NET and other items such as Routing in ASP.NET MVC).

BundleConfig has one static method called RegisterBundles, which lists all the files to be minified/bundled. This is called in the global.asax.cs App_Start method. There is no reason you have to stick with this convention, but I can't see an immediate problem with it so I suggest using it.

Let's take a look at what is going on in the RegisterBundles method. The following example (code removed for brevity) shows the creation of two types of bundles: a ScriptBundle containing two Microsoft AJAX JavaScript files and a StyleBundle containing site.css.

```
public static void RegisterBundles(BundleCollection bundles)
{
  bundles.Add(new ScriptBundle("~/bundles/MsAjaxJs").Include(
            "~/Scripts/WebForms/MsAjax/MicrosoftAjax.js",
            "~/Scripts/WebForms/MsAjax/MicrosoftAjaxWebForms.js"));

  bundles.Add(new StyleBundle("~/Content/css").Include("~/Content/site.css"));
}
```

I think it's pretty self-explanatory how this API works—the only parameters you may be wondering about are the "~/bundles/MsAjaxJs" and "~/Content/css" values. These provide a path that your bundle should be referenced at. When you want to use your bundles, you simply reference the bundles as in the following (note MVC has a similar syntax):

```
<%: Styles.Render("~/Content/css", "~/Content/moreCss") %>
<%: Scripts.Render("~/bundles/MsAjaxJs") %>
```

But there is one more thing to be aware of—the use of minified and bundled files can make debugging harder, so files will only be bundled and minified when you are not running in debug mode. This can be modified in web.config as shown here:

```
<compilation debug="true"></compilation>
```

Or you can also use the BundleTable.EnableOptmizations API if you need programmatic control.

It would be tedious to add each file in a directory, so the Bundles API also has an IncludeDirectory method. But you may be wondering in what order ASP.NET will bundle your scripts and CSS files? By default, files are bundled alphabetically. ASP.NET does, however, understand the dependencies for some popular libraries—the bundler is smart enough to know that jQuery needs to be bundled before jQueryUI.

The bundler even understands common naming conventions and will always place reset.css and normalize.css first when combining CSS files.

Creating Your Own Transforms

If you want to use your own bundling or minification mechanism, the Optimization extensions allow you to do this too by implementing the IBundleTransform interface.

Let's create a simple custom bundler that replaces a string in JavaScript files to demonstrate how to do this:

1. Create a new class called TestTransform and add the following code:

```
using System.Web.Optimization;

public class TestTranform : IBundleTransform
    {
        public void Process(BundleContext context, BundleResponse response)
        {
```

```
            response.Content = response.Content.Replace("replace me", "Yep your custom bundler
works!");
            response.ContentType = "text/css";
        }
    }
```

2.   Now open Global.asax and register the new transform:

```
var testBundle = new Bundle("~/bundles/testMinify").Include("~/scripts/test.js");
testBundle.Transforms.Add(new TestTranform());
bundles.Add(testBundle);
```

3.   Reference your bundle and transform with a script tag in our aspx or master file as shown below:

```
<%: Scripts.Render("~/bundles/testMinify") %>
```

4.   Finally, create a new JavaScript file in the root of the script directory and add the following code:

```
alert('replace me');
```

5.   Now open the site and an alert box should be shown with the replaced text.

More Useful Possibilities of Bundling/Minification

Custom bundlers and minifiers can be used for any pre-processing you might want to do on JavaScript or CSS files. For example, at the Build 2012 conference, Mads Kristensen (Microsoft Web Platform Program Manager) showed a creative example of overriding the minification process to compile CoffeeScript to JavaScript. For further information on this, please refer to http://channel9.msdn.com/Events/BUILD/BUILD2012/SAC-837T.

Validation and XSS Changes

XSS (cross-site scripting) is a well-known attack where unvalidated user input is directly output onto a web page, unencoded, and run. For example, imagine if the following script were submitted to a forum site and then output unencoded (it would be run for each user that visited the site!):

```
<script>alert('do something bad')</script>
```

Or even the much worse:

```
<script>window.location='http://www.justinbiebermusic.com/'</script>
```

XSS attacks can, however, be much more serious as they can be used to hijack another user's session cookie, and as a result, allow the attacker to make requests in the context of another user.

For more information on XSS, please refer to www.owasp.org/index.php/Cross-site_Scripting_(XSS) and www.blackhat.com/presentations/bh-usa-09/VELANAVA/BHUSA09-VelaNava-FavoriteXSS-SLIDES.pdf.

ASP.NET Validation

By default, ASP.NET will try to validate submitted requests for potential attacks such as XSS. At some point, you have probably seen this kick in and a screen similar to the one shown in Figure 6-2.

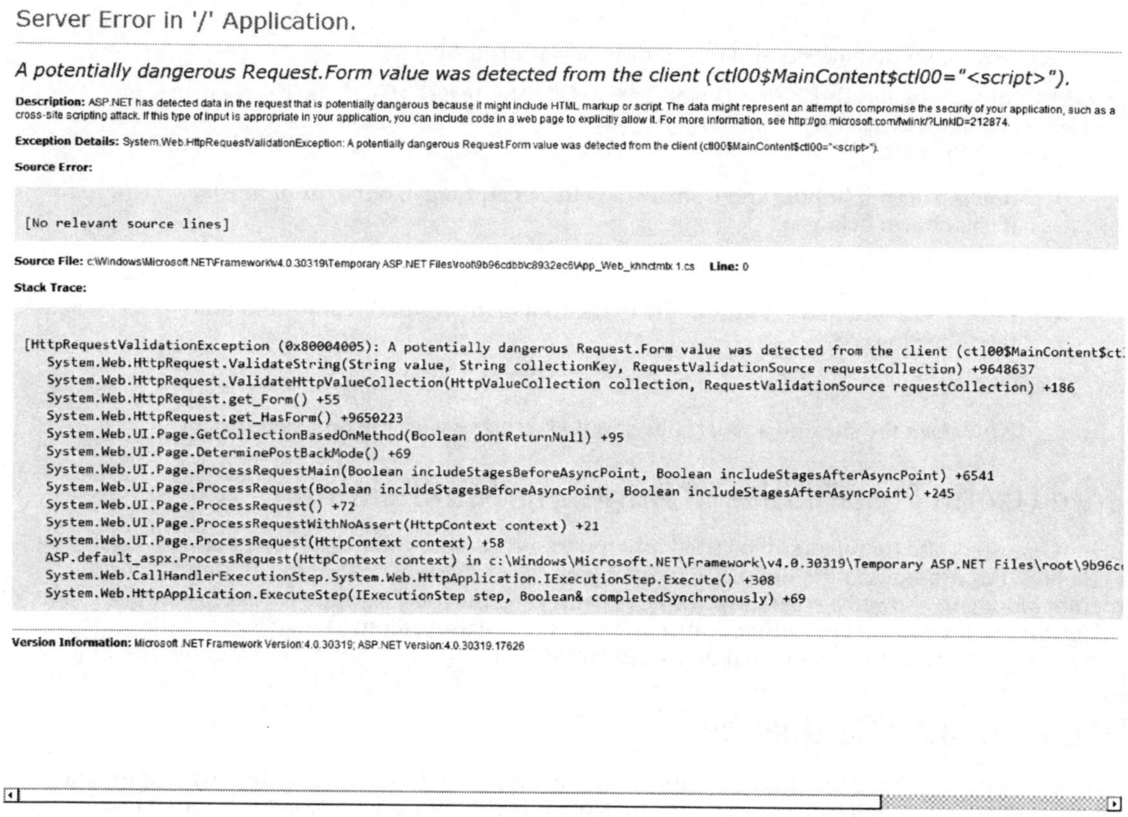

Server Error in '/' Application.

A potentially dangerous Request.Form value was detected from the client (ctl00$MainContent$ctl00="<script>").

Description: ASP.NET has detected data in the request that is potentially dangerous because it might include HTML markup or script. The data might represent an attempt to compromise the security of your application, such as a cross-site scripting attack. If this type of input is appropriate in your application, you can include code in a web page to explicitly allow it. For more information, see http://go.microsoft.com/fwlink/?LinkID=212874.

Exception Details: System.Web.HttpRequestValidationException: A potentially dangerous Request.Form value was detected from the client (ctl00$MainContent$ctl00="<script>").

Source Error:

```
[No relevant source lines]
```

Source File: c:\Windows\Microsoft.NET\Framework\v4.0.30319\Temporary ASP.NET Files\root\9b96cdbb\c8932ec6\App_Web_khhdmtx1.cs   **Line:** 0

Stack Trace:

```
[HttpRequestValidationException (0x80004005): A potentially dangerous Request.Form value was detected from the client (ctl00$MainContent$ctl
   System.Web.HttpRequest.ValidateString(String value, String collectionKey, RequestValidationSource requestCollection) +9648637
   System.Web.HttpRequest.ValidateHttpValueCollection(HttpValueCollection collection, RequestValidationSource requestCollection) +186
   System.Web.HttpRequest.get_Form() +55
   System.Web.HttpRequest.get_HasForm() +9650223
   System.Web.UI.Page.GetCollectionBasedOnMethod(Boolean dontReturnNull) +95
   System.Web.UI.Page.DeterminePostBackMode() +69
   System.Web.UI.Page.ProcessRequestMain(Boolean includeStagesBeforeAsyncPoint, Boolean includeStagesAfterAsyncPoint) +6541
   System.Web.UI.Page.ProcessRequest(Boolean includeStagesBeforeAsyncPoint, Boolean includeStagesAfterAsyncPoint) +245
   System.Web.UI.Page.ProcessRequest() +72
   System.Web.UI.Page.ProcessRequestWithNoAssert(HttpContext context) +21
   System.Web.UI.Page.ProcessRequest(HttpContext context) +58
   ASP.default_aspx.ProcessRequest(HttpContext context) in c:\Windows\Microsoft.NET\Framework\v4.0.30319\Temporary ASP.NET Files\root\9b96c
   System.Web.CallHandlerExecutionStep.System.Web.HttpApplication.IExecutionStep.Execute() +308
   System.Web.HttpApplication.ExecuteStep(IExecutionStep step, Boolean& completedSynchronously) +69
```

Version Information: Microsoft .NET Framework Version:4.0.30319; ASP.NET Version:4.0.30319.17626

Figure 6-2. Potentially dangerous request submitted

You could be forgiven for thinking that ASP.NET will prevent all XSS attacks. Unfortunately, this isn't the case.

■ **Warning** Attempting to circumvent ASP.NET protection on live web sites is very probably illegal, so don't do it!

Unfortunately, ASP.NET's protection mechanisms are fairly easily circumvented (see www.procheckup.com/vulnerability_manager/documents/document_1258758664/bypassing-dot-NET-ValidateRequest.pdf), and there is a mind-blowing number of ways to format input and produce an XSS attack. (See http://ha.ckers.org/xss.html.) Thus, it is vital that you never trust any input from a user and always make sure you encode any output.

Other Issues with ASP.NET Validation

ASP.NET validation can also sometimes get in the way if users want to be able to enter certain characters such as "<" or ">". As an example, I worked on a medical system where staff would often use characters such as "<" and ">" to denote ranges of laboratory values. In certain combinations, the characters "<" and ">" will cause ASP.NET's validation checks to fail, which led to some unhappy medical staff not being able to enter data how they wanted!

Prior to ASP.NET 4.5, if you wanted to ensure staff could always enter data in this format, you had little choice but to turn validation off at a page or site level.

So now we that we know the issues with the existing model, let's see how ASP.NET 4.5 improves things.

New Shiny ASP.NET 4.5 Validation Mode!

ASP.NET 4.5 validation mode is enabled by default in ASP.NET 4.5 sites and in web.config with the following key:

```
<httpRuntime requestValidationMode="4.5" />
```

When operating in 4.5 validation mode, a number of new features are enabled such as lazy validation, the ability to access raw unvalidated data without triggering the validation mechanisms, and new integrated AntiXSS functionality!

Lazy Validation

When the validation mode is set to 4.5, submitted data using *Server Controls* (standard HTML form elements will still trigger failure) will only be validated when and if it's actually used. Consequently, if a submitted data contains potentially dangerous values but you never actually use it, then ASP.NET will not throw a nasty, potentially dangerous, request error.

Raw Unvalidated Data

ASP.NET 4.5 provides the ability for you to access the raw form, cookies, QueryString, and URL data without triggering validation with the new unvalidated collections:

```
Request.Unvalidated.Cookies["myValue"]
Request.Unvalidated.QueryString["myValue"]
Request.Unvalidated.Form["myValue"]
```

■ **Warning** When you use this method, you are on your own and must remember to perform your own checks!

135

ValidateRequestMode

Validation can now be disabled at control level with the ValidateRequestMode property:

```
<asp:TextBox ValidateRequestMode="Disabled" runat="server"></asp:TextBox>
```

AntiXSS

ASP.NET 4.5 has beefed up protection against XSS attacks by incorporating a more advanced protection mechanism based on the open source AntiXSS libraries. The AntiXSS libraries provide superior encoding and protection by using a whitelist-based model (specifying the values that are allowed rather than those that are not allowed), and they contain additional security and encoding features.

ASP.NET 4.5 sites and applications use AntiXSS encoding by default by specifying the following option in web.config:

```
<httpRuntime ...
  encoderType="System.Web.Security.AntiXss.AntiXssEncoder, System.Web,
    Version=4.0.0.0, Culture=neutral, PublicKeyToken=b03f5f7f11d50a3a" />
```

AntiXSS routines are now used by default for the following methods in ASP.NET 4.5:

- CssEncode

- HtmlEncode

- HtmlFormUrlEncode

- HtmlAttributeEncode

- XmlAttributeEncode

- XmlEncode

- UrlEncode

- UrlPathEncode (new)

You can also, of course, use the various AntiXSS methods individually if you need more control. For example:

```
<%=System.Web.Security.AntiXss.AntiXssEncoder.HtmlEncode("<script>alert('I wont run as im
encoded!');</script>", false)%>
```

Let's talk to Barry Dorrans, the original developer of AntiXSS and author of *Wrox's Beginning ASP.NET Security*, about AntiXSS and XSS attacks.

Barry Dorrans and AntiXSS

AntiXSS was originally developed as a separate open source project, wasn't it?

> *Yes. And it still is. The open source project provides more encoding options—the core encoders were taken into the framework (Alex: Barry also mentioned AntiXSS has additional VBScript, Javascript, and the two LDAP encoders that are not present in the framework version). AntiXSS will be updated and enhancements pulled from*

.NET 4.5, and .NET will take enhancements from AntiXSS as well for the code encoders.

Any general advice on how to protect against XSS attacks?

Don't trust input. This doesn't just mean data from forms, but data from your database, as there's a risk it may have been compromised, or data from a request such as cookies or headers. All of these can be changed by an attacker, and all should be validated and encoded before output. Additionally, encode correctly. If you're outputting to JavaScript, use the JavaScript encoder. If your JavaScript is going to insert HTML, then you need to HTML encode first, then JavaScript encode, before outputting it into your page.

Any new features in AntiXSS that you would like to highlight to readers?

AntiXSS now supports .NET 4.0's encoder swapping, so you can switch between the original .NET encoder and the AntiXSS encoder (either the built-in 4.5 version or the stand-alone version) with the flick of a config setting.

Hmm … time to move on to unobtrusive validation …

Unobtrusive Validation

ASP.NET 4.5's unobtrusive validation significantly reduces the amount of JavaScript that is generated inline when using ASP.NET's validation controls.

Let's see this in action by comparing the two modes. First, add a textbox and validation control to a page:

```
<asp:TextBox ID="txtFirstname" runat="server"></asp:TextBox>
        <asp:RequiredFieldValidator runat="server" ControlToValidate="txtFirstname"
ErrorMessage="Required"></asp:RequiredFieldValidator>
```

Check out all the funky validation code this small addition generates:

```
<script type="text/javascript">
//<![CDATA[
var Page_Validators =  new Array(document.getElementById("ctl02"));
//]]>
</script>
<script type="text/javascript">
//<![CDATA[
var ctl02 = document.all ? document.all["ctl02"] : document.getElementById("ctl02");
ctl02.controltovalidate = "txtFirstname";
```

```
ctl02.errormessage = "Required";
ctl02.evaluationfunction = "RequiredFieldValidatorEvaluateIsValid";
ctl02.initialvalue = "";
//]]>
</script>

<script type="text/javascript">
//<![CDATA[

var Page_ValidationActive = false;
if (typeof(ValidatorOnLoad) == "function") {
    ValidatorOnLoad();
}

function ValidatorOnSubmit() {
    if (Page_ValidationActive) {
        return ValidatorCommonOnSubmit();
    }
    else {
        return true;
    }
}
        //]]>
</script>
And
<script type="text/javascript">
//<![CDATA[
function WebForm_OnSubmit() {
if (typeof(ValidatorOnSubmit) == "function" && ValidatorOnSubmit() == false) return false;
return true;
}
//]]>
</script>
```

Ugh—and this is the slightly cut-down version! Luckily, we can reduce this in ASP.NET 4.5 by enabling the new unobtrusive validation mode (enabled by default in 4.5 sites and applications). When unobtrusive validation is enabled, additional HTML5 data attributes are added to controls to hold the meta information about how validation should work and the generated script is much reduced:

```
<input name="txtFirstname" type="text" id="txtFirstname" />
        <span data-val-controltovalidate="txtFirstname" data-val-errormessage="Required"
id="ctl02" data-val="true" data-val-evaluationfunction="RequiredFieldValidatorEvaluateIsValid"
data-val-initialvalue="" style="visibility:hidden;">Required</span>
```

If for some reason you don't want to use the new validation mode, you can turn it off in a number of places.

- Web.config:

```
<add name="ValidationSettings:UnobtrusiveValidationMode" value="None" />
```

- Programmatically:

```
ValidationSettings.UnobtrusiveValidationMode =
        UnobtrusiveValidationMode.WebForms;
```

- At page level:

```
Page.UnobtrusiveValidationMode = System.Web.UI.UnobtrusiveValidationMode.WebForms;
```

Async

One of the big themes in ASP.NET 4.5 is better support for asynchronous scenarios with the introduction of `Await` and `Async` keywords. It's worth noting that previous versions of ASP.NET contain async functionality such as async pages and interfaces for writing async handlers and modules (although their examples and documentation are a bit lacking).

For more information, please refer to `http://msdn.microsoft.com/en-us/magazine/cc163463.aspx`.

Async in ASP.NET 4.5

ASP.NET 4.5 contains several new APIs and changes that allow you to utilize async functionality in your web applications. But first, some of you may be wondering why you might want async support at all.

By default, ASP.NET has access to a (configurable) number of threads to services site requests. If all of these threads are doing something (e.g., awaiting a response from a remote server), then your web server won't be able to respond to new requests and probably will start throwing Server Unavailable messages, leaving your users to look up amusing cat videos on YouTube.

Many ASP.NET applications function marvelously until they hit a certain number of requests, and then performance can degrade very quickly. Apart from throwing more hardware at the problem or optimizing code, we can try to be more efficient in utilizing resources.

If you have certain types of requests that have to wait on an external resource, you can essentially give back the thread to service other requests (until a response is received).

Of course, you could still end up with a situation where you tie up all the threads on a machine waiting for requests. In which case, you may want to consider other possibilities such as a non-blocking message/queue-based system.

When to Use Async to Improve Performance in ASP.NET

There are no hard and fast rules for determining when async functionality should be used, and it is vital that when making any changes, you measure their effect by benchmarking your application before and after changes are made. As a rough guide, you can consider implementing async functionality when the following situations are true:

- Your users are getting server unavailable errors.

- You have task(s) that are not CPU intensive and wait on a remote resource such as a service or database.

- The task being performed is not really short—the overhead of maintaining the async model and context switching could actually make things worse for very fast tasks.

So now that we have a (simplified) view of why you might want to do this, let's see how ASP.NET 4.5 can help us out.

Async HttpModule

It was possible in previous versions of ASP.NET to develop async modules and handlers, but documentation and examples were very scarce. ASP.NET 4.5 makes this much easier.

The example below shows how to create an asynchronous HttpModule that will call the Digg REST API (http://developers.digg.com/version2/digg-getall) asynchronously and output a string of JSON onto each web page the user requests:

```
using System.Threading.Tasks;
using System.Net;

public class TestHttpModule:IHttpModule
{

        public void Init(HttpApplication context)
        {
            EventHandlerTaskAsyncHelper helper = new
EventHandlerTaskAsyncHelper(ScrapeHtmlPage);
            context.AddOnPostAuthorizeRequestAsync(helper.BeginEventHandler,
helper.EndEventHandler);
        }

        private async Task ScrapeHtmlPage(object caller, EventArgs e)
        {
            WebClient client = new WebClient();
            var result = await
client.DownloadStringTaskAsync("http://services.digg.com/2.0/digg.getAll");
            //process here
            System.Web.HttpContext.Current.Response.Write(result);
        }


        public void Dispose()
        {

        }
    }
```

Note how we used the new EventHandlerTaskAsyncHelper class to wrap the Begin and End methods out of a task object, which avoided the need to worry about any implementation detail.

If you are playing with this example, remember to register the module in web.config:

```
<system.webServer>
    <modules>
      <add name="WebApplication4.TestHttpModule" type="WebApplication4.TestHttpModule"/>
    </modules>
  </system.webServer>
```

HttpTaskAsyncHandler

Previously if you wanted to develop an async handler, you would have to implement the IHttpAsyncHandler interface (see http://madskristensen.net/post/How-to-use-the-IHttpAsyncHandler-in-ASPNET.aspx). ASP.NET 4.5 introduces a new abstract class called `HttpTaskAsyncHandler` that hides a lot of the complexity from you.

HttpResponse, BeginFlush, and EndFlush

If you are sending a very large response to a user, it is necessary to periodically call the `HttpResponse.Flush` to stop memory usage becoming too high. ASP.NET 4.5 augments the `HttpResponse` class with new `BeginFlush` and `EndFlush` methods to allow you to perform blocks of flushing and not overuse OS resources.

GetBufferlessInputStream

ASP.NET 4 introduced a method called `GetBufferlessInputStream` to retrieve a stream object from a request. (See `http://george2giga.com/tag/file-upload/` for an example.) This method, however, was synchronous and would occupy a thread for the entire request. ASP.NET 4.5 adds `BeginRead` and `EndRead` methods to the `GetBufferlessInputStream` method to allow chunked reading and releasing of resources between read calls.

GetBufferedInputStream

New to ASP.NET 4.5 is the `GetBufferedInputStream`, which is similar to `GetBufferlessInputStream` but also saves a copy of the request internally (the same place that Form, Files data is kept). This is cool as it allows you to use results in downstream pages, modules, and handlers.

WebSockets

Web applications are becoming increasingly sophisticated, and it is common to need to communicate with various services.

There are a number of options to accomplish this task with, probably the most popular being to continually poll a server with XHR requests. Other alternatives exist that delay disconnections. These can be tricky to implement and don't scale well (sometimes worse than polling as they keep a connection open), so they aren't used as much.

HTTP isn't really an ideal protocol for performing frequent requests for the following reasons:

- It's not optimized for speed, and it utilizes a lot of bandwidth for every request with various headers, and the like, sent with each request.

- To keep an application up-to-date, many requests must be sent.

- It provides limited cross-domain support (relying on workarounds such as JSONP `http://remysharp.com/2007/10/08/what-is-jsonp/`).

- Firewalls and proxies sometimes buffer streaming / long-polling solutions, increasing latency.

- Long-polling and streaming solutions are not very scalable.

WebSockets is a new technology that attempts to resolve some of these limitations by:

- Sending the minimum amount of data necessary

- Making more efficient usage of bandwidth

- Providing cross-domain support

- Still operating over HTTP so it can transverse firewalls and proxies

- Working with some load balancers (TCP l4)

- Providing support for binary data (Note: some JavaScript implementations don't currently support this.)

- Providing a full duplex communication channel

When would WebSockets be a suitable protocol for your application? You might want to consider using WebSockets in the following scenarios:

- Games

- Real-time data

- Chat applications

- News tickers

There is a nice set of demos at www.html5rocks.com/en/tutorials/websockets/basics/ and an interesting article that compares a WebSockets and polling solution in terms of latency and throughput at http://websocket.org/quantum.html.

WebSockets Pitfalls

WebSockets is a relatively new protocol that has already undergone a number of versions as various issues are addressed. Addressing these problems is important as support across browsers varies.

At the time of writing, WebSockets (in some form) can be used by the following browsers (check http://caniuse.com for the most up to date information):

- IE10

- Chrome 13+

- Firefox 7

- Safari 5+

- Opera 11+

Earlier implementations of WebSockets had some security issues, so your connections may work but they are not secure. (Firefox disabled support in Firefox 4 and 5 for this reason.)

The other issue that you may encounter is that some older proxy servers don't support the HTTP upgrade system that WebSockets uses to connect, so some clients may be unable to connect.

ASP.NET 4.5 WebSockets Support

ASP.NET 4.5 introduces a number of APIs for working with WebSockets. If you find you need more control than the ASP.NET API's offers, then look into WCF because it has also been updated.

Before we begin, there are a couple of requirements for using ASP.NET WebSockets API:

- Application must be hosted on IIS 8 (available only with some version of Windows 8—please note IIS Express currently does not work).

- WebSockets protocol feature must be installed (IIS option).

- ASP.NET 4.5 must be in use.

- A compatible browser on the client must be present. (IE10 or Chrome will work fine at time of writing.)

- It would help if your Chinese birth animal were the horse.

Currently, Microsoft has no plans to release WebSockets support for earlier versions of IIS. Consequently, if you plan to run it on Windows Server 2008, you are going to have to look at other options such as `http://superwebsocket.codeplex.com/`. Alternatively you could look at the SignalR library from Microsoft, which is designed for developing async applications and providing WebSockets (and fallback) support: `https://github.com/SignalR/SignalR/wiki/WebSockets`.

Hello, WebSockets Example!

I am going to assume that you are already working with some version of Windows 8 that has IIS and ASP.NET 4.5 installed. The other thing we are going to need to do is make sure IIS has the WebSockets protocol feature installed (this is in the add/remove programs bit):

1. First, create a new empty ASP.NET project called WebSockets.

2. Add the NuGet package Microsoft.Websockets.

3. Pull down the latest jQuery library and put it in a scripts directory (I am using 1.7.2). Note: jQuery isn't necessary; it just saves a bit of tedious event and manipulation code.

4. Now add a file called `index.htm` and enter the following code:

```
<!doctype html>

<head>

<script src="Scripts/jquery-1.7.2.min.js" type="text/javascript"></script>

<script type="text/javascript">

$(document).ready(function () {

var name = prompt('what is your name?:');

var url = 'ws://' + window.location.hostname + window.location.pathname.replace('index.htm',
'ws.ashx') + '?name=' + name;

alert('Connecting to: ' + url);

ws = new WebSocket(url);

ws.onopen = function () {
```

```
$('#messages').prepend('Connected <br/>');

$('#cmdSend').click(function () {

ws.send($('#txtMessage').val());

$('#txtMessage').val('');

});

};

ws.onmessage = function (e) {

$('#chatMessages').prepend(e.data + '<br/>');

};

$('#cmdLeave').click(function () {

ws.close();

});

ws.onclose = function () {

$('#chatMessages').prepend('Closed <br/>');

};

ws.onerror = function (e) {

$('#chatMessages').prepend('Oops something went wront <br/>');

};

});

</script>

</head>

<body>

<input id="txtMessage" />

<input id="cmdSend" type="button" value="Send" />

<input id="cmdLeave" type="button" value="Leave" />

<br />
```

```
<div id="chatMessages" />

</body>

</html>
```

5. To create an HttpHandler, add a new generic handler to the project called ws.ashx and enter the following code:

```
using System;

using System.Collections.Generic;

using System.Linq;

using System.Web;

using Microsoft.Web.WebSockets;

namespace WebSockets

{

public class ws : IHttpHandler

{

public void ProcessRequest(HttpContext context)

{

if (context.IsWebSocketRequest)

context.AcceptWebSocketRequest(new TestWebSocketHandler());

}

public bool IsReusable

{

get

{

return false;

}

}
```

```
        }

    }
```

6. Finally, you need to create something to handle the WebSockets connection (TestWebSocketHandler, that is created in the AcceptWebSocketRequest method). Create a new class called TestWebSocketHandler and enter the following code:

```
using System;

using System.Collections.Generic;

using System.Linq;

using System.Threading;

using System.Web;

using Microsoft.Web.WebSockets;

namespace WebSockets

{

public class TestWebSocketHandler : WebSocketHandler

{

private static WebSocketCollection clients = new WebSocketCollection();

private string name;

public override void OnOpen()

{

this.name = this.WebSocketContext.QueryString["name"];

clients.Add(this);

clients.Broadcast(name + " has connected.");

}

public override void OnMessage(string message)

{

clients.Broadcast(string.Format("{0} said: {1}", name, message));

}
```

```
public override void OnClose()

{

clients.Remove(this);

clients.Broadcast(string.Format("{0} has gone away.", name));

}

}

}
```

7. That's all you need. Now you can compile the project and run it in a compatible browser (IE10 or the latest Chrome will do fine), making sure you are hosting your project from IIS (project properties if you are not) and the site/application is operating in integrated pipeline mode.

8. Once you have run it up, you will be prompted to provide a name. An alert box will then indicate the end point of your application (ws://localhost/.. Note: The secure HTTPS version is wss://.)

9. Now open up a different browser via WebSockets (see Figure 6-3).

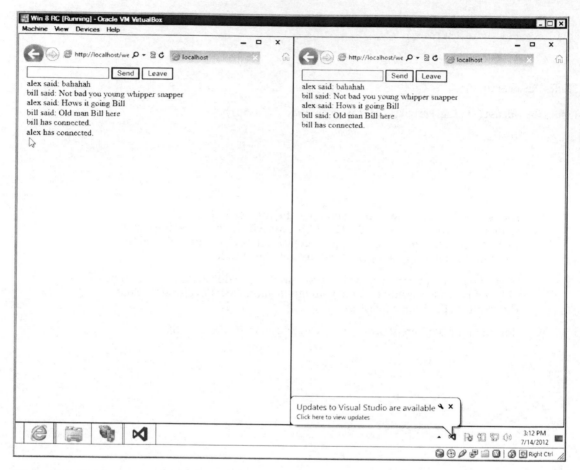

Figure 6-3. WebSockets example running

Performance Improvements

Microsoft says that combined use of ASP.NET 4.5 and Windows 8 can improve web application startup time by up to 35 percent (www.asp.net/vnext/overview/whitepapers/whats-new#_Toc_perf).

A number of performance enhancements have been made that will affect ASP.NET applications performance:

- Shared assemblies

- Multi core JIT compilation

- Precompilation

- Optimized GC

- Prefetcher

Shared Assemblies (ASP.NET 4 & VS2012)

If you have a number of web sites hosted on a server, it's quite likely that many of them also use the same libraries. For example, several sites may reference NHibernate assemblies. When a web server first starts up, having many copies of the same libraries slows everything down as each one must be individually processed, read, and loaded.

VS2012 introduces a new command line tool that replaces individual assemblies with a link to a single copy of an assembly, making this process much quicker. If a site references a specific version of an assembly, the symbolic link will be replaced by the actual assembly.

To use the shared assemblies, you must use the command-line tool aspnet_intern.exe, which comes as part of the VS2012 SDK, to process assemblies on the server (you can also use this feature within ASP.NET 4 if you apply the following update: http://support.microsoft.com/kb/2468871).

When aspnet_intern is run, it will, by default, process assemblies that appear in more than three places. (This is configurable using the minrefcount option.)

Let's see this in action now:

1. Open a command prompt and go to C:\Program Files (x86)\Microsoft SDKs\Windows\v8.0A\bin\NETFX 4.0 Tools.

2. Use the following command to look at all aspnet_interns options:

```
aspnet_intern /?
```

3. Run the following command to get a report of assemblies that would benefit from interning without actually interning:

```
aspnet_intern -mode analyze -sourcedir
"C:\Windows\Microsoft.NET\Framework\v4.0.30319\Temporary ASP.NET Files" > c:\internReport.txt
```

4. Run the following command to intern assemblies to the folder C:\CommonASP:

```
aspnet_intern -mode exec -sourcedir
"C:\Windows\Microsoft.NET\Framework\v4.0.30319\Temporary ASP.NET
Files" -interndir C:\CommonASP
```

Microsoft suggests setting up a weekly scheduled task to do this.

Multi Core JIT Compilation (4.5)

When a site first starts up, individual assemblies must be JIT compiled by the framework. ASP.NET 4.5 speeds up this work by dividing compilation across multiple cores. This feature is enabled by default in ASP.NET 4.5, but it may be turned off in web.config as shown below:

```
<system.web>
    <compilation profileGuidedOptimizations="None"  />
</system.web>
```

GC Compilation Optimized for Memory

To a certain extent, previous versions of ASP.NET allowed you to configure and tweak how the garbage collector worked (http://learn.iis.net/page.aspx/50/aspnet-20-35-shared-hosting-configuration/).

ASP.NET 4.5 introduces a new profile setting for those running servers, hosting many sites that groups these tweaks together. To enable this setting, copy the following setting to the aspnet.config file at Windows\Microsoft.NET\Framework\v4.0.30319\aspnet.config:

```
<configuration>
  <runtime>
    <performanceScenario value="HighDensityWebHosting"  />
```

Prefetcher (Windows 8 and ASP.NET 4.5 only)

Recent versions of Windows include a technology known as Prefetcher (http://en.wikipedia.org/wiki/Prefetcher), which reduces disk-read time by maintaining an index of recently used files.

Until now, Prefetcher was not available in server editions of Windows because it was mainly aimed at client applications. Prefetching, however, can reduce launch time for individual sites. To enable Prefetching for individual sites, run the following command from a Visual Studio command prompt:

```
sc config sysmain start=auto
reg add "HKEY_LOCAL_MACHINE\SYSTEM\CurrentControlSet\Control\Session Manager\Memory
Management\PrefetchParameters" /v EnablePrefetcher /t REG_DWORD /d 2 /f
reg add "HKEY_LOCAL_MACHINE\Software\Microsoft\Windows NT\CurrentVersion\Prefetcher" /v
MaxPrefetchFiles /t REG_DWORD /d 8192 /f
net start sysmain
```

You must then add the following switch to your web site:

```
<configuration>
  <system.web>
    <compilation enablePrefetchOptimization="true" />
  </system.web>
</configuration>
```

Precompile

VS2012 allows you to precompile a web site before deployment or publishing to reduce startup time. To enable this option, right-click on Project, select Properties, and then go to the Package/Publish Web tab and select the checkbox that reads "Precompile this application before publishing."

Miscellaneous Changes

You should also be aware of the following changes in VS2012 affecting ASP.NET users.

IIS Express

In VS2012, IIS Express is now the default web server for testing your applications. IIS Express has all the main features of its bigger brother, but it doesn't require administrator rights for most tasks, it is not run a service, and it can be used by multiple users on the same machine. Refer to http://learn.iis.net/page.aspx/868/iis-express-overview/ for more information.

Enable CDN Fallback

The Script Manager control will now fall back to a local version of referenced scripts if they are not loaded successfully from the CDN. For more information on the EnableCDN feature, please refer to http://weblogs.asp.net/infinitiesloop/archive/2009/11/23/asp-net-4-0-scriptmanager-improvements.aspx.

Routing Changes

An update was made to IIS 7 to natively enable routing functionality on Windows 7 SP1. Previously it was necessary to add a setting called runAllManagedModulesForAllRequests to your web.config file to enable this. The new web site templates in Visual Studio 12 do not include this setting, which means that it is false by default. Thus, if you run one of the new project templates on a machine without the aforementioned update applied, then routing won't work. To resolve this problem, simply add the setting to web.config:

```
<configuration>
  <system.webServer>
    <modules runAllManagedModulesForAllRequests="true">
    </modules>
  </system.webServer>
</configuration>
```

HttpRequest.Abort

HttpRequest.Abort is a new method that forcibly terminates an HTTP connection.

New APIs for Better Async Support

A number of new APIs have been introduced for better Async support such as HttpResponse.ClientDisconnectedToken, HttpRequest.TimedOutToken, and HttpContext.ThreadAbortOnTimeout. These APIs allow you to be notified of client disconnection or timeout and control the time before ASP.NET aborts a request. Unfortunately there is no information on these at the time of writing.

New APIs for Extending Web Forms Compilation

Microsoft has also introduced new APIs for customizing how ASP.NET works. Again, very little information is available on these APIs, but I wanted to make you aware of them. A new class called ControlBuilderInterceptor has been created that should allow you to customize Web Forms output to some degree, and a new method called TemplateParser.ParseTemplate will allow the creation of a template instance from ASPX markup.

AN INSIDER'S OPINION

I asked ASP.NET MVP Malcolm Sheridan what his favorite features are in ASP.NET 4.5 and ASP.NET MVC 4:

The best feature for me in the inbuilt asynchronous controllers. Making this super easy is a winner for me. The inbuilt bundling and mini fixation of JavaScript and CSS files are compelling also.

Conclusion

ASP.NET 4.5 contains a number of useful features. Probably the biggest game changer is support for model and declarative binding. New async support and improvements to validation are also very welcome and will benefit all users.

CHAPTER 7

■ ■ ■

ASP.NET MVC 4

ASP.NET MVC 4 contains improved project templates, a new API for serving up different views under certain conditions, a number of tweaks to Razor syntax, better support for async scenarios, and improved integration with Entity Framework.

■ **Note** We won't be discussing the new ASP.NET Web API in this chapter (a brand-spanking new way of building RESTful services) since it has its very own chapter because we thought it was so awesome. Head over to Chapter 8 for more information.

Upgrading to MVC 4

MVC 4 will happily run alongside ASP.NET MVC version 3 and .NET 4/VS2010. You can thus experiment and create MVC 4 projects without fear of breaking your old applications. But when the time comes to move to the juicy new v4 stuff, how do you migrate your existing v3 projects to MVC 4?

There are three main methods of upgrading to MVC 4:

- Copy existing content into a new MVC 4 project

- Manually upgrade the project

- Utilize the MVC 4 NuGet package

■ **Note** For the latest information on the upgrade process, please refer to http://www.asp.net/whitepapers/mvc4-release-notes.

Copy Existing Content into a New MVC 4 Project

To upgrade your application by copying content, simply perform the steps below:

1. Create a new MVC4 project ensuring you match the existing project name, namespace options, etc.

2. Copy all the code, content, controllers, views, and scripts (plus any pictures of cats!) you may have into the new project.

3. Add additional project and assembly references.

4. Copy any web.config changes you have made.

The main advantage of upgrading with this method is that it's very straightforward. The downside, however, is that by creating a completely new project, you will lose file change history in source control systems and will probably upset various build processes you may have set up. If these things are important to you, then you are probably better off performing a manual upgrade so let's look at how to do that now.

Manually Upgrade the Project

To perform a manual upgrade is a bit more involved than the previous method (and a little tedious).

First, we need to make some changes in web.config to tell our site to reference the new ASP.NET MVC 4 assemblies.

Open up all the web.config files in your project and replace any lines that read as the following:

```
System.Web.Mvc, Version=3.0.0.0
System.Web.WebPages, Version=1.0.0.0
System.Web.Helpers, Version=1.0.0.0
System.Web.WebPages.Razor, Version=1.0.0.0
```

With their MVC 4 counterparts:

```
System.Web.Mvc, Version=4.0.0.0
System.Web.WebPages, Version=2.0.0.0
System.Web.Helpers, Version=2.0.0.0,
System.Web.WebPages.Razor, Version=2.0.0.0,
```

Now open the root web.config file and update the webpages:Version appSettings key to the string "2.0.0.0":

```
<appSettings>
  <add key="webpages:Version" value="2.0.0.0" />
<appSettings>
```

In the root web.config file, add a new PreserveLoginUrl key entry:

```
<appSettings>
  <add key="webpages:Version" value="2.0.0.0" />
  <add key="PreserveLoginUrl" value="true" />
<appSettings>
```

Now delete any references to System.Web.MVC (v3). In Solution Explorer, remove the following assembly references:

*   System.Web.Mvc (v3.0.0.0)

*   System.Web.WebPages (v1.0.0.0)

- System.Web.Razor (v1.0.0.0)

- System.Web.WebPages.Deployment (v1.0.0.0)

- System.Web.WebPages.Razor (v1.0.0.0)

Now add references to the new versions of these assemblies:

- System.Web.Mvc (v4.0.0.0)

- System.Web.WebPages (v2.0.0.0)

- System.Web.Razor (v2.0.0.0)

- System.Web.WebPages.Deployment (v2.0.0.0)

- System.Web.WebPages.Razor (v2.0.0.0)

In Solution Explorer, unload your MVC project as we are going to make some changes to the project file; this won't work if the solution is open (and kittens will die!).

1. Open the project file (it should be called YourProjectName.csproj) and replace any references of the ProjectTypeGuids E53F8FEA-EAE0-44A6-8774-FFD645390401 with E3E379DF-F4C6-4180-9B81-6769533ABE47.

2. Save the changes you have made and reload the project.

3. Finally, if your application or its references uses any assemblies compiled against the previous version of MVC, tell these to use MVC4 by adding binding redirect entries such as the following:

```
<configuration>

  <runtime>
    <assemblyBinding xmlns="urn:schemas-microsoft-com:asm.v1">
      <dependentAssembly>
        <assemblyIdentity name="System.Web.Helpers"
            publicKeyToken="31bf3856ad364e35" />
        <bindingRedirect oldVersion="1.0.0.0" newVersion="2.0.0.0"/>
      </dependentAssembly>
      <dependentAssembly>
        <assemblyIdentity name="System.Web.Mvc"
            publicKeyToken="31bf3856ad364e35" />
        <bindingRedirect oldVersion="1.0.0.0-3.0.0.0" newVersion="4.0.0.0"/>
      </dependentAssembly>
      <dependentAssembly>
        <assemblyIdentity name="System.Web.WebPages"
            publicKeyToken="31bf3856ad364e35" />
        <bindingRedirect oldVersion="1.0.0.0" newVersion="2.0.0.0"/>
      </dependentAssembly>
    </assemblyBinding>
  </runtime>
</configuration>
```

Utilize the MVC4 NuGet Package

You can upgrade MVC 3 projects by applying the AspNetMvc package. To do this simply run the following command from NuGet Package Manager Console: Install-Package AspNetMvc (please refer to the appendix for more information on NuGet). For more information on this package please refer to http://nuget.org/packages/aspnetmvc.

Razor Enhancements

Microsoft has made some welcome tweaks to the Razor engine that simplify some common scenarios and make code a little more readable, which can only be a good thing, right?

Tilde Syntax (~)

The first change allows you to use the tilde (that weird ~ character) in URL paths to avoid the need to use path-mapping helper methods such as Url.Content. This change means that if you wanted to create a link to a JavaScript file instead of writing the reference, use the Url.Content helper method:

```
<script src="@Url.Content("~/MyScripts/Something.js")"></script>
```

You can now simply write:

```
<script src="~/Scripts/Site.js"></script>
```

Much nicer!
Razor will resolve this syntax with all standard HTML attributes.

Null and Boolean Handling

The second syntax change simplifies the scenario where you don't want to write something at all when a model property is null—it's harder than you might think!

```
<div @{if (Model.myTestProperty != null)
   { <text>class=not-null</text> } }>
   Content
</div>
```

It's actually pretty common to need to do this as you might only want to add a CSS class to an element if a model property is not null.
With MVC 4, this can now be written as the following:

```
<div class="@Model.myTestProperty">Content</div>
```

The syntax also works with boolean types so if a value is false, the checked attribute will not be generated as in the example below:

```
<input checked="@Model.IsSelected" type="checkbox" />
```

It is worth noting that in the final release, Microsoft plans to render empty strings when writing values into data attributes as the .NET team feels this would be the expected behavior.

Razor and Bundle Syntax

Razor has added new syntax for referencing minified CSS and JavaScript files:

```
@Styles.Render("~/Content/pinkPoodleStyle/css")
@Scripts.Render("~/MyScripts/js")
@Styles.Render("~/Content/pinkPoodleStyle/css", "~/Content/MellowYellow/css")
```

An advantage of using this syntax, in addition to readability, is that Razor will ensure that just one version of the file is referenced even if the scripts are referenced multiple times, for example, in separate partial views.

New Default Project Templates

The screenshot below shows the default ASP.NET MVC site template you are probably very familiar with:

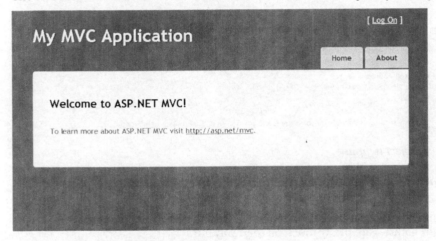

Figure 7-1. MVC 3 default design template

MVC 4 has completely revamped this template:

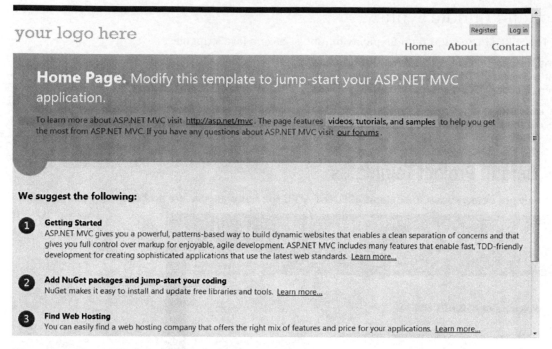

Figure 7-2. New MVC default project template

In addition to a much better-looking design, there are a number of other interesting aspects to take note of:

- Microsoft Ajax script references have been removed. (I think we can all now agree the Microsoft Ajax libraries are pretty much on their way out.)

- jQuery libraries have been updated to latest version (at the time of writing anyway!).

- knockout.js (a way of binding data) and Modernizr libraries (tests support for different features) are now included.

- Semantic markup is used.

- The template utilizes a viewport meta tag that makes it display better on mobile devices.

- The template is easier to customize due to use of razor sections.

- JavaScript is used to provide a superior user experience for logging in and registration.

- The markup and styling ensure site looks good in various resolutions or mobile devices (see below screenshot where I have reduced the browser window's size).

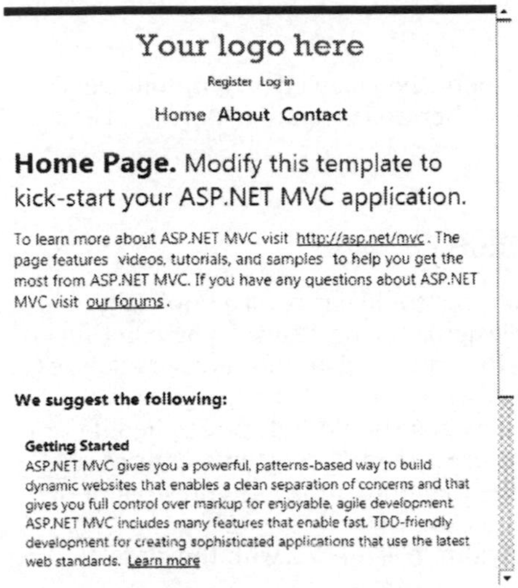

Figure 7-3. The new project templates looks good even under smaller resolutions.

Improved Support for Mobile Development

Mobile optimized sites are likely to become increasingly important with many businesses and analysts predicting that mobile visitors will soon exceed desktop users for many sites:

> *The browsing experience of smart phones continues to improve with advances in technology and speed of access. We believe that it's very likely that mobile devices could become the preferred method of accessing the Internet in the future. Morgan Stanley predicts that by 2014 access from mobile devices will exceed that of the desktop.*

> www.morganstanley.com/institutional/techresearch/pdfs/Internet_Trends_041210.pdf

In fact, Google believes mobile development is so important that whenever they develop a new product, they first develop a mobile version (http://venturebeat.com/2010/04/12/eric-schmidt-mobile-first/). Thus, it's quite likely, even if you are not doing any mobile design work now, that you will have to at some point in the future.

ASP.NET MVC has always been a good choice to develop a mobile site with the ability to have full control over the HTML generated and its extensible nature. ASP.NET MVC 4 contains a number of enhancements aimed at mobile development that improves this even further.

But before we delve into the MVC specific features, let's review quickly some of the issues around mobile development as these will put some of these changes in context.

Developing a Mobile-optimized Site

Generally, a website developed for the desktop will not look very good when viewed on a mobile device. With a few simple modifications, however, these sites can display rather well on mobile devices. Let's take a look at some common techniques and methods.

Utilize Flow Layouts and Responsive Design Practices

Explaining flow layout and responsive design techniques and practices could easily fill a book (a good start is http://www.abookapart.com/products/responsive-web-design). At a basic level, you can think of flow layout techniques as not using fixed width and heights so a site scales well at different screen sizes and resolutions and thus also hopefully different devices.

Media queries are a CSS3 feature that allows you to specify rules that should only be applied if the browser matches certain conditions such as minimum and maximum screen sizes. Media queries are commonly used on mobile-optimized sites to override default rules that don't look right on smaller screens and to apply landscape/portrait versions of pages.

The below example shows a media query that only applies a width to elements with the class content and *only* on screens less than 600 pixels wide:

```
@media screen and (max-width: 600px) {
        .content {
        width: 500px;
        }
}
```

You can also use media queries on your style sheet references:

```
<link rel="stylesheet" media=" (min-device-width: 800px)" href="example.css" />
```

There are a number of options for media queries; please consult https://developer.mozilla.org/en/Mobile/Viewport_meta_tag for further examples.

■ **Note** Media queries are a good (and the only!) alternative for creating landscape/portrait versions of sites for mobile Internet Explorer browser.

Addition of Viewport Meta Tag

By default, most mobile devices will display a page in zoomed-out mode that probably isn't what the majority of your visitors are going to want. For example, a site displayed in zoomed-out mode on a mobile device might look something like the screenshot below:

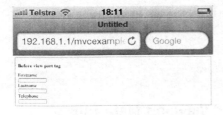

Figure 7-4. Website before viewport meta tag added

Hmm … not so good! We can fix this problem by adding a special viewport meta tag to tell devices not to zoom out the display of the web page, and it will instead look like this:

Figure 7-5. Website after viewport meta tag added

Following is an example viewport meta tag that will tell mobile browsers not to zoom out when displaying the content:

```
<meta name="viewport" content="width=device-width" />
```

These techniques are employed within the new MVC template files.

Limitations of Responsive Design, Flow Layout, and Viewport Meta Tags

These techniques can greatly assist making a site usable on a mobile device, but they have their limitations:

- Very complex screens won't display very well on a mobile device so you might want to present information differently to mobile-device users.

- Some designs may be too complex to be overridden.

- You might need to display different content depending on device type. (For example, for low-end devices just plain text, whereas cutting-edge smart phones get a much more interesting version.

- You might want to give users the option to display both desktop and mobile-optimized versions.

There are thus times when you are really going to want to serve up an entirely different UI for mobile users. MVC makes this relatively easy to do.

In previous versions of MVC, it was possible to override MVC's default view engine to allow you to serve different views for the same action depending on certain conditions. This could then allow you to give mobile users different views and potentially make use of the same controller and models. I have seen and used this technique on a number of projects, and it worked very successfully. For more information on this and a possible implementation, please refer to: http://www.hanselman.com/blog/ABetterASPNETMVCMobileDeviceCapabilitiesViewEngine.aspx.

MVC 4 improves on this further as it now has this feature out of the box with an easy to use API. Let's take a look at the new DisplayMode functionality.

DisplayMode

The DisplayMode functionality allows you to serve different views dependent on specific conditions and saves you from having to implement this functionality yourself (see above). This API is ideal to allow you to create a mobile version of a specific site, but don't think you are restricted to this purpose as it could also be used wherever you want to serve up a different layout to users—e.g., to create different site themes or layouts.

We will now create a simple example that displays a different view depending on the browser's user-agent string. The user-agent string is sent as part of every HTTP request and describes the user's browser (and generally OS).

Below is the user-agent that Chrome (v16) sends a webserver from my machine:

```
User-Agent: Mozilla/5.0 (Windows NT 6.1; WOW64) AppleWebKit/535.7 (KHTML, like Gecko)
Chrome/16.0.912.77 Safari/535.7.
```

If you look at the above example, it might surprise you to see that it also contains names of other browsers/rendering engines. Historically, some browser manufacturers would do this as some (bad) site developers would perform simple string matches when checking for a browser and redirect users that didn't use the specific browser targeted. The browser manufacturers knew this and wanted to avoid this scenario so they added additional entries.

■ **Note** Keep this example in mind when you are writing your DisplayMode API matching rules—writing simple user-agent string matching code probably won't work that well. Instead if you are using this technique for mobile development, you will probably want to use a device database for identifying individual devices/sets of devices. You could, for example, use a product from a company such as 51 degrees (http://51degrees.mobi/).

However, in order to keep things simple, we will just check for the presence of testbrowser in the user-agent string.

Open up Global.asax and in the Application_Start method, add the following code:

```
DisplayModeProvider.Instance.Modes.Insert(0, new DefaultDisplayMode("testbrowser")
        {
            ContextCondition = (context => context.Request.UserAgent.IndexOf
                ("testbrowser", StringComparison.OrdinalIgnoreCase) >= 0)
        });
```

Now we need to create a separate view for our testbrowser users. MVC follows a convention when determining which view to serve for which display mode it is operating in:

```
ViewName.DisplayModeName.cshtml
```

Thus, if you had created a display mode called testbrowser and met the conditions for this mode, MVC would serve you the view index.testbrowser.cshtml in preference to index.cshtml. If you haven't created a separate testbrowser version of a view, then the default will be displayed. MVC will also use this model when working with partial views and layout files. For example partial views @Html.Partial("_MyPartial") will render _MyPartial.testbrowser.cshtml and Layout files will render _Layout.testbrowser.cshtml.

Let's continue with our example by creating a new view called index.testbrowser.cshtml and add some text to indicate this is the testbrowser view and not the standard one.

Something like "hey idiot this is the testbrowser view" will do just fine!

■ **Note** MVC also contains inbuilt support for serving mobile views using ASP.NET's mobile detection features. To use, simply create views in the format ViewName.Mobile.cshtml, and you don't even need to set up the display mode as above! It should be noted the inbuilt ASP.NET mobile detection features don't work so well with some mobile-device emulators so the Display Mode API could be a good fix of these limitations.

Changing Browser User-Agent

To demonstrate the new display mode, we will need the ability to change our browser's user-agent string. In Internet Explorer 9, you can modify the user-agent string using IE's inbuilt development tools (instructions below). There are also a number of extensions for other browsers:

- https://addons.mozilla.org/en-US/firefox/addon/user-agent-switcher/ (Firefox)

- http://spoofer-extension.appspot.com/ (Chrome)

Modifying User-Agent in Internet Explorer 9

Let's create a new user-agent string in IE9:

1. Open IE9 (good start!).

2. Press F12 to bring up the development tools.

3. Go to the Tools menu and then select Change user agent string ➤ Custom.

4. Add "testbrowser" as the name and value of the new user-agent string.

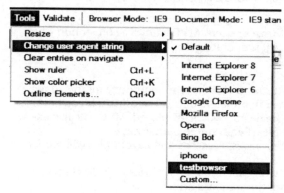

Figure 7-6. Adding a new user-agent in IE9 dev tools

We are all set to test our new display mode, so run up the MVC site and the "standard" view should be shown.

Now use the user-agent switcher in IE9 to change the user-agent, refresh the screen, and you should see this overridden view is instead shown—hurray!

Browser Overriding

MVC 4 contains a number of APIs to allow you to pretend a specific device was accessing the site. These APIs could be useful for allowing the user to switch to a non-mobile view or for testing your application. Note that using these APIs only has an effect on layout, views, and partial views and will not affect any other ASP.NET Request.Browser related functionality.

The overridden browser is stored in a cookie. (Note: According to documentation, you can replace the BrowserOverrideStores.current provider—sorry no information yet.)

I have listed the override methods below. (Note: these are contained within the System.Web.WebPages namespace as extension methods on HttpContextBase.)

- HttpContext.SetOverriddenBrowser() - allows you to set the user-agent string to a specific value

- HttpContext.GetOverriddenUserAgent() – gets the overridden value (or actual if not overridden)

- HttpContext.GetOverriddenBrowser() - returns HttpBrowserCapabilitiesBase object of overridden browser that can be used with ASP.NET APIs such as IsMobile

- HttpContext.ClearOverriddenBrowser() – removes any overridden user agent for current request

New Mobile Application Project Template and jQuery Mobile

MVC4 contains a new mobile site template utilizing the popular jQuery mobile framework (JQM to its friends) and containing important settings such as the viewport meta tag described earlier.

The below screenshot shows the default template accessed from my iPhone:

Figure 7-7. Mobile Application ASP.NET MVC default template

As you can see, this is a great way of beginning to explore mobile site development and jQuery mobile. But why would you use such a framework in the first place? Well, you certainly don't have to (and in many cases probably shouldn't!), but JQM (and don't think that this is the only mobile framework around) provides the following features:

- Tries to take care of various niggly display issues across various types of devices

- Provides an abstraction over various device actions such as a user rotating a device, swiping, and other gestures

- Hijacks the loading of links and performs these calls with AJAX, which makes for a nicer experience

- Takes care of browser history management—this becomes more complex when Ajax is used to load pages as you want to present an intuitive experience to your users

- Contains various controls such as sliders and buttons similar in look and feel to those on an iPhone (because in my experience most clients seem to think a mobile site should look like an iPhone app—websites are different from iPhone native apps!).

jQuery.Mobile.MVC

As we've seen, JQM is a framework for making mobile development easier. Microsoft has released a NuGet package to allow you to easily set up jQuery mobile in your MVC4 applications.

To install the package, simply run the following command from the NuGet package console window (Tools ➤ Other Windows ➤ NuGet package console):

```
Install-Package jQuery.Mobile.MVC
```

Installing the package will make a number of changes including registering different mobile display modes, creating a view switcher component, and installing of JQM specific views.

Async Controller Actions

In previous versions of ASP.NET MVC, you could avoid tying up ASP.Net threads by using Async controllers. For more information on why you might want to do this, please refer to the async section in the ASP.Net chapter (Chapter 6).

Prior to MVC 4, if you wanted to create an async controller action, you had to change your controller to inherit from AsyncController and write code similar to the following (the following downloads and outputs the HTML from Google's home page):

```
public class TestController : AsyncController
    {
        public void DoSomethingAsync()
        {
            AsyncManager.OutstandingOperations.Increment();
        var wc = new WebClient();
            wc.DownloadStringCompleted += (s, e) =>
            {
                if (!e.Cancelled && e.Error == null)
                {
                    AsyncManager.Parameters["html"] = e.Result;
                }
```

```
            AsyncManager.OutstandingOperations.Decrement();
        };
        wc.DownloadStringAsync(new Uri("http://www.google.com"));
    }
    public ActionResult DoSomethingCompleted(string html)
    {
        return Content(html);
    }
}
```

Bit verbose, eh? MVC 4 makes this very much easier (and more readable) and allows you to write controller actions that return Task<ActionResult>, which works well with .NET 4.5's async functionality:

```
public class NewController : Controller
{
    public async Task<ActionResult> Index()
    {
        var webClient = new WebClient();
        string html = await webClient.DownloadStringTaskAsync("http://www.google.com");
        return Content(html);
    }
}
```

Much nicer!

EF Database Migration Support

MVC4 contains inbuilt support for Entity Framework (EF) database migration features that were introduced in Entity Framework 4.3. The database migration features make it very easy to keep track of database schema changes and programmatically apply them. Let's see how this integrates with ASP.NET MVC.

1. Create a new ASP.NET MVC 4 project.

2. Create a new class called Person in the models folder with the following code:

```
public class Person
{
    public int Id { get; set; }
    public string FirstName { get; set; }
}
```

3. Right-click on the controllers folder and select Add Controller.

4. Change the template to MVC controller with read/write actions and views, using Entity Framework as in Figure 7-8 below:

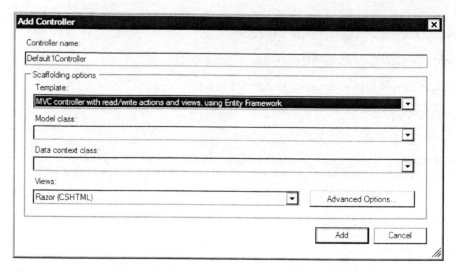

Figure 7-8. New EF template support

5. Select Person as the model class.

6. On data context, select <New data context..> and rename it to PersonContext.

7. Click OK.

MVC will generate scaffolding create, update, and delete views and controller code for the Person class.

Now open the Package Manager console (View ➤ Other windows ➤ Package manager console) and run the following command:

```
Enable-Migrations
```

This will create a new Migrations folder within your application containing a file called configuration.cs. At the time of writing, configuration.cs will contain something similar to the following:

```
protected override void Seed(MvcApplication10.Models.PersonContext context)
    {
        //  This method will be called after migrating to the latest version.

        //  You can use the DbSet<T>.AddOrUpdate() helper extension method
        //  to avoid creating duplicate seed data. E.g.
        //
        //    context.People.AddOrUpdate(
        //      p => p.FullName,
        //      new Person { FullName = "Andrew Peters" },
        //      new Person { FullName = "Brice Lambson" },
        //      new Person { FullName = "Rowan Miller" }
        //    );
        //
    }
```

Now compile and run the project and Visual Studio will create a database in the project's App_data directory based on this class.

Now let's add a new property to the Person class:

```
public string LastName { get; set; }
```

OK, time to apply this change to our database. Open the Package Manager console and enter the following command:

```
add-migration LastName
```

Entity Framework will generate update code for the property added in the Migrations folder with the format todaysdate_migrationname.

You can then apply your migration by running the update-database command from the Package Manager console.

Azure Support

ASP.NET MVC 4 supports the Azure 1.6 SDK and has been updated to deploy the required assemblies automatically. It also contains updated membership, profile, and session providers for use with Azure.

Miscellaneous Enhancements

MVC 4 contains the following other enhancements:

- The MVC JSON serializer has been replaced with the popular open source Json.NET serializer

- New App_Start directory contains routing, bundling, and filter configuration (see ASP.net chapter for further details)

- Controllers can be added to any folder rather than the standard structure from the IDE.

- New AllowAnonymous attribute that allows you to secure a controller with the Authorize attribute but still expose individual methods to anonymous users

- HTML.TextBox has additional overload that accepts a format parameter and calls String.Format

- HTML.Label related methods now allow you to specify html attributes as a parameter

- New URL helper methods for working with Web API (URL.HttpRouteURL)

- New properties on controller class – Profile & ViewEngineCollection (and a few Async related properties)

- New HTML.Value, HTML.ValueFor & HTML.ValueForModel methods

Future Enhancements

At the time of writing, ASP.NET MVC 4 has not been officially released, but Microsoft says it is planning to make a number of other changes that I want to make you aware of (for the most up-to-date list of changes, please consult: http://aspnet.codeplex.com/wikipage?title=ASP.NET%20MVC%204%20RoadMap).

- Editor, display templates, and HTML helpers will have improved HTML5 support, e.g., TextBoxFor when used with a DateTime model property will render an input element with the type set to date.

- Project templates will be updated to support logging into sites such as Facebook using oAuth and OpenID.

- Project creation will be speeded up (it's a bit slow as of the RC!).

- There will be a new empty MVC project template (similar to ASP.NET empty project).

- New Entity Framework Scaffolding for Web API will be added.

Single Page Applications and Recipes

During the beta release, Microsoft released a preview of a project type called Single Page Application (SPA). SPA is a way of structuring applications using a single page and loading content dynamically with the aim of an improved user experience, and it is often used on mobile sites. SPA is not expected to be included with MVC 4 release, but it will be available separately as a NuGet package. For more details, please refer to: http://www.asp.net/single-page-application.

Microsoft also released a preview of a feature called Recipes. Recipes was designed for automate tedious tasks. For more information, please refer to: http://haacked.com/archive/2011/09/21/writing-a-recipe-for-asp-net-mvc-4-developer-preview.aspx and http://channel9.msdn.com/events/BUILD/BUILD2011/TOOL-803T.

Microsoft indicates that it doesn't intend to release Recipes feature with MVC4, and it's likely to change considerably from the preview. So, for now, simply be aware you are likely to have a method to automate some tedious tasks programmatically in the future.

Conclusion

MVC developers will have no difficulty getting a grip on ASP.NET MVC4's new features. These features help further cement ASP.NET MVC's place as the choice of platform for future Microsoft web development.

■ ■ ■

CHAPTER 8

Windows Communication Foundation and Web API

In this chapter, you will be introduced to all the changes that have been made in .NET 4.5 with respect to Windows Communication Foundation (WCF). These changes include the use of async-await from the client side, improvements made to WCF configuration, and the inclusion of new bindings—HttpsBinding and UdpBinding. In addition, you will also learn about Web API, which is the new way of creating RESTful services.

You finish the chapter learning about WebSockets, which is another addition made to WCF to help in establishing a true bidirectional communication via sockets over the web that doesn't have the overhead of frequent request-response.

Support for Async Calls

As you have already learned from the previous chapters, .NET 4.5 supports async-await calls, and this support extends to WCF as well. When you create a Service Reference to a service from Visual Studio, the async calls are automatically generated for you in the proxy.

For example, the proxy code generated by the SvcUtil tool for an async call on a simple HelloWorld method will look like the following:

```
public System.Threading.Tasks.Task<string> HelloWorldAsync() {
        return base.Channel.HelloWorldAsync();
}
```

And, if you are calling this method in an event handler, say for a button pressed event, your code would look something like this –

```
private async void OkButton_Click(object sender, EventArgs e)
{
    var proxy = new Service1Client();
    textBox.Text = await proxy.HelloWorldAsync();
}
```

This code ensures that the thread doesn't wait until the call to the WCF service finishes.

Configuration Improvements

In the previous versions of WCF, the configuration file that was auto-generated tended to look complex. This was due to the fact that when Visual Studio uses SvcUtil to create, all the default values of the bindings were present in the configuration file as well. For example, a simple wsHttpBinding on the client would look like the following:

```
<configuration>
    <system.serviceModel>
        <bindings>
            <wsHttpBinding>
                <binding name="WSHttpBinding_IService1" closeTimeout="00:01:00"
                    openTimeout="00:01:00" receiveTimeout="00:10:00" sendTimeout="00:01:00"
                    bypassProxyOnLocal="false" transactionFlow="false"
hostNameComparisonMode="StrongWildcard"
                    maxBufferPoolSize="524288" maxReceivedMessageSize="65536"
                    messageEncoding="Text" textEncoding="utf-8" useDefaultWebProxy="true"
                    allowCookies="false">
                    <readerQuotas maxDepth="32" maxStringContentLength="8192"
maxArrayLength="16384"
                        maxBytesPerRead="4096" maxNameTableCharCount="16384" />
                    <reliableSession ordered="true" inactivityTimeout="00:10:00"
                        enabled="false" />
                    <security mode="Message">
                        <transport clientCredentialType="Windows" proxyCredentialType="None"
                            realm="" />
                        <message clientCredentialType="Windows"
negotiateServiceCredential="true"
                            algorithmSuite="Default" />
                    </security>
                </binding>
            </wsHttpBinding>
        </bindings>
        <client>
            <endpoint
address="http://localhost:8732/Design_Time_Addresses/HelloWorld/Service1/"
                binding="wsHttpBinding" bindingConfiguration="WSHttpBinding_IService1"
                contract="ServiceReference1.IService1" name="WSHttpBinding_IService1">
                <identity>
                    <dns value="localhost" />
                </identity>
            </endpoint>
        </client>
    </system.serviceModel>
</configuration>
```

Clearly, this doesn't help in readability of the configuration file. In Visual Studio 2012, when SvcUtil is used to generate the proxy and the configuration file, the default values are taken out and the equivalent configuration file will look like the following:

```
<configuration>
   <startup>
        <supportedRuntime version="v4.0" sku=".NETFramework,Version=v4.5" />
   </startup>
   <system.serviceModel>
        <bindings>
            <ws2007HttpBinding>
                <binding name="WS2007HttpBinding_IService1" />
            </ws2007HttpBinding>
        </bindings>
        <client>
            <endpoint
address="http://localhost:8733/Design_Time_Addresses/HelloWorldService/Service1/"
                binding="ws2007HttpBinding" bindingConfiguration="WS2007HttpBinding_IService1"
                contract="ServiceReference1.IService1" name="WS2007HttpBinding_IService1">
                <identity>
                    <userPrincipalName value="Mahesh-XPS\Mahesh" />
                </identity>
            </endpoint>
        </client>
   </system.serviceModel>
</configuration>
```

Tooltips, IntelliSense, and Validation Improvements

When you edit in the configuration file in Visual Studio, you are able to see the tooltips for properties, as shown in Figure 8-1. These tooltips are taken from the WCF configuration documentation and are quite handy while editing the configuration file manually.

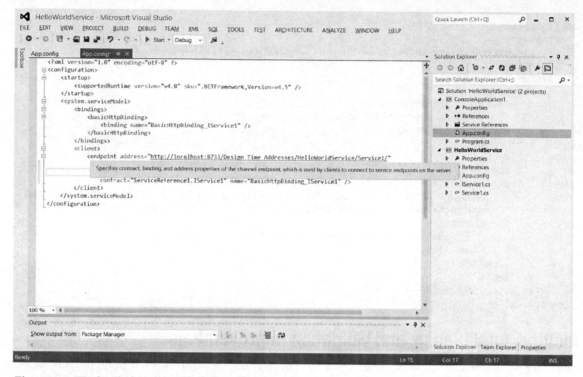

Figure 8-1. Tooltip help on configuration files

Another change in the configuration editor is better IntelliSense support. For instance, when you are trying to type the binding type, you get prompted with all the available options, as shown in Figure 8-2.

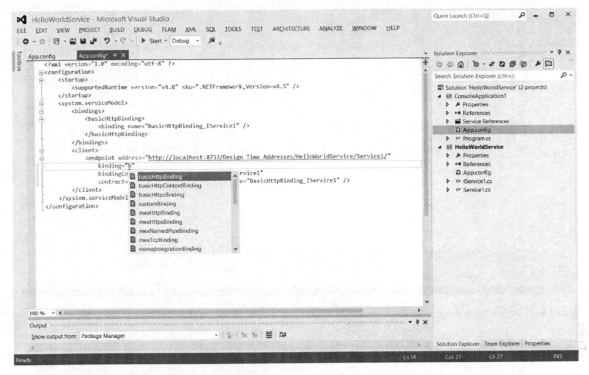

Figure 8-2. IntelliSense in Configuration Editor

This is not the only area of improvement—you will also see IntelliSense pop up when you are typing in a service name, contract name, binding or behavior configuration name, and so on. This allows you to avoid typos when you are manually typing in the information.

Regarding typos, if you do end up typing the wrong behavior or binding configuration name by mistake, Visual Studio will automatically pick up the validation error and display it for you, as shown in Figure 8-3.

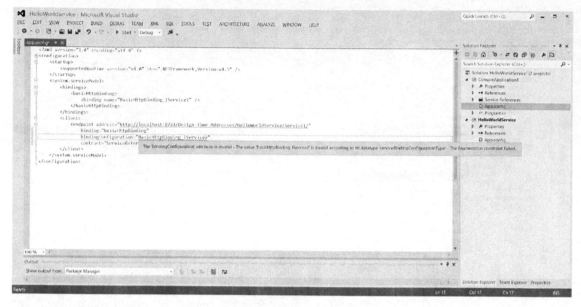

Figure 8-3. Validation errors in Configuration Editor

Universal Datagram Protocol Support

Before .NET 4.5, the main transport protocol that was supported out of the box was TCP. Universal Datagram Protocol (UDP) is a protocol that bypasses the handshake between the two connection points, thus speeding up data transfer rates but with a trade-off on other important things such as security, reliability, ordering of messages, and data integrity. The main reason for using UDP binding is for transmitting quick fire-and-forget messages to the service.

There are plenty of examples on how to get UDP working with older versions of WCF, but the process involves a bit of work on your side. However, with .NET 4.5, you can use a binding called UdpBinding. UdpBinding cannot be hosted on IIS or WAS, and the code to self host a simple service using UdpBinding:

```
class Program
{
    [ServiceContract]
    public interface IUdpService
    {
        [OperationContract]
        void SendMessage(string message);
    }

    public class UdpService : IUdpService
    {
        public void SendMessage(string message)
        {
            //Do something
            Console.WriteLine("Message: {0}", message);
```

```
        }
    }

    static void Main(string[] args)
    {
        using(var serviceHost = new ServiceHost(typeof(UdpService), new
Uri("soap.udp://localhost:40000")))
        {
            serviceHost.AddServiceEndpoint(typeof(IUdpService), new UdpBinding(),
string.Empty);
            serviceHost.Open();

            Console.WriteLine("Press any key to close service...");
            Console.ReadLine();
        }
    }
}
```

The URI scheme for UDP binding starts with soap:udp:// as seen in the previous code. To use UdpBinding in your service, you need to add a reference to the assembly System.ServiceModel.Channels in addition to System.ServiceModel. The client code using UdpBinding looks like the following:

```
    var channelFactory = new ChannelFactory<IUdpService>(new UdpBinding(),
        new EndpointAddress(new Uri("soap.udp://localhost:40000")));

    var proxy = channelFactory.CreateChannel();
    proxy.SendMessage("Hello there");
```

BasicHttpsBinding

If you need to use the basicHttpBinding in a secure environment, you will most likely run it over a secure HTTPS connection in WCF. To do that, you need to set the security mode to Transport, which needs to be done by customizing the binding in the configuration file:

```
<bindings>
    <basicHttpBinding>
        <binding name="customHttpsBinding">
            <security mode="Transport">
                <transport clientCredentialType="None"/>
            </security>
        </binding>
    </basicHttpBinding>
</bindings>
```

In .NET 4.5, rather than create your own custom binding, you can use the newly added BasicHttpsBinding. An example of such a binding being set in configuration is shown below:

```
<services>
  <service name="Sample.HelloWorldService">
    <host>
      <baseAddresses>
        <add baseAddress = "https://.../HelloWorldService/" />
      </baseAddresses>
```

```
    </host>
    <endpoint address="" binding="basicHttpsBinding" contract="Sample.IHelloWorldService"/>
  </service>
</services>
```

■ **Note** Starting from WCF 4.0, if you create a service without specifying any endpoints, the runtime will automatically add endpoints for you. In WCF 4.5, if you host your service in IIS and configure IIS to use SSL, the runtime will automatically create endpoints for both HTTP (`BasicHttpBinding`) and HTTPS (`BasicHttpsBinding`).

Compression

In WCF 4.5, you can now compress the contents of your message when you use binary encoding. To make use of this, you need to set the `CompressionFormat` property, which can either be set to `Deflate` or `GZip`. The following is a sample configuration for enabling `GZip` compression:

```
<customBinding>
    <binding name="GZipBinding">
        <binaryMessageEncoding compressionFormat ="GZip"/>
        <httpTransport />
    </binding>
</customBinding>
```

Enabling compression is really useful where the network bandwidth is an issue, but you have to keep in mind that it puts an additional load on the CPU that could lead to adverse effects.

■ **Tip** Remember that you need to enable compression on both the server and the client side. If you don't do that, you will end up getting a `ProtocolException`.

SOAP, REST, AND WCF

When WCF was first introduced in .NET 3, the emphasis was to make it completely WS-* compliant. What this meant was that the protocol it mainly supported was SOAP. SOAP is a highly mature protocol that is widely used. However, it is not the only one—REST has gained popularity due to its simplicity and ability to be used across all platforms. A new binding called `WebHttpBinding` was added in .NET 3.5 to help build RESTful services.

The WCF REST Starter Kit was also introduced soon after to build on the support for REST in WCF. This starter kit never made it into a production release, but some of its content was absorbed into .NET 4.

With .NET 4.5, a lot more of the content from the WCF REST Starter Kit has now been added. But the most important change is that the content has now been moved from the WCF libraries over to ASP.NET.

~~WCF~~ ASP.NET Web API

The pre-beta release of the Web API was packaged as part of WCF, and it was also called WCF Web API. But there was no need for it to be part of WCF—the Web API relies more on the HTTP protocol and verbs, and it does not use SOAP protocol at all. With the beta, Microsoft moved the API out of WCF into ASP.NET and rebranded it as ASP.NET Web API. However, it doesn't change the way it works. But, first, you need to understand how REST operates before you delve into how to use the new Web API.

A Quick Introduction to REST

REST stands for *Representational State Transfer*. It was an idea floated by Roy Fielding. Roy Fielding, for those who don't know, was one of the principal authors of the HTTP protocol. Strictly speaking, REST is not really a protocol or specification—it is actually an architectural style and is used for representing resources on the net. The representation of a book, for instance, could look something like this: http://someuri/book/9781430243328, where 9781430243328 is the ISBN of the book. When you access the URL, you could effectively get the details of the book in some format such as Plain Old XML (POX) or JSON.

So, what does REST fix? And why do we really need it? To answer these questions, we need to look at the SOAP protocol, which is what we currently use in WCF. SOAP is good and there are various standards built around it, but if you look into a simple message sent via SOAP, you will realize that it is heavy in nature. To call a simple GetBookDetails method in a service, the SOAP message would need to be formatted to look like the following:

```
<s:Envelope xmlns:s="http://schemas.xmlsoap.org/soap/envelope/">
  <s:Header>
    <Action s:mustUnderstand="1"
xmlns="http://schemas.microsoft.com/ws/2005/05/addressing/none">http://tempuri.org/IBookServic
e/GetBookDetails</Action>
  </s:Header>
  <s:Body>
    <GetBookDetails xmlns="http://tempuri.org/">
      <isbn>9781430243328</isbn>
    </ GetBookDetails >
  </s:Body>
</s:Envelope>
```

If you start using some of the WS-* protocols for things such as securing the payload or authentication, the message gets even bigger and more complex. The equivalent call using REST would be a simple URL such as http://someurl/book/9781430243328. The response to this URL would look something like the following, which is a lot more readable than a SOAP response:

```
<book>
    <isbn>9781430243328</ isbn >
    <title>Introducing .NET 4.5</title>
    <publisher>APRESS</publisher>
    <authors>
       <author>Mackey, Alex</author>
       <author>Tulloch, William</author>
```

```
        <author>Krishnan, Mahesh</author>
    </authors>
</book>
```

■ **Note** *SOAP*, which originally stood for *Simple Object Access Protocol*, is just referred to as *SOAP* and is no longer an acronym—a clear indication that it is no longer simple. And in spite of all the talk about standards, interop is still a big issue while using SOAP.

One of the main advantages of using REST is the ability to perform CRUD (Create, Read, Update, and Delete) operations on resources using just HTTP verbs. Table 8-1 shows how the verbs can be used for CRUD operations.

Table 8-1. HTTP verbs and their equivalent CRUD operations

Verb	Operation
GET	Used to retrieve either a single resource or multiple resources
POST	Used to insert a resource
PUT	Used to update an existing resource
DELETE	Used to remove an existing resource

HttpClient Class in the System.Net.Http Library

The HttpClient class was introduced with the now obsolete WCF REST Starter Kit mentioned earlier. It is primarily used to work with HTTP requests and their responses, which come in handy when you are working with REST services. Unlike the original version from the REST Starter Kit, the HttpClient shipped with .NET 4.5 supports async calls as shown in the following code snippet:

```
public async void CallRestService(string url)
{
    try
    {
        using (var client = new HttpClient())
        {
            var response = await client.GetStringAsync(url);

            //Do something with the response
        }
    }
    catch (HttpRequestException e)
    {
        //Do something with exception
```

```
    }
}
```

The class also contains methods to send common HTTP verbs such as Get, Put, Post, and Delete when calling a URL. This is very useful for REST calls, and some of the useful methods are shown in Table 8-2.

Table 8-2. HttpClient methods

Method	Notes
GetAsync	Sends a GET request to the URL
PutAsync	Sends a PUT request to the URL
PostAsync	Sends a POST request to the URL
DeleteAsync	Sends a DELETE request to the URL

Creating an ASP.NET Web API Service

To create a simple RESTful service for a resource of books using ASP.NET Web API, follow these steps:

1. Create a new project from Visual Studio by choosing File ➤ New ➤ Project.

2. In the New Project dialog box, choose a Web Project template from the list on the left side and select ASP.NET MVC 4 Web Application from the list of templates. Type in a suitable name for the project, as shown in Figure 8-4.

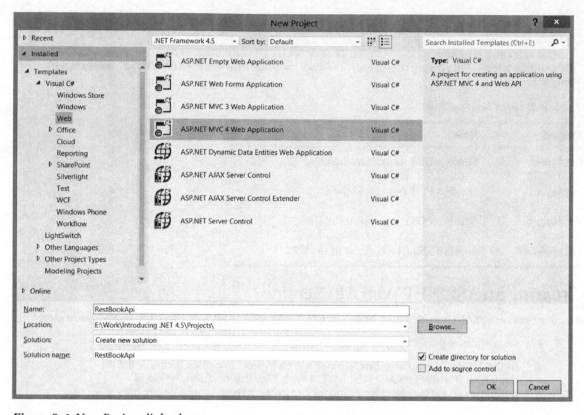

Figure 8-4. New Project dialog box

3.   A new ASP.NET MVC 4 Project dialog box will appear, as shown in Figure 8-5.
     Select Web API from the list of templates and press OK. This will create an
     MVC project that you can use to create RESTful services.

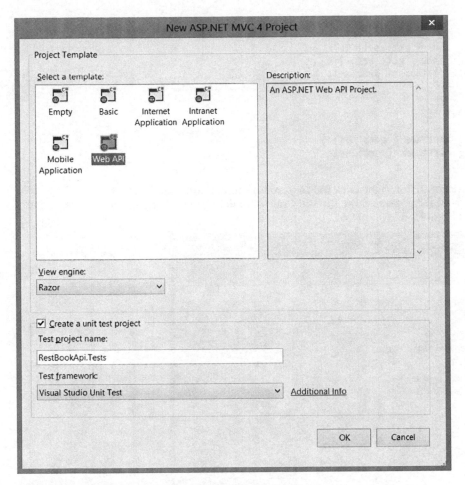

Figure 8-5. New ASP.NET MVC 4 Project dialog box

4. You will see several folders that are automatically created in the Solution
    Explorer (such as Controllers, Model, and Views), along with several files. You
    need to create your own model that holds the data structure of a Book object
    and a controller that will hold the logic for the REST service.

5. To create a model, right-click the Models folder in the Solution Explorer and
    select Add ➤ New item from the menu. The Add New Item dialog box will
    appear.

6. Using the dialog box, create a new class called Book and use the following code
    snippet to create a class for Book and Author in the Book.cs file:

```
public class Book
{
    public string Isbn { get; set; }
    public string Title { get; set; }
    public Author[] Authors { get; set; }
}

public class Author
{
    public string LastName { get; set; }
    public string FirstName { get; set; }
}
```

7. To create the controller, right-click the Controllers folder and choose Add ➤ Controller from the popup menu. An Add Controller dialog box will open up, as shown in Figure 8-6.

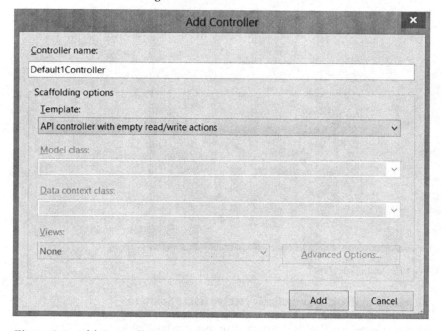

Figure 8-6. *Add Controller dialog box*

8. In the Add Controller dialog box, change the name of the controller to BooksController and choose the Template API controller with empty read/write actions. Press OK to create the controller. The class auto-generated by Visual Studio will look the following code:

```
public class BooksController : ApiController
{
    // GET /api/books
    public IEnumerable<string> Get()
```

```
    {
        return new string[] { "value1", "value2" };
    }

    // GET /api/books/5
    public string Get(int id)
    {
        return "value";
    }

    // POST /api/books
    public void Post(string value)
    {
    }

    // PUT /api/books/5
    public void Put(int id, string value)
    {
    }

    // DELETE /api/books/5
    public void Delete(int id)
    {
    }
}
```

■ **Note** The code template creates entry points to do basic CRUD operations, but the return values are strings and the id used to access objects are integers. In our simple example, we want to make use of the class Book and the ISBN string as identifiers.

9. Replace the BooksController code in the file with the following code:

```
public class BooksController : ApiController
{
    Dictionary<string, Book> bookDictionary =
        new Dictionary<string, Book> {
            {
                "9780470524657",
                new Book
                {
                    Title = "Silverlight for Dummies",
                    Isbn = "9780470524657",
                    Authors = new Author[] {
                        new Author { FirstName = "Mahesh", LastName = "Krishnan"},
                        new Author { FirstName = "Philip", LastName = "Beadle"},
                    },
                }
```

```
            },
            {
                "9781430243328",
                new Book
                {
                    Title = "Introducing .NET 4.5",
                    Isbn = "9781430243328",
                    Authors = new Author[] {
                        new Author { FirstName = "Mahesh", LastName = "Krishnan"},
                        new Author { FirstName = "Alex", LastName = "Mackey"},
                        new Author { FirstName = "William", LastName = "Tulloch"},
                    },
                }
            },

        };

    // GET /api/books
    public IEnumerable<Book> Get()
    {
        return bookDictionary.Values;

    }

    // GET /api/books/5
    public Book Get(string id)
    {
        try
        {
            return bookDictionary[id];
        }
        catch (Exception e)
        {
            throw new HttpResponseException(new
HttpResponseMessage(HttpStatusCode.NotFound));
        }
    }

    // POST /api/books
    public void Post(Book book)
    {

    }

    // PUT /api/books/5
    public void Put(string id, Book value)
    {
    }

    // DELETE /api/books/5
    public void Delete(string id)
    {
```

```
        }
    }
```

This code creates some sample data for the controller and implements the two `Get` methods. When a call to the URL `http://.../api/books` is made, the controller will return a list of books, and when a call is made with a specific ISBN, such as `http://.../api/books/9781430243328`, only that book will be returned.

10. To compile the code, you need to ensure that the right namespaces are included at the top of the file. Make sure you replace `RestBookApi` with the actual namespace of the project:

```
using System.Net;
using RestBookApi.Models;
```

11. Run the application by pressing F5 and check the two URLs out. Depending on the type of browser you use, you may get a JSON output or an XML output. The output shown in Figure 8-7 shows the URL being called from the Chrome browser.

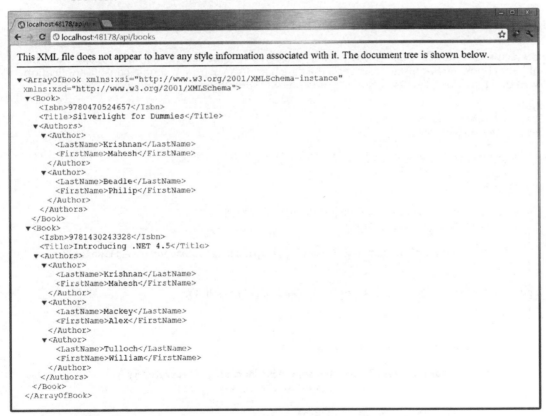

Figure 8-7. Chrome browser showing results of a REST service call

Choosing the Right Return Format

The type of browser or client you use to access the REST service determines what format the data is returned. *But, how does the Web API know what format to send based on the client?* The answer to that lies in the requests header—more specifically, the Accept header—that is passed in the request to the server. If you inspect the request headers in a tool such as Fiddler or the Developer tools in Internet Explorer, you will be able to see these values, as shown in Figure 8-8.

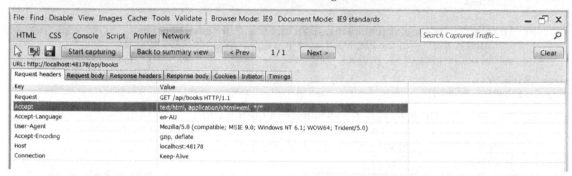

Figure 8-8. *The Accept header showing the MIME text the browser will accept*

If you change the values of the Accept header, you can direct the server to send the response in the format of your choosing. For instance, to send the data back in XML from a simple console application using the HttpClient class discussed earlier, your code will something like the following code:

```
using System;
using System.Net.Http;
using System.Threading.Tasks;

namespace RestClient
{
    class Program
    {
        static string baseAddress = "http://localhost:48178/";
        static void Main(string[] args)
        {
            CallRestServiceAsync(string.Format("{0}/api/books/", baseAddress)).Wait();
        }

        public static async Task CallRestServiceAsync(string url)
        {
            try
            {
                using (var client = new HttpClient())
                {
                    client.DefaultRequestHeaders.Add("Accept", "text/xml");
                    var response = await client.GetStringAsync(url);

                    Console.WriteLine(response);
                }
```

```
            }
            catch (HttpRequestException e)
            {
                Console.WriteLine(e.Message);
            }
        }
    }
}
```

This code allows you to plug in your own set of media formatters on the server that can be used to customize the return type. To create your own media formatter, you need to derive a class from BufferedMediaTypeFormatter and implement the WriteToStream override. You also need to specify the supported MIME type and overrides called CanWriteType and CanReadType, which is used to determine whether the object type you are serializing is supported. The following is a sample CsvFormatter that is used to serialize IEnumerable<Book>:

```
using System;
using System.Collections.Generic;
using System.IO;
using System.Net.Http.Formatting;
using System.Net.Http.Headers;
using RestBookApi.Models;

namespace RestBookApi
{
    public class CsvFormatter : BufferedMediaTypeFormatter
    {
        public CsvFormatter()
        {
            SupportedMediaTypes.Add(new MediaTypeHeaderValue("text/csv"));
        }

        public override bool CanReadType(Type type)
        {
            return false;
        }

        public override bool CanWriteType(Type type)
        {
            return typeof(IEnumerable<Book>).IsAssignableFrom(type);
        }

        public override void WriteToStream(Type type, object value, Stream stream,
HttpContentHeaders contentHeaders)
        {
            var books = value as IEnumerable<Book>;
            if (books != null)
            {
                var writer = new StreamWriter(stream);
                writer.WriteLine("Isbn, Title");
```

```
        foreach (var book in books)
        {
            writer.WriteLine("{0}, {1}", book.Isbn, book.Title);
        }
        writer.Flush();



    }
  }
 }
}
```

■ **Note** This is a very simple example of a CSV media formatter. When you implement your own formatter, you not only check if the object that needs to be serialized is a type of IEnumerable<Book>, but also if a Book object is passed to it. In addition, you would also do more work on the actual WriteToStream method to make sure that the Author objects are serialized. If you wish to read the data passed on to you, you would also implement the ReadFromStream method.

After you've added this class to your project, you also need to register this formatter in your global configuration. You can do this in the Application_Start method in the Global.asax.cs file:

```
public class WebApiApplication : System.Web.HttpApplication
{
    …
    protected void Application_Start()
    {
        …
        GlobalConfiguration.Configuration.Formatters.Add(new CsvFormatter());
    }
    …
}
```

Error Handling

When you are working with simple HTTP request/responses, which is what Web API is all about, error messages become nothing more than HTTP status codes on a web response. Some common HTTP status codes are shown in Table 8-3.

Table 8-3. Some common HTTP codes and their descriptions

HTTP Code	Description
200	OK

HTTP Code	Description
201	Created
400	Bad Request
404	Not Found
409	Conflict
500	Internal Server Error
501	Not Implemented

This concept doesn't change when working with errors in Web API. A simple exception of type HttpResponseException is thrown with the corresponding HttpStatusCode enumeration inside an HttpResponseMessage object. For example, if a book with the requested ISBN is not found, then you throw an exception:

```
//Isbn not found…?
throw new HttpResponseException(new HttpResponseMessage(HttpStatusCode.NotFound));
```

Implementing the Full Set of CRUD Operations

If you want to complete the full range of CRUD operations, you need to implement the Put, Post, and Delete methods in the BookController class. Let's start with the insert first. A very simple implementation for the Post, which is an insert operation, would like the following:

```
// POST /api/books
public void Post(Book book)
{
    bookDictionary[book.Isbn] = book;
}
```

Although this will work, there are a couple of issues with the implementation. REST API should reply to a POST message for insert with a status code of 201 (Created), rather than the default 200 (OK), which is what the Web API sends. In addition, the result of the creation (which is, effectively, a copy of the newly created data) is sent back to the client along with the URI where the newly created resource can be found. To address these issues, the actual implementation of the Post needs to change to look similar to the following code snippet:

```
// POST /api/books
public HttpResponseMessage<Book> Post(Book book)
{
    bookDictionary[book.Isbn] = book;
    var response = Request.CreateResponse ( HttpStatusCode.Created);
    string uri = Url.Route(null, new { id = book.Isbn });
    response.Headers.Location = new Uri(Request.RequestUri, uri);
    return response;
}
```

To add the update routine, the Put method in the controller class needs to be changed to something like the following code:

```
// PUT /api/books/5
public void Put(string id, Book value)
{
    if(bookDictionary.ContainsKey(id))
        bookDictionary[id] = value;
    else
        throw new HttpResponseException(new
HttpResponseMessage(HttpStatusCode.NotFound));

}
```

Notice that if the ISBN is not found, an HttpResponseException with the HttpResponseMessage set to HttpStatusCode.NotFound is thrown.

To implement Delete, the code snippet will look similar to the following:

```
// DELETE /api/books/5
public void Delete(string id)
{
    if(bookDictionary.ContainsKey(id))
        bookDictionary.Remove(id);
}
```

Routing

How does the Web API know that when the URL is http://.../api/books, the BooksController *should be used?* If you are already familiar with ASP.NET MVC, you probably already know the answer. ASP.NET MVC uses a routing table to keep track of what controllers and what actions to invoke when a URL is called. The Web API hooks on to the same routing table. When Visual Studio code generated files for you, it automatically added the routing logic for you in the RouteConfig.cs file. If you open the file, you will notice the following lines added to the RegisterRoutes method:

```
routes.MapHttpRoute(
    name: "DefaultApi",
    routeTemplate: "api/{controller}/{id}",
    defaults: new { id = RouteParameter.Optional }
);
```

When a client calls the URL http://.../api/books/12345, the Web API adds Controller to the value in the {controller} part in the route template, which, in this case, is books (and so the BooksContoller is used).

The next question is *How does the Web API know which method to call?* The answer to that is quite simple. It depends on a combination of the HTTP method used in the URL and the method present in the controller class. Table 8-4 demonstrates how it works.

Table 8-4. HTTP verbs/methods and their corresponding controller methods

HTTP Method	Controller Method
GET	Any method that starts with `Get`. If the `{id}` parameter is present, a `Get` method that takes a parameter is called. Examples are `Get()`, `GetBooks()`,`Get(string isbn)`, `GetBooks(string isbn)`.
POST	Any method that starts with `Post`, such as `Post(Book book)` and `PostBook(Book book)`.
PUT	Any method that starts with `Put`, such as `Put(string isbn, Book value)`, and `PutBook(string isbn, Book value)`.
DELETE	Any method that starts with `Delete`, such as `Delete(string isbn)` and `DeleteBook(string isbn)`.

■ **Tip** If you have a method that starts with `Get` in your controller, but you do not want the Web API to use it, just put the `NonAction` attribute in front of the method.

Using Attributes for the Actions

Sometimes using just convention to figure out what action to call, or rather what method to call, just doesn't cut it. You may want to use your own method names. The way to get Web API to figure out what HTTP method maps to what method in the controller is by way of attributes that you attach to these methods.

For instance, if you want to call your method `LoadBooks` instead of `GetBooks`, you need to add the `HttpGet` attribute to the method:

```
[HttpGet]
Public Books[] LoadBooks()
{
    …
}
```

Table 8-5 shows the attribute for the corresponding HTTP method.

Table 8-5. Attributes and their corresponding HTTP methods

Attribute	Http	Method
HttpGet		Get
HttpPost	Post	HttpPost

Attribute	Http	Method
HttpPut		Put
HttpDelete	Delete	HttpDelete

Filtering, Sorting, and Paging

As REST calls are just URLs, it gives us a wonderful opportunity to use query strings to start filtering data, sorting data in a certain order, and even introducing paging. Microsoft introduced a standard way of doing this in a protocol called *OData*, which stands for *Open Data*. To enable Web API to use OData, you need to install the NuGet Package Microsoft.AspNet.WebApi.OData. Web API uses the query parameters that are part of the OData protocol to implement filtering, sorting, and paging. To make use of these features, you need to return an IQueryable<T> rather than an IEnumerable<T> in your Get functions.

For instance, the example of Get we have used to return all the Book objects would change to something like the following:

```
// GET /api/books
public IQueryable<Book> Get ()
{
    return bookDictionary.Values.AsQueryable();
}
```

Once this is done, you would be able to use query parameters such as the following ones:

- http://.../api/books?$filter=Title%20eq%20'Silverlight%20for%20Dummies'—This will filter the results and bring only books whose title equals *Silverlight for Dummies*.

- http://...api/books?$top=10—This will bring in the top ten items.

- http://...api/books?$skip=10—This will skip the first ten items and bring the rest.

- http://.../api/books?orderby=Title—This will order the results by title.

- http://.../api/books?orderby=Title%20desc—This will order the results by title in descending order.

■ **Tip** You are not restricted by just one query parameter. You can use a combination of the query parameters to get the data you are looking for. The format of the query strings that are used in OData can be found at http://www.odata.org/developers/protocols/uri-conventions.

WebSockets

Currently, when a web browser, or any other client for that matter, connects to a server via HTTP protocol, it is in a simple request/response format. Although this is just fine for most scenarios, it fails when the server needs to repeatedly send live data (such as share prices or sports scores and updates) back to the client. One way to overcome this is through polling (and a variation of it called *long-polling*). Another way is through live streaming.

These approaches have several drawbacks—prominent among them being the large amounts of data being sent back and forth across the network. And these solutions don't scale well, either.

One of the solutions to fix this is to establish a socket connection via the web through which web browsers can connect to the server and have full-duplex, bidirectional communication. This new protocol is called *WebSockets*. It works with the client and server using the HTTP protocol to exchange information and establish a handshake. Once done, it is used to set up a proper sockets connection, which can then be used to send information both ways anytime—client to server and server to client. And the data sent between the two can either be in binary or text.

Enabling the Server to Support WebSockets

To create WebSockets binding in the server, you need to user either NetHttpsBinding or NetHttpBinding, depending on whether the transport needs to be secure or not.

■ **Note** WebSockets does not work on older versions of the Windows operating system. You need Windows 8 or higher for it to work, as it requires IIS 8.

Follow these steps to create a simple service that runs long-running operations and provides feedback to the client on progress:

1. Create a new WCF Service Library project in Visual Studio 2012 and call it WebSocketsExample (or any other name, but use the name suggested so that the namespace will be the same as the example).

2. Delete the IService1.cs and Service1.cs file that gets automatically generated.

3. Press Shift+Alt+C to add a new class to the project and call the filename LongRunningService.cs.

4. Replace the content of the file with the source code as shown:

```csharp
using System.ServiceModel;
using System.Threading;

namespace WebSocketsExample
{
    [ServiceContract(CallbackContract = typeof(IProgressCallbackService))]
    public interface ILongRunningService
    {
        [OperationContract(IsOneWay = true)]
        void DoLongRunningOperation();
    }

    [ServiceContract]
```

```
public interface IProgressCallbackService
{
    [OperationContract]
    void UpdateProgress(int percentageComplete);
}

[ServiceBehavior(ConcurrencyMode = ConcurrencyMode.Reentrant)]
public class LongRunningService : ILongRunningService
{
    public void DoLongRunningOperation()
    {
        for (var i = 0; i <= 100; i += 10)
        {
            Thread.Sleep(1000);
            try
            {
                OperationContext.Current.GetCallbackChannel<IProgressCallbackService>().
                    UpdateProgress(i);
            }
            catch (CommunicationException)
            {
                //Ignore communication exception in this simple implementation
                //Handles the client closing down the connection
            }
        }
    }
}
```

This code snippet creates a service called LongRunningService that takes about ten seconds to run (which we've implemented with a Thread.Sleep method). At the end of each second, it calls a method in the call back service to provide with an update of the progress.

5. Open the App.config file in the project and change the service name to WebSocketsExample.LongRunningService. Then replace the default basicHttpBinding binding in the service endpoint to NetHttpBinding and add a bindings section for netHttpBinding. These changes are shown in bold:

```
…
<services>
    <service name="WebSocketsExample.LongRunningService">
    …
    <!-- Service Endpoints -->
    <!-- Unless fully qualified, address is relative to base address supplied above -->
    <endpoint address="" binding="netHttpBinding"
contract="WebSocketsExample.ILongRunningService" bindingConfiguration="WebSocketsBinding">
…
    </services>
    <bindings>
      <netHttpBinding>
        <binding name="WebSocketsBinding" >
```

```
    <webSocketSettings transportUsage="WhenDuplex"/>
    </binding>
  </netHttpBinding>
</bindings>
<behaviors>
...
```

6. Running the application from Visual Studio should now run the service from WCF Service Host.

Accessing WebSockets Service from within .NET

Typically, WebSockets services are called from within a browser (using JavaScript). But, to access the service from within a .NET client, you can create a simple console application to the same solution and add a service reference pointing to the service you just created. Then change the default Program.cs file to call the service as shown in the following code:

```
using System;
using System.ServiceModel;
using WebSocketsClient.ServiceReference1;

namespace WebSocketsClient
{
    class CallbackContract : ILongRunningServiceCallback
    {
        public void UpdateProgress(int percentageComplete)
        {
            Console.WriteLine("Progress indicator: {0}", percentageComplete);
        }
    }
    class Program
    {
        static void Main(string[] args)
        {
            var callbackContext = new InstanceContext(new CallbackContract());
            var proxy = new ServiceReference1.LongRunningServiceClient(callbackContext);
            proxy.DoLongRunningOperation();
            Console.ReadLine();
        }

    }
}
```

This looks like any other WCF duplex implementation, but the app.config file will contain all the binding to make it use WebSockets.

■ **Tip** The address for WebSockets starts with ws://. You can open app.config on the client project to check this out.

Conclusion

This chapter introduces you to all the changes that have been made to WCF in .NET 4.5. The biggest change, in my opinion, comes from the addition of the Web API. The Web API lets you create REST services with ease from an ASP.NET MVC project template. The bulk of the Web API used to be part of WCF in earlier preview releases on Visual Studio 2012, but it was eventually pulled out and made part of ASP.NET. If you think about it, it does make sense since the REST services are more closely aligned to exposing services across the web.

Support for async calls and the introduction of WebSockets are also important changes in WCF and are covered in the chapter. In addition, WCF 4.5 introduces a number of changes such as support for UDP, a new binding called BasicHttpsBinding, and support for compression. The chapter also talks about the improvements made in Visual Studio and (WCF) that make their configuration a lot easier.

■ ■ ■

CHAPTER 9

Working with Data

In this chapter, we are going to look at what has changed in terms of working with data in .NET 4.5 and Visual Studio 2012. Most of the action is around Entity Framework, but there have also been some changes made to the SqlClient data provider around streaming and asynchronous programming. Also with this release we see the introduction of LocalDb.

LocalDb

With Visual Studio 2012 (and SQL Server 2012), there is a new version of SQL Server Express call SQL Server Express LocalDb, or LocalDb for short. LocalDb has been created specifically for developers providing the same T-SQL, programming surface, and client-side providers as SQL Server Express but without having to install and manage a full instance of SQL Server Express or SQL Server.

Creating a Database with LocalDb

From within Visual Studio 2012, there are a few different ways that a LocalDb database can be created depending on the job at hand. The thing to be aware of is that the location of the resulting .mdf file differs depending on which method you use.

From the SQL Server Object Explorer

Within Visual Studio, open the new SQL Server Object Explorer (Ctrl +\,Ctrl +s) and click on the Add SQL Server icon. When the Connect to Server dialog box displays, enter (localdb)\v11.0 as the server name and click Connect. Right-click on the localdb icon (see Figure 9-1) and select New Query.

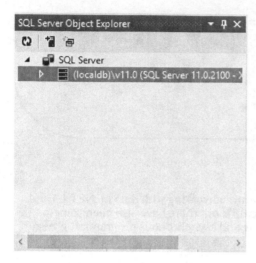

Figure 9-1. SQL Server Object Explorer

The simplest command to create a database is the following:

```
Create database TestDb1
```

This will create a new .mdf file which will be located in c:\Users\user-name (type %userprofile% in the File Explorer address bar to get there). This is probably not the best place to store your database files, so the Microsoft recommendation when creating database files is to specify the location. Enter the following and click the Execute button:

```
Create database TestDb1 on (name='TestDb1',  filename='c:\DbFiles\TestDb1.mdf')
```

While you are in the SQL Server Object Explorer, you can also create a new database by right-clicking on the Databases folder just below the localdb icon and select "Add New Database". A new database gets created but this time, if you go looking for it, the .mdf and .ldf files will be located in the folder C:\Users\user-name\AppData\Local\Microsoft\Microsoft SQL Server Local DB\Instances\v11.0.

Creating a New Database Project

With the release of SQL Server 2012, a new set of database developer tools for Visual Studio was released, and these tools have been integrated into Visual Studio 2012. These tools make use of LocalDb to allow developers to do database development offline without having to have a full version of SQL Server installed.

When you create a new SQL Server database project, as part of the project, two things happen in relation to LocalDb:

- First, a new instance folder is created under C:\Users\user-name\AppData\Local\Microsoft\Microsoft SQL Server Local DB that will be named after the solution in which you have created the project. This folder will contain the system databases, logs, and so forth.

- Second, within the project a folder named Sandbox will be created (select Show All Files to see it), which will contain the .mdf file that you will work against and which takes the name of the project.

If you want to access this database from another project, the data source for the connection string will be (localdb)\<solution name>.

Adding a Database to an Application

If you are using a file-based database as part of your application, you can add a new database by selecting Add ➤ New Item, and then from the Data node select Service-based Database. This will create a LocalDb .mdf file within the project folder and add the corresponding connection string to the app.config file.

SqlClient Data Provider

With .Net 4.5 some new features, both small and large, have been added to SqlClient. Some of these are in line with the release of SQL Server 2012 or are to catch-up with SQL Server 2008, especially around support for sparse columns. Probably the two new additions that will have the most impact are the implementation of the Task Parallel Library (TPL) to provide a more robust model for handling data asynchronously, and the inclusion of streaming support for unstructured data.

In this next section, we will take a brief look at this two new features as well as the new SqlCredential class and finish off with a short summary of some of the other changes that are part of this release.

Asynchronous Programming

Previously, asynchronous programming with the SqlClient data provider was achieved by adding Asynchronous Processing = true to the connection string and using SqlCommand.BeginExecuteNonQuery() or SqlCommand.BeginExecuteReader(). These methods still exist in .NET 4.5 (though you no longer need the asynchronous command in the connection string), but like elsewhere in the framework, the TPL has been implemented in SqlConnection, SqlCommand, SqlDataReader, and SqlBulkCopier (as well as their underlying abstract classes) to provide asynchronous versions of existing synchronous methods.

The new methods follow the standard pattern of appending Async to the method name so, for example, SqlConnection.Open() now has as a corresponding asynchronous method SqlConnection.OpenAsync(). A full list of all the new methods can be found at http://msdn.microsoft.com/en-us/library/hh211418(v=vs.110).aspx.

The following contrived example demonstrates some of the async methods that are available. If you want to try the code, modify the connection string to point to the database of your choice and modify the select statement accordingly.

```
class Program
{
  public static void Main()
  {
    string connString = "Data Source=(local); Initial Catalog=DummyDb; Integrated
Security=SSPI";
    var cts = new CancellationTokenSource();
```

```
        using (var conn = new SqlConnection(connString))
        {
            var command = new SqlCommand("WAITFOR DELAY '00:00:05';select FirstName from
FakePeople", conn);
            ExecuteNonQueryAsync(conn, command)
              .ContinueWith(t =>
                {
                    Console.WriteLine("Start reader");
                    command.ExecuteReaderAsync(cts.Token)
                      .ContinueWith(async t2 =>
                        {
                            if (t2.Status == TaskStatus.Canceled)
                                Console.WriteLine("Read was cancelled");
                            while (await t2.Result.ReadAsync())
                                Console.WriteLine(t2.Result[0]);
                        });
                    Console.WriteLine("Do something else while getting the results");
                });

            Console.WriteLine("Waiting...");
            Console.ReadKey();
        }
    }

    public static async Task<int> ExecuteNonQueryAsync(SqlConnection conn, SqlCommand cmd)
    {
        await conn.OpenAsync();
        Console.WriteLine("Connection open");
        await cmd.ExecuteNonQueryAsync();
        Console.WriteLine("Query completed");
        return 1;
    }
}
```

Streaming

We have clearly reached a point where databases store more than just dates, numbers, and strings. Documents, images, media files, and the like are part of the wonderful world of data that our applications need to retrieve and store. In recognition of this, streaming support to and from SQL Server has been added to support scenarios involving unstructured data that is stored on the server. This addition should simplify writing applications that stream data by not having to fully load the data into memory, and it will also improve the scalability of the middle-tier applications especially in cases that require interaction with SQL Azure.

To facilitate streaming from SQL Server, new methods have been added to the DbDataReader and implemented in SqlDataReader. These methods include the following:

- IsDbNull()

- GetFieldValue()

- GetFieldValueAsync()

- GetStream()

- GetTextReader()

- GetXmlReader()

For streaming to SQL Server, the SqlParameter class has been modified so that it can accept and react to Stream, XmlReader, and TextReader objects depending on the SqlDbType you are targeting.

Combined with the new asynchronous methods in SqlClient, it will become easier to manage moving unstructured data between applications and SQL Server. If you are interested in exploring this further, some simple but reasonably comprehensive examples can be found at http://msdn.microsoft.com/en-us/library/hh556234(v=vs.110).aspx.

SqlCredential

Even though we all know integrated security is always the preferred option when connecting to a database, there are cases (SQL Azure springs to mind) when you need to use a username and password. In these cases, we needed to keep the username and password with the connection string, which left them vulnerable to being exposed in a crash dump or a page file in a page swap. With .NET4.5, this problem can now be mitigated with the use of the SqlCredential class.

The SqlCredential class exposes just two properties, UserId and Password, the latter of which is of the type SecureString. The SqlConnection has, in turn, been modified and now has a Credential property of the type SqlCredential as well as a modified constructor that takes an instance of SqlCredential as a parameter. Here is an example of how it can be used:

```
private void LoginButton_Click(object sender, RoutedEventArgs e)
{
  var connString = "Data Source=(local);Initial Catalog=DummyDb";
  var password = PasswordText.SecurePassword;
  password.MakeReadOnly();

  var sqlCredential = new SqlCredential(UsernameText.Text,password);
  string message = "Successfully logged in";
  try
  {
    using (var connection = new SqlConnection(connString,sqlCredential))
    {
      connection.Open();
    }
  }
  catch (Exception ex)
  {
    message = "failed to log in";
  }

  MessageBox.Show(message);
}
```

The key thing to note is that the SqlCredential constructor will only allow you to pass an instance of SecureString that has been marked as read only.

A blog post from the ADO.NET team that covers this in a bit more detail can be found at http://blogs.msdn.com/b/adonet/archive/2012/03/09/safer-passwords-with-sqlcredential.aspx.

And the Other Stuff

In order to round off this section on the SqlClient, here is quick list of some of the other changes and features you will find with this release of the framework:

- Support for high availability, disaster recovery is available. Always On Availability Groups is a feature that was introduced with SQL Server 2012. If you are using SQL Server 2012 and have this feature enabled with SqlClient, on the connection property you can now specify the availability group listener for an availability group or a SQL Server 2012 Failover Cluster Instance. For more information, see http://msdn.microsoft.com/en-us/library/hh205662(v=vs.110).aspx.

- Connection failures will now be logged in the extended events log.

- SqlClient now supports extended protection.

- Sparse columns, a feature that was added in SQL Server 2008, are now supported in SqlClient. In addition, if you use the method SqlDataReader.GetSchemaTable(), you can check if a column is a sparse column or not by checking its IsColumnSet property.

- When TrustServerCertificate is false and Encrypt is true, the connection attempt will fail unless the server name or IP address specified in the SQL Server's SSL certificate exactly matches the one used in the connection string.

Entity Framework

Writing about what is new in the Entity Framework (EF) in .NET 4.5 is not as simple as it looks. The main reason is that the EF team is gradually working toward removing the Entity Framework from the .NET Framework so that they can provide a more responsive release cycle. The consequence of this is that even though there have been some new EF features added to .NET 4.5, other features such as code-first and DbContext (which were released in EF 4.1) have not been rolled into it and are still only available via the EF NuGet package.

The simplest way to install EF 5.0 NuGet package, which requires .NET 4.5, is to open the Package Manager Console and enter the following command:

```
Install-Package EntityFramework
```

This will install the latest version of the Entity Framework.

Support for Enums

One of the criticisms that have been leveled at the Entity Framework has been its lack of support for enums. With the release of .NET4.5, enums are now supported and can be implemented using either Code, Model, or Database First workflows. In the following example, we will use code-first to create our entities.

1. First, create a new console application project, ensuring it targets the .NET 4.5 Framework, and then add the EF 5.0 NuGet package.

2. Next, add a new class and call it Employee. Open the resulting Employee.cs file and add the following code:

```
public class Employee
{
  public int Id { get; set; }
  public string FirstName { get; set; }
  public string LastName { get; set; }
  public Positions Position { get; set; }
}

public enum Positions
{
  CEO,
  CTO,
  SeniorDeveloper,
  Developer,
  Tester
}

public class EmployeesContext: DbContext
{
  public DbSet<Employee> Employees { get; set; }
}
```

3. Next, open up the `Program.cs` file and modify the `Main()` method using the following code as a guide:

```
static void Main(string[] args)
{
  using (var context = new EmployeesContext())
  {
    context.Employees.Add(new Employee
      {
        Position = Positions.CEO,
        FirstName = "James",
        LastName = "Brown"
      });
    context.Employees.Add(new Employee
      {
        Position = Positions.CTO,
        FirstName = "Sly",
        LastName = "Stone"
      });
    context.SaveChanges();
    var ceo = context.Employees.Where(e => e.Position == Positions.CEO)
                          .FirstOrDefault();
    if (ceo != null)
      Console.WriteLine("The CEO is {0} {1}", ceo.FirstName, ceo.LastName);
    else
      Console.WriteLine("No CEO was found");
    Console.ReadKey();
  }
}
```

As you can see, it is a fairly painless process using enums with the Entity Framework both in terms of using them when persisting data and in LINQ queries. Setting them up in Model First or Database First requires a few more steps but again provides exactly the same functionality. If you are interested in a Model First example take a look at this blog post: http://msdn.microsoft.com/en-us/library/hh770088(v=vs.103).aspx.

■ **Note** If this is your first look at the code-first workflow, you may be wondering where the database is. When the NuGet package is installed, it checks which database server is installed and then uses a configuration setting to set the default database server for creating databases from the code-first workflow. If SqlExpress is running, it will be used. Otherwise, LocalDb will be used. If you are using LocalDb with the previous example, you can find the database by opening the SQL Server Object Explorer, click on the add new server icon, in the Connect to Server dialog box enter (localdb)\v11.0, and click connect. In the SQL Server Object Explorer expand the Databases node below the LocalDb node and you should see the database that was created.

Support for Multi-Result Stored Procedures

In the past, with Entity Framework you could call a stored procedure that had multiple result sets, but it would only return the first result set. This has been changed in EF 5, and it is now possible to access all the result sets returned by a stored procedure. There is one catch though. This feature, though supported by EF's plumbing, is not exposed as an option by the modeling tools so that the only way to actually implement it is by manually editing the EDMX.

To show what is involved, we will walk through a simple implementation. You can follow along working against you own database or, if you want, you can download the database project for the sample database used here by going to http://tinyurl.com/7grkrys and downloading the file AirTavelDb.zip or the completed solution containing the code for this and the next two sections: entityFrameworkExamples.zip.

■ **Note** The following setup for this example is basically the same for the next two sections so we will go into more detail here.

---

1. You need to set up a few things to begin. First, create a new console project and call it MultiResultStoredProcExample.

2. Next, open the Package Manager Console window and install the latest Entity Framework package:

Install-Package EntityFramework

3. Now add a new entity data model and name it AirTravel and click the button labeled Add.

4. On the Choose Model Contents dialog box, select Generate from database and click Next and then select the connection for the `AirTravelDb`. If you are using LocalDb for the database you will probably need to add a new connection. To do this, click on the New Connection button and in the Connection Properties enter `(localDb)\<YourSolutionNameHere>`. Click Refresh and then select the database name.

5. In the next screen (Figure 9-2), where you select the database objects you want, drill down into the stored procedures node and select the stored procedure `AMeaninglessStoredProc`, change the model namespace to `AirTravelModel`, and click the Finish button.

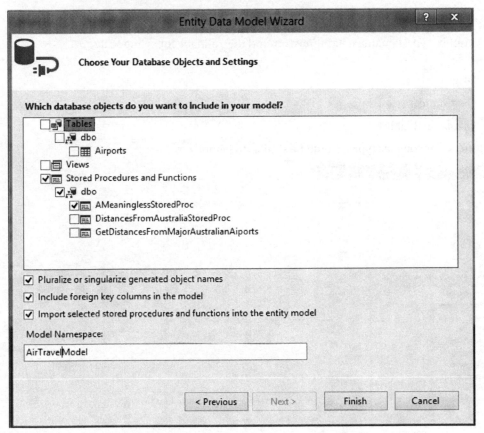

Figure 9-2. Selecting the stored procedure

At this point, you should have an empty designer, but since you didn't select any tables, that's okay.

6. To be able to work with the DbContext API, you need to get the DbContext Generator template. Right-click on the designer and select "Add Code Generation Item…" from the context menu.

7. Now right-click on the designer and select Model Browser from the context menu. In the Model Browser window opening the Complex Types folder, you should find a class called AMeaninglessStoredProc_Result. This complex type was generated off the data returned from the first result set in your stored procedure. To better represent the data being returned, rename it AustralianInternationalAirports.

8. Next, open the Function Imports folder. You want to rename the function import AMeaninglessStoredProc so right-click on it and select Edit. In the dialog box that displays, rename the function to AustralianAirportsAndDistances.

9. Finally, since a complex type wasn't generated for your second result set, you need to create one. Right-click on the Complex Types folder and select Add New Complex Type. Rename it PointToPoint and then add the following scalar properties:

    •   Origin: string

    •   Destination: string

    •   Distance: double

Once that is done, your complex types should be similar to Figure 9-3.

Figure 9-3. *Model Browser after editing*

Now, at this point, if you called the function AustralianAirportsAndDistances, you would only get one result set back. So that you can return both result sets, you will now need to edit the EDMX:

10. Right-click on `AirTravel.edmx`, select Open With, and then select XML (Text) Editor.

11. Next, you need to edit the function import in the CSDL content. Look for the following XML:

```
<FunctionImport Name="AustralianAirportsAndDistances"
ReturnType="Collection(AirTravelModel.AustralianInternationalAirports)">
  <Parameter Name="AirportCode" Mode="In" Type="String" />
</FunctionImport>
```

12. Now you need to modify this so that the function will return both result sets. Update this section to the following:

```
<FunctionImport Name="AustralianAirportsAndDistances" >
  <ReturnType Type="Collection(AirTravelModel.AustralianInternationalAirports)"/>
  <ReturnType Type="Collection(AirTravelModel.PointToPoint)"/>
  <Parameter Name="AirportCode" Mode="In" Type="String" />
</FunctionImport>
```

13. Next, you need to add a new result mapping for your `PointToPoint` complex type to the function import mapping. Scroll down to the C-S mapping content section and update the `FunctionImportMapping` so it matches this:

```
<FunctionImportMapping FunctionImportName="AustralianAirportsAndDistances"
FunctionName="AirTravelModel.Store.AMeaninglessStoredProc">
<ResultMapping>
  <ComplexTypeMapping TypeName="AirTravelModel.AustralianInternationalAirports">
    <ScalarProperty Name="Id" ColumnName="Id" />
    <ScalarProperty Name="AirportCode" ColumnName="AirportCode" />
    <ScalarProperty Name="AirportName" ColumnName="AirportName" />
    <ScalarProperty Name="Latitude" ColumnName="Latitude" />
    <ScalarProperty Name="Longitude" ColumnName="Longitude" />
  </ComplexTypeMapping>
</ResultMapping>
<ResultMapping>
  <ComplexTypeMapping TypeName="AirTravelModel.PointToPoint" >
    <ScalarProperty Name="Origin" ColumnName="Origin"/>
    <ScalarProperty Name="Destination" ColumnName="Destination" />
    <ScalarProperty Name="Distance" ColumnName="Distance" />
  </ComplexTypeMapping>
</ResultMapping>
</FunctionImportMapping>
```

When that is all done, you can now retrieve both result sets. The following code will give you an idea of how it is done (see Figure 9-4 for the output):

```
static void Main(string[] args)
{
  string distinationAirportCode = "NRT"; //Narita airport;
  using (var context = new AirTravelDbEntities())
  {
    var result = context.AustralianAirportsAndDistances(distinationAirportCode);
    foreach (var ap in result)
```

```
    {
        Console.WriteLine("{0}: {1}, {2}", ap.AirportCode, ap.Latitude, ap.Longitude);
    }
    Console.WriteLine();
    //to get the second result we need to call GetNextResult()
    var result2 = result.GetNextResult<PointToPoint>();
    foreach (var ptp in result2)
    {
        Console.WriteLine("{0} -> {1}: {2} km", ptp.Origin, ptp.Destination, ptp.Distance);
    }
  }
  Console.ReadKey();
}
```

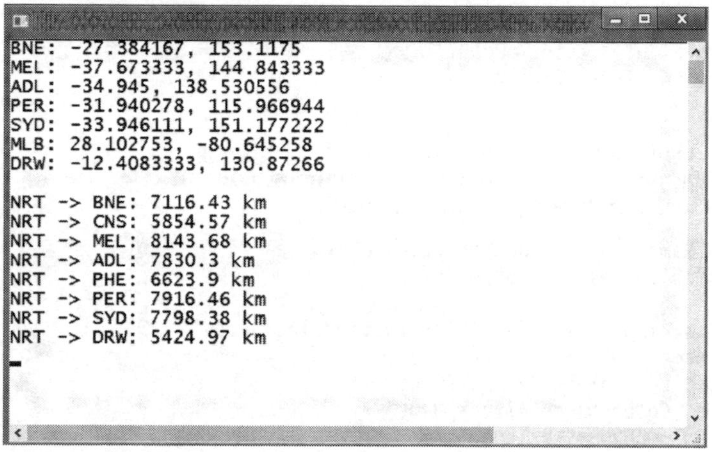

```
BNE: -27.384167, 153.1175
MEL: -37.673333, 144.843333
ADL: -34.945, 138.530556
PER: -31.940278, 115.966944
SYD: -33.946111, 151.177222
MLB: 28.102753, -80.645258
DRW: -12.4083333, 130.87266

NRT -> BNE: 7116.43 km
NRT -> CNS: 5854.57 km
NRT -> MEL: 8143.68 km
NRT -> ADL: 7830.3 km
NRT -> PHE: 6623.9 km
NRT -> PER: 7916.46 km
NRT -> SYD: 7798.38 km
NRT -> DRW: 5424.97 km
```

Figure 9-4. Output from both result sets

At the time of writing, it is clear that this feature is not as easy to use as should be, but it can be done. If you are thinking of using of it, plan ahead before implementing it.

Working with Spatial Data Types

Spatial data types, which were introduced with SQL Server 2008, are now supported in the Entity Framework with the classes DbGeography and DbGeometry in the namespace System.Data.Spatial. This means you can store and query against the spatial data types Geometry and Geography, whether you take a code-first, model-first, or database-first approach to constructing your entities.

The real power that comes with the inclusion of these classes is that using them with LINQ provides an easy way to perform complex spatial calculations against the database since all of the properties and methods associated with the SQL spatial data types are exposed through the corresponding EF classes.

To give you a small taste of what this means, in the following excerpt we want to find all of the airports within 15 kilometers from a given location. (Note: If you are following on from the previous example you will need to add the Airports table as an entity to the model. Otherwise, this example is included in the completed solution mentioned earlier.)

```
static void Main(string[] args)
{
  var newYorkLocation = DbGeography.FromText("Point( -74.006605 40.714623)");
  var searchDistanceInMeters = 15000;
  using (var context = new AirTravelDbEntities())
  {
    var airports = from a in context.Airports
                   where a.Location.Distance(newYorkLocation) < searchDistanceInMeters
                   select new { airportName = a.AirportName,
                   Code = a.AirportCode,
                   Distance = Math.Round(a.Location.Distance(newYorkLocation).Value/1000,2) };
    Console.WriteLine("Aiports within {0} kilometres of New York:", searchDistanceInMeters /
1000);
    foreach (var airport in airports)
    {
      Console.WriteLine("{0} ({1}) {2} km", airport.airportName,
airport.Code,airport.Distance);
    }

    Console.ReadKey();
  }
}
```

The SQL generated by the LINQ query looks like this:

```
SELECT
1 AS [C1],
[Extent1].[AirportName] AS [AirportName],
[Extent1].[AirportCode] AS [AirportCode],
ROUND(([Extent1].[Location].STDistance(@p__linq__2)) / cast(1000 as float(53)),
2) AS [C2]
FROM [dbo].[Airports] AS [Extent1]
WHERE ([Extent1].[Location].STDistance(@p__linq__0)) < @p__linq__1
```

As you can in the SQL statement that is generated by Entity Framework the method `Distance()` on the geography object `Location` is translated to the `STDistance` comparative method in SQL.

Table-Value Function Support

Though this will only work with a database-first workflow, you can now add table-value functions (TVFs) to your entity data model. When you import a table-value function, Entity Framework, as it does for stored procedures, will create an import function and a complex type that will map to the schema of the table returned. Where TVFs have the advantage over stored procedures is that the import function created for the TVF is composable, which means that you can use LINQ and Entity SQL against them.

For the following example, we will use the `AirTravel` database we used in the previous two sections.

1. If you are creating a new solution, import the `AirTravelDb` project.

2. Add a new console window project.

3. Add a new ADO.NET Entity Data Model and select Generate from Database.

4. When you are prompted to select database objects, drill down into the Stored Procedures and Functions node and select GetDistancesFromMajorAirports.

5. From the Data Model Designer page, open the Model Browser.

6. Open the Complex Types folder and rename the class GetDistancesFromMajorAustralianAiports_Result to DistancesFromAustralianAirports (you don't have to do this, it's just a little neater).

7. Return to the Solution Explorer and open the Program.cs file and add the following code to the Main() method:

```
using (var context = new AirTravelDbEntities())
{
  var result = context.GetDistancesFromMajorAustralianAiports("NRT")
          .Where(a => a.StartPointAirportCode == "BNE" || a.StartPointAirportCode == "MEL");
  foreach (var item in result)
  {
    Console.WriteLine("{0} -> {1}: {2} km", item.StartPoint, item.EndPoint, item.Distance);
  }
  Console.ReadKey();
```

If you now run application, you should get the output in Figure 9-6.

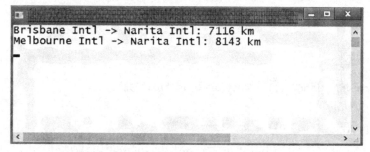

Figure 9-6. *Output from table function example*

As you can see, it is fairly easy to implement a table-value function in Entity Framework that allows you to use it directly in a LINQ query—definitely an advantage over using stored procedures.

Performance

Using any ORM will introduce overhead to data access. With this in mind, the ADO.NET team has made improving the performance of Entity Framework one of their goals with this release (see the ADO.NET team blog at http://blogs.msdn.com/b/adonet/archive/2012/02/14/sneak-preview-entity-framework-5-0-performance-improvements.aspx). One of the ways the team has improved performance is by introducing automatic compilation of LINQ to Entities queries.

Up until this version, when you created a LINQ to Entity the Entity Framework would walk the expression tree generated by the compiler to translate it into SQL. This process involved some overhead, especially for complex queries, and would be repeated every time the query was called. You could reduce this overhead by using the CompiledQuery class, which would allow you to compile the query once, returning you a delegate that pointed to the compiled version in the Entity Framework cache. The problem with this is that you had to know about it and you needed to explicitly implement it.

With the introduction of the auto-compiled LINQ queries feature, every LINQ query you execute gets automatically compiled and placed in the query cache. Therefore, every time you run the query, it will be retrieved from the cache negating the need to go through the compilation process again.

Entity Model Designer

Not a lot has changed with the designer, but in VS2012 you find will the following new features:

- **Multiple diagrams per model**. Especially for complex models, this feature will be useful since it allows you to visualize subsections of the overall model.

- **Assign colors to shapes**. Shapes in the designer can now be assigned different colors, which again is useful when dealing with complex models. To change the color of a shape, select it and then in the properties window under the Diagram node, you will see the property Fill Color where you can change the color from either the dropdown palette or by directly entering the RGB values for the color you want.

- **Batch import of stored procedures**. In VS 2010, you could load multiple stored procedures when creating your model, but then for each stored procedure you had to explicitly create a function import and complex type for each one. Not a problem if you only have a few to contend with, but increase that number by any reasonable amount, and you have a lot more work on your hands. With VS2012, the Entity Framework will now not only import the stored procedures (and functions) in one hit, but it will also create corresponding function imports and associated complex types.

Conclusion

It is very few developers who do not interact in some way or form with data and for a lot of us this usually means working with SQL Server, which is what everything in this chapter essentially leads back to. The question is whether these new features that we have covered in this chapter help or hinder us.

When developing applications, the question of what comes first—the database or the application—has tended, whichever position you took, to cause friction. The addition of LocalDb (and the associated SQL Server Data Tools that have been included in VS 2012) has the potential to change the way we think about this by providing a more iterative and flexible approach to both application and database development. Another area where LocalDb will be an interesting option is integration and functional testing. Coupled with the inclusion of a database project, spinning up and initializing data independent of a SQL Server instance may reduce some of the frustration that testing against a shared SQL Server instance can cause.

The changes to the SqlClient Data Provider, with the introduction of asynchronous and streaming support, will ensure that data access does not become the thorn in the side of developing responsive applications.

Finally, there is the Entity Framework. Having gotten off to a rocky start when it was first introduced, it is clear that the ADO.NET team is putting in the work to make it a viable option in the ORM space.

■ ■ ■

Windows Azure

In this chapter, you will be introduced to Microsoft's cloud platform—Windows Azure—and how you can create applications that run in this platform. After a brief introduction to the cloud, you first learn about Web Sites, Cloud Services, and Virtual Machines. You then learn about table storage and blobs, which are used to store data in Azure. You finish off the chapter by learning about Windows Azure's SQL Database, which is the Azure version of Microsoft SQL Server.

The Cloud

So, what is the cloud? To understand it, you need to take a step back and think about how the Internet is represented in a lot of design and architecture documents. That's right—it is drawn as a cloud. And that is precisely what the cloud is—the Internet. Aside from being a metaphor for the Internet, the cloud is used as a shortened form for *cloud computing*. And cloud computing is nothing but computing power/services available on the Internet.

Cloud providers, such as Microsoft and Amazon, provide the customer the ability to store large amounts of data, run web applications, and do heaps of other things in the cloud. These providers run their infrastructure in their datacenters.

So, what is the difference between a regular datacenter and a cloud offering? Typically, cloud offerings are run out of very large datacenters and provide the following advantages that smaller datacenters find hard to match:

- No upfront cost to set up the services

- Low running cost, some of it charged by the hour

- Elasticity on demand (in other words, the ability to scale up and down easily and quickly)

- High availability and reliability

- Maintenance, upgrades, patches, and so forth are automatically taken care of in lots of cases

- Seemingly infinite computing power and resources at your disposal

---

CLOUD MODELS

Cloud computing usually falls into three separate models—Infrastructure as a Service (IaaS), Platform as a Service (PAAS), and Software as a Service (SaaS).

Infrastructure as a Service (IaaS)

In this offering, cloud providers provide infrastructure, such as computers, as a service to consumers. These computers are provided in a virtualized environment, and users can spin up any number of "virtual machines" they want. They can then install whatever operating system they want and run any applications they want in them. Companies such as Amazon are big players in this space, and Microsoft has now made a big push into this space with their *Virtual Machine* and *Virtual Network* offering.

Platform as a Service (PaaS)

In the IaaS offering, consumers will have to manage the operating system, install patches, and do a lot of maintenance—this could be a lot of hard work. What if the service provider did all this for you and, in turn, all you had to do was write your applications in a certain way? This is what PaaS does. These cloud providers provide a platform, in which you can run your applications, and while doing so, you lose some of the flexibility you had in the IaaS offering, but you exchange it for other gains. For instance, things such as infrastructure setup, maintenance, upgrades, and load balancing will be taken care of by the service provider. Microsoft Azure with their *Cloud Services* offering provides this service. The beauty about Microsoft's PaaS offering is that you can leverage on existing .NET knowledge and code you already have. You will be able to migrate existing applications or create new ones to run in the Azure platform with minimal effort. Microsoft is also making every effort to make this platform available to people using other languages and frameworks (such Java and node.js).

Software as a Service (SaaS)

In the SaaS offering, you will be provided with the software itself offered as a service to customers. Typical software that is offered in this fashion is Customer Relationship Management (CRM), Human Resources Management (HRM), Accounting, and so on. Microsoft's Office 365 falls in to the SaaS offering, and Microsoft charges customers based on the number of accounts they have. SalesForce is also another popular SaaS product.

The Windows Azure Platform

As I mentioned earlier, Windows Azure is Microsoft's cloud platform. If you are running an application in Microsoft Azure, it means that your application is running in one of Microsoft's six datacenters around the world—Microsoft has two in the United States, two in Europe, and two in Asia. These datacenters are extremely big and host tens of thousands of servers, have multiple levels of redundancy, and are extremely secure (physically).

Execution Models

One of the main uses of Azure is to host applications in the cloud and execute them. The Azure platform provides three ways in which you can execute applications (what Microsoft refers to as execution models):

- Virtual machines
- Web Sites
- Cloud Services

Virtual Machines

Windows Azure allows you to create virtual machines (VMs) based on images you've created (or ones readily available from Microsoft) as and when you need them. This is Microsoft's IaaS offering, and not only can you create these VMs on demand, you only pay for what you use—cost is calculated on an hourly basis, and if you don't need any VMs, you can just shut them down and not pay for them. VMs hosted in the cloud allow you to set up machines the way you want them—with the right configuration and software.

Web Sites

You can use the cloud to do a variety of things such as store large amounts of data or leverage the highly scalable nature of the cloud to do massive number crunching, but one of the most common uses is to simply move your existing web site to it. By moving your web site to the cloud, you not only make the web site highly scalable and available, you also bring down your hosting costs. The Web Site offering from Windows Azure fills this basic need—to host your web application. Windows Azure will automatically take care of things such as running multiple instances of the site on different servers (if you want to) and taking care of load balancing. Think of it as your web farm in the cloud.

Web sites offer a much simpler solution to run your web site compared to creating a VM, configuring IIS, and worrying about infrastructure details.

Cloud Services

Web sites are great to run simple web applications that currently run on IIS but that don't require additional software or configuration. Sometimes, however, your needs could be a lot more complex—such as the need to have administrative privilege or the desire to run tasks in the background in a scalable way. In such cases, Web Sites may just not cut it and your VM role may be an overkill. This is where Cloud Services come in to play. Currently, Cloud Services provide two roles under which your application can run—a web role and a worker role.

A web role is used to run a web application. You can think of it as being similar to the Web Sites' offering, but something with a lot more control—and like a web site, you can also run multiple instances of a web role to make it highly scalable. A worker role is used to run code in the background, and you can think of it as being similar to a Windows service—but running in the cloud— and again, you can run multiple instances of it, which makes it highly scalable.

Data Management in Azure

The execution models—VMs, Web Sites, and worker/web roles—are used to run code in Azure, but most applications also need to persist data to be useful. The main ways to work with data in Azure include the following:

- Table storage

- Blobs

- SQL Database

■ **Note** Apart from using these built-in ways to store and retrieve data, you can also create a VM that provides other mechanisms to handling data such as running an instance of database (this is not limited to just SQL Server—you can also run something like MySQL on it) or running a NoSQL database such as Raven DB or Mongo DB.

Storage in Azure is highly redundant—Microsoft keeps three copies of the same data in a single datacenter, and you can choose to do geo-replication of tables and blobs. What this means is that if you have geo-replication enabled, Microsoft will automatically replicate the data to another datacenter in the same region. So, if your data is stored in the north central datacenter in the United States, Azure will automatically copy it to the south central datacenter.

Table Storage

Windows Azure Table Storage Service, or Tables for short, is used to store structured data. If you have been doing programming for a while or have studied computer science, you immediately think, "Oh, relational database!" at the mention of table storage, but you couldn't be more wrong. A relational database contains a database schema, which defines how the data is stored, and the data itself is stored in rows and columns within a table. Each entity in a Relation Database System (RDBMS) has its own table, and there are concepts such as indexes, joins, and SQL queries.

Apart from the reuse of the word *table*, Windows Azure Table Storage Service and relational databases are quite different. So different that it is referred to as a *NoSQL* database. In table storage, a single table can contain multiple entities. You still have the concept of rows, but instead of fixed columns for a table, you have a set of properties. You can think of these properties as nothing more than name-value pairs. Like an RDBMS, tables also provide basic CRUD (Create, Read, Update, and Delete) functionality, which is available via RESTful web services. A much easier way to work with tables is using WCF Data Services. With WCF Data Services, you can query the data using LINQ and perform inserts, updates, and deletes just like you would do with entities stored in a relational DB.

Each Windows Azure account can have any number of tables in it, and each table can contain any number of entities in the form of rows. Each row is, however, limited to 255 properties. Some of these properties are mandatory and need to exist for each entity:

- **Partition Key**: This identifies how the data is partitioned. How you decide what the unit of partition is depends on your application. It is not uncommon to partition the same data in several ways.

- **Row Key**: This identifies the unique key for the entity within the partition.

- **Timestamp**: This is used to determine when the entity was created and updated. This is used mainly for concurrency locking.

WHY DO YOU NEED PARTITION KEYS?

You may be able to uniquely identify an entity using its row key alone. *So, why do you need partition keys?* Partition keys are really important for scalability in Windows Azure. Entities that have the same partition key will be stored together in Azure, and this really helps performance. Whenever you access table storage, you should make it a point to include the partition key. Under the hood, Azure looks at usage patterns of partitions and does some optimizations. It may do things like split up the table (physically) based on the partition and store it in different storage nodes.

Partition keys also provide transaction support for table storage—you can do multiple updates, inserts, and deletes in an atomic fashion as long as the rows involved use the same partition key.

Blobs

Blobs are nothing more than files that are needed by your application—the only difference is that instead of being stored in the local file system, they are stored in a central place. Blobs, whose name stands for *binary large objects*, are accessed through a URL, and if the name of the storage account is called dotnetbook, the blobs stored in that account can be found in the URL http://dotnetbook.blob.core.windows.net. Windows Azure provides facilities to upload and read whole blobs or even parts of these blobs.

So, why not just use files stored locally, like you do currently? In other words, why use blobs? You have to remember that when you are working with Web Sites or Cloud Services, you have multiple instances running, which means you are running these on different VMs. If you create a file locally in one VM, it may not be available in the other VM, which is not very useful. By creating it as a blob, it is centrally available to all roles.

There are two types of blobs in Azure—block blobs and page blobs. Block blobs are made up of a sequence of blocks (<= 4MB in size). Breaking it up into these smaller chunks makes reading and writing of blobs easier. Currently, block blobs have a maximum size of 200GB.

Page blobs can be as large as 1TB, and they are made up of pages. You can do random read/writes to these pages. If you are dealing with smaller files, such as text files or images, you will end up working with just block blobs.

You can also have as many blobs as you want per account. Each blob is actually held in a container, which is nothing more than a logical grouping. So, effectively, each account can contain any number of containers and each container contains any number of blobs.

For example, you may have an account called dotnetbook, which holds containers called images and documents and samples, and under images you may store blobs with the name logo.png, bkgrnd.jpg, and image.png. The document container may contain document blobs under the names Azure.docx and Metro.docx. Figure 10-1 shows how the URL for the blob is created for the image blobs in this example.

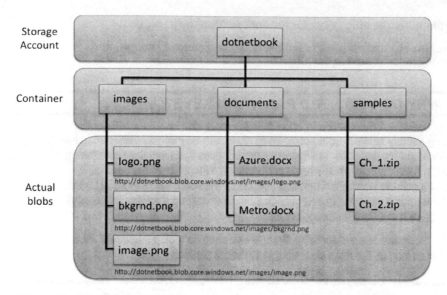

Figure 10-1. *URL for blobs*

As blobs are nothing more than standard URLs, they can be quite useful for storing application files such as images, CSS files, and JS files. One advantage of doing it this way rather than being deployed with the other project files is that these files can be exposed via the Azure Content Delivery Network (CDN). CDNs are servers placed closer to your own networks that help in caching content closer to where you are accessing it.

To delve into it a bit further, there are currently only six Azure datacenters around the world where your blob can be stored. But Azure also has 24+ datacenters, which spread across the world hosting CDNs where the content of these blobs can be cached. To understand CDNs better, let's take the example of trying to access an image from, say, Sydney, Australia, with the image being hosted in Singapore. If you were using a CDN to cache the image, the content would be served out of a CDN node in Sydney, but the traffic doesn't have to make a round-trip all the way to Singapore.

SLOBS VS. BLOBS

A friend of mine once jokingly asked , "Hey, if *blobs* are the new names for files in Azure, why didn't Microsoft call table storage *slobs*?"

Slobs are usually associated with being unattractive and crude—I can wholeheartedly say that table storage is actually a very attractive option. What makes it very attractive is the fact that table storage is highly scalable, performs really well, and is relatively inexpensive. If you are thinking about some kind of data store to store large amounts of structured data and also want it to be fast, table storage is where you would put it. Blobs, on the other hand, can store really, really large amounts of data (that is usually unstructured) in a single file.

SQL Database

If you have an existing application, chances are you have a relational database of some sort where your data is stored. If you are using a Microsoft stack, chances are this database is SQL Server. The Azure platform's equivalent of SQL Server in the cloud is SQL Database, which was formerly known as SQL Azure. This database makes migrating an existing relational database to the cloud easy.

SQL Database may be similar to its SQL Server counterpart, but you will find that there are a lot of differences between SQL Server and SQL Database running on Azure, some of which are included in the following list:

- Database size in SQL Database cannot be greater than 150GB.

- Some query commands do not work in SQL Database.

- SQL Database will terminate long-running query operations.

- You need to have a clustered index in SQL Database.

- SQL Database does not support .NET CLR data types, encrypted columns, FILESTREAM, distributed transactions, full text search, and so on.

A comprehensive list of all the differences can be found at http://msdn.microsoft.com/en-us/library/windowsazure/ff394115.aspx.

In spite of these differences, working on SQL Database is quite easy if you are already working with SQL Server. You will be able to use familiar API from ADO.NET, run queries in SQL, and create entities using Entity Framework. In fact, switching over to SQL Database running on Azure from SQL Server in some cases is all about just changing the connection string!

TABLES VS. SQL DATABASE

If you are confused as to where you would want to store your structured data—in Tables or SQL Database—don't be. Here are some simple tips to help in your decision-making:

If you are migrating data stored in an existing SQL server database to the cloud, choose SQL Database. You may have to rewrite a large portion of your application if you switch it to start using Tables instead.

If your database size exceeds 150GB, you may not be able to use SQL Database. Federation using SQL Database and installing SQL Server in a VM are options (both of which are outside the scope of discussion of this book). Using Tables is also an option, but may require a lot of changes to your application.

If you are starting your application from scratch or you don't mind rewriting the data access layer in your application, then you could consider Tables. If cost, performance, and scalability are important, then Tables are a good choice. Tables are also great for redundancy.

Messaging

Applications sometimes need to communicate with each other. The Windows Azure platform provides a couple of ways to facilitate this communication:

- Queues
- Service Bus

Queues

A queue is a place where messages are held, and queues are used to exchange information between different applications. When one application needs to communicate with another, it creates a message and places it in a queue. The other application keeps looking at the queue for new messages and when one arrives, it picks it up to do some processing.

The best way to explain queues is through an example. If you've got a web application that uploads large images as blobs and a worker role that creates thumbnails from these images, you need to signal the worker role as soon as the image is loaded from the web application. You also need to tell the worker role the name of the image and where it is located. The web application puts this information in a message and posts it to a queue. The worker role keeps polling the queue for messages and as soon as it sees the message, it gets the message from the queue and starts working on creating the thumbnails. Once completed, the worker role should delete the message from the queue. If something goes wrong before the message is deleted, Azure restores the message to the queue. The worker role can then process it again.

Queue sizes are currently limited to 64K, and as with table storage and blobs, Azure provides a RESTful API and an SDK to work with queues.

Service Bus

Service Bus is another mechanism provided by Azure to help applications communicate. Service Bus also provides a queuing mechanism, but unlike the queues mentioned in the previous section, a single message in a queue can be consumed by multiple applications. This is achieved via a Publish/Subscribe mechanism. Service Bus also provides a relay service that allows a service to be made available even when a firewall is present.

Wait, There Is More ...

We've discussed execution models, data management, and messaging in Windows Azure. The platform is not limited to just these features. It contains a lot more elements—things to help with caching, identity management, networking, media services, and many more. The site http://www.windowsazure.com/ is a good starting point to learn more about these additional services.

However, the things discussed in the previous sections are most likely to be the most commonly used elements in Windows Azure and the ones you would use to get started on the platform. Therefore, these are the only components covered in this book. We also don't cover Service Bus apart from the introduction in the previous section.

Getting Started with Azure

Now that we've covered the basics of Windows Azure, let's see what you need to begin coding. The Azure SDK, at the time of writing, is ver 1.7, and you can download it from https://www.windowsazure.com/en-us/develop/net/. NuGet packages for the Azure SDK bits are also available (see http://nuget.org/profiles/azure-sdk). Windows Azure Tools for Microsoft Visual Studio will install everything you need to develop applications in Windows Azure.

In addition, the Azure SDK also provides you with emulators, which, although not the same as the real environment, can help you run and debug applications locally.

Alternatively, you can open Visual Studio 2012 and select File ➤ New ➤ Project… This will bring up the New Project dialog box as shown in Figure 10-2. Select Cloud from the left panel in the dialog box, choose Get Windows Azure SDK for .NET, and press OK. If you have already installed the Windows Azure SDK, you will see the available project types instead of the Get Windows Azure SDK for .NET option.

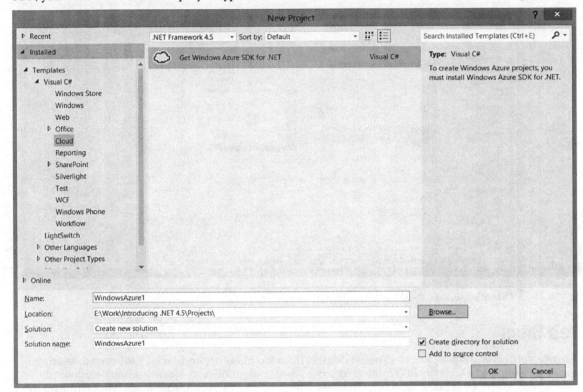

Figure 10-2. New project dialog box

This action will open up the necessary page to download and install the right tools as shown in Figure 10-3. The tools will be installed using the Web Platform Installer. The Windows Azure SDK for .NET contains the Windows Azure Tools for Microsoft Visual Studio, which allow you to do the following things right out of Visual Studio:

- Create new Windows Azure projects from the newly installed project templates

- Start the Compute and Storage Emulator from Visual Studio and run your projects there

- Use the Server Explorer to explore Azure compute and storage instances (and the emulators)

- Deploy your application directly to Azure from new menus

In addition, the SDK also installs Windows Azure Client Libraries for .NET, which contains libraries to talk to Windows Azure.

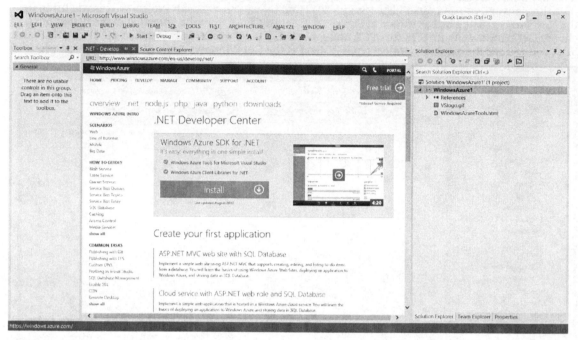

Figure 10-3. *Download page for Windows Azure*

Web Sites

If you currently have a simple web site that doesn't have too many dependencies (not even a database), then deploying it to a web site in Windows Azure is quite straightforward. Having databases does not make it too complex—it just means that there are a few more steps to go through, such as setting up the database in the cloud and changing connection strings. But for the sake of simplicity, let's try to move a simple ASP.NET MVC application across to Azure.

Before you jump into Visual Studio to deploy your application, you need to create a web site using the Windows Azure Management Portal. To do that, navigate to http://manage.windowsazure.com using a browser. The management portal has had a refresh at the same time SDK 1.7 was released. While the old version was written in Silverlight, the new version is in plain HTML—what this means is that you can even access it from your iPad or mobile phone if you want to. If you don't have an account on Windows Azure, you can go through the steps of creating a new account using your Windows Live ID. (Don't worry if you don't have a Windows Live ID—you can create one for free.)

At the time of writing, Microsoft provided users with a 90-day trial to try Windows Azure without having to pay for it. If you have an MSDN subscription, you can use that too as it has a certain amount of free Azure credits per month. Once you've created an account, you can go to http://manage.windowsazure.com to start creating web sites, services, and databases in the cloud. Figure 10-4 shows the Windows Azure Portal.

Figure 10-4. The Windows Azure Management Portal

To create a new web site, click CREATE AN ITEM under ALL ITEMS, and then choose WEB SITE from the options provided in the NEW panel when it slides up. You will be prompted with options to do a QUICK CREATE, CREATE WITH DATABASE, or FROM GALLERY. Choose QUICK CREATE and type in a unique URL, as shown in Figure 10-5. Then press CREATE WEB SITE to create a new web site—this web site is actually a placeholder where you can deploy your ASP.NET application.

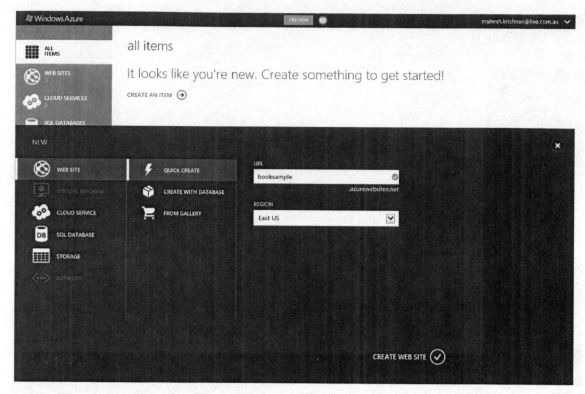

Figure 10-5. The NEW panel for creating items such as a web site

Deploying Your ASP.NET Application to an Azure Web Site

To deploy your ASP.NET application to Windows Azure, follow these steps:

1. Open up Windows Azure Portal to bring up the list of Web Sites that are available. You should see the web site created from the previous section, as shown in Figure 10-6.

Figure 10-6. Newly created web site in the portal

2. Click the name of the web site that you want to install your ASP.NET application on. This will take you to a detailed view of the web site. This screen allows you to configure the web site in a number of ways.

3. From the Dashboard tab, click Download publish profile to download the .publishsettings file that can be used from Visual Studio.

4. From Visual Studio, open the ASP.NET project that you want to deploy to the Azure web site.

■ **Note** At the time of writing, Windows Azure web sites do not support .NET 4.5, but this should be fixed eventually. You can change the framework version from the Configure tab in the portal.

5. Right-click the project from the Solution Explorer and choose Publish… from the drop-down menu. This brings up the Publish Web dialog box as shown in Figure 10-7.

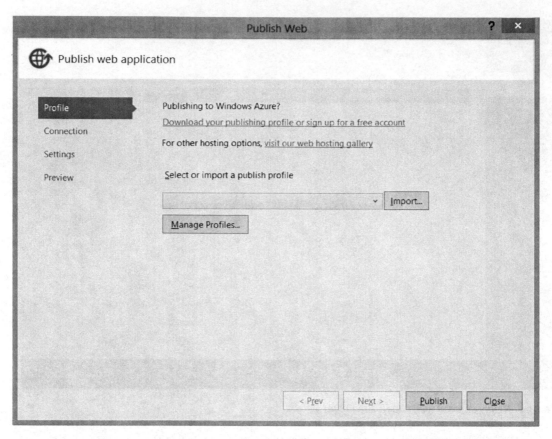

Figure 10-7. Dialog box to publish a web site to Azure

6. Press Import… button and from the File Open dialog box choose the
   .publishsettings file that you just saved from the Windows Azure Portal. This
   will automatically import all the settings that you need to publish to Azure as
   shown in Figure 10-8. (If you haven't previously downloaded a
   .publishsettings file, you can click the link Download your publishing profile
   or sign up for a free account to download it.)

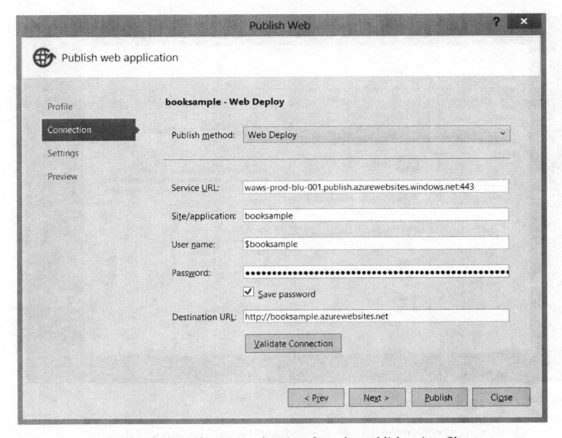

Figure 10-8. Dialog box showing the imported settings from the .publishsettings file

7. Press Publish in the dialog box to publish the application to Windows Azure and also to launch it in your browser.

Deploying Other Web Sites such as WordPress to Azure

Windows Azure is not limited to just hosting ASP.NET web sites. In fact, you can host sites created using even non-Microsoft technologies such as PHP—Drupal and WordPress being two popular content management systems written using PHP. To create a WordPress blog in your site, follow these steps:

1. From the Windows Azure Management Portal, go to the WEB SITES section and click CREATE A WEB SITE.

2. From the options, choose FROM GALLERY. This brings up the Find Apps for Azure window as shown in Figure 10-9.

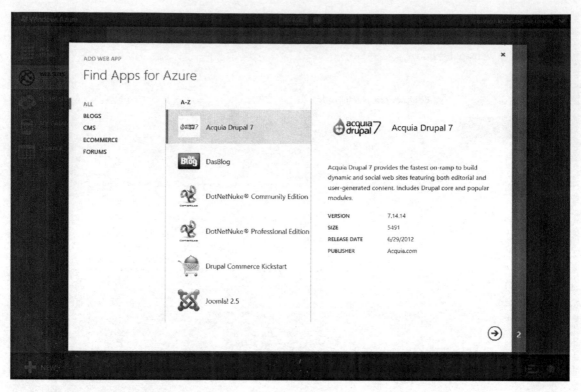

Figure 10-9. Find Apps For Azure

3.　Click on BLOGS option on the side. This should list WordPress as one of the options. Click on WordPress and press the next arrow. This takes you to the Configure Your App step as shown in Figure 10-10.

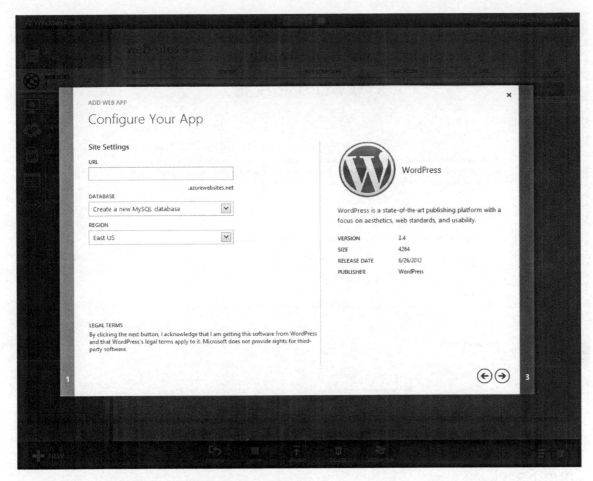

Figure 10-10. Configuring WordPress application

4. Type in a unique URL for the site and press the next arrow.

5. This takes you to CREATE NEW DATABASE step. Leave the defaults as they are, check the option to agree to the terms and conditions, and press the check mark button. This deploys a new WordPress site to the newly created web site on Windows Azure.

6. Once the application is deployed, you can click on the URL to take you to the newly created WordPress site, as shown in Figure 10-11. As you are entering the site for the first time, you will be prompted to enter a few pieces of information (such as site title and password) before you create an actual WordPress site.

Figure 10-11. The last step in setting up a WordPress site on Azure

Cloud Services

When you want more control over your cloud projects, you need to start using Cloud Services to deploy your application. To see how it works, let's start by creating a simple project by following these steps:

1. Select File ➤ New ➤ Project… from the menu or press Ctrl+Shift+N. This will bring up the New Project dialog box. Set the type of template to Cloud and select Windows Azure Cloud Service as the project template. Set the name of the project to HelloCloud and press OK. The New Windows Azure Cloud Service dialog box will be displayed, as shown in Figure 10-12.

■ **Note** At the time of writing, only .NET Framework 4 is supported. Make sure that you select the right framework version for the project template to show up.

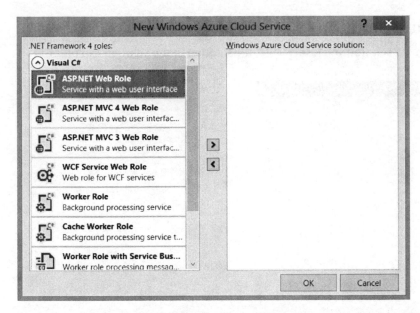

Figure 10-12. Adding new roles in the New Windows Azure Cloud Service dialog box

2. Double-click ASP.NET Web Role from the list of roles displayed. This will add an item to the Windows Azure cloud service solution list.

3. Right-click the WebRole1 item from the Windows Azure cloud service solution list and select Rename from the menu. Rename WebRole1 to something more meaningful such as HelloAzureWebApp.

4. Press OK to create the solution and all the projects in it.

5. Press F5 to run the application. You will notice a window displaying that the application is being run in the local Windows Azure Debugging environment, followed by the actual web application being displayed in a browser. That's it—you've created and run your first Windows Azure application!

▪ **Note** The Windows Emulator needs to run with elevated privilege. You might have to restart Visual Studio and run it as Administrator if you don't have the right permissions.

Looking into the Azure Solution

If you expand all the projects in the solution you just created, the solution in the Solution Explorer will show up as shown in Figure 10-13.

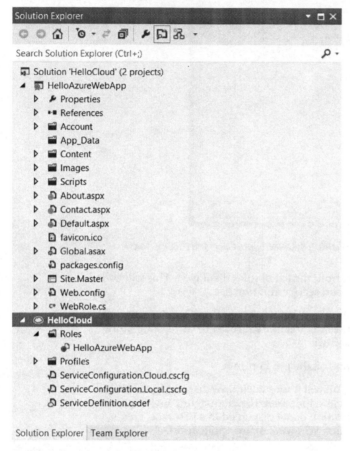

Figure 10-13. Solution Explorer showing the Azure project HelloCloud

You will notice that there are actually two projects in the solution—the HelloAzureWebApp and HelloCloud. The HelloAzureWebApp is nothing but a standard ASP.NET Web Forms application. It contains nothing that is specific to Azure. (Actually, I lie. There is some Azure specific stuff in there, such as the WebRole.cs file, but more about that later.)

The second project HelloCloud is the project that gets deployed into the cloud. Notice that this project has a folder called Roles. The ASP.NET project that needs to be deployed into the cloud exists here as a role. In addition, you will see three separate files:

- ServiceConfiguration.Cloud.cscfg: This file contains configuration information needed to run the web role in the cloud (in other words, in the actual Azure datacenter).

- **ServiceConfiguration.Local.cscfg**: This file contains configuration information needed to run the web role in the local Azure debugging environment.

- **ServiceDefinition.csdef**: This file contains service configuration definition, such as what the service configuration file contains and the endpoints under which the different roles in your cloud application run.

You do not have to worry too much about these files because they get modified automatically when you set things up interactively. Right-click the HelloAzureWebApp role in the Solution Explorer and select Properties. A properties window will open up as shown in Figure 10-14.

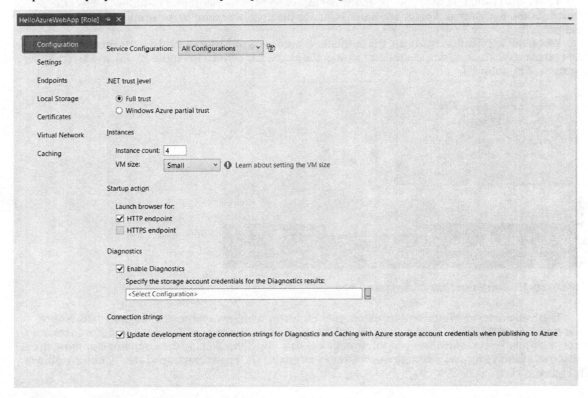

Figure 10-14. *Properties window for a role*

You will notice how you can set various options including how many instances of the role you want to run and what VM size to use. If you click the Settings tab, you will see existing settings used by the application. You can add any number of properties over here that you would want to configure at runtime, such as time-out values or environment-specific values.

Storage and Compute Emulators

It is not practical for you to deploy your application to the Azure datacenter and test it over there every time you make a change, no matter how small. The solution offered by Microsoft to solve this problem is an emulator environment that simulates the production Windows Azure and storage environments.

In fact, there are two emulators—one for Azure Compute and one for Azure Storage. These emulators mimic their Azure counterparts and allow you to run your applications on your own desktop. As a bonus, you also get to set breakpoints, step through code, inspect variables, and all those nice things you do when you debug your application from Visual Studio.

To see the emulators in action, open the HelloAzureWebApp role's property window. (Select the role from Solution Explorer and press Alt+Enter.) Change the instance count in the properties window to 4 and press F5.

When the application starts up, the emulator is automatically started, and it ends up as an icon in the system tray. Right-click the emulator icon in the status bar (shown in Figure 10-15) and select Show Compute Emulator UI.

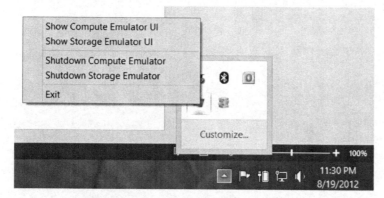

Figure 10-15. *Emulator icon in the system tray*

This will open the Windows Azure Compute Emulator window, as shown in Figure 10-16. Notice that under the HelloCloud application, the HelloAzureWebApp is shown, and under it four instances are shown. Similarly, you can also open the storage emulator by right-clicking the emulator icon from the Windows system tray and selecting Show Storage Emulator UI. The storage emulator window is shown in Figure 10-17.

■ **Note** The storage emulator actually stores data in a SQL Server Express instance in your local machine. You can open up your database using a tool such as SQL Server Management Studio and have a look at how the data is stored. You can also start modifying data stored in the tables directly, but I wouldn't recommend it. There are other ways to do it, which are covered later in this chapter.

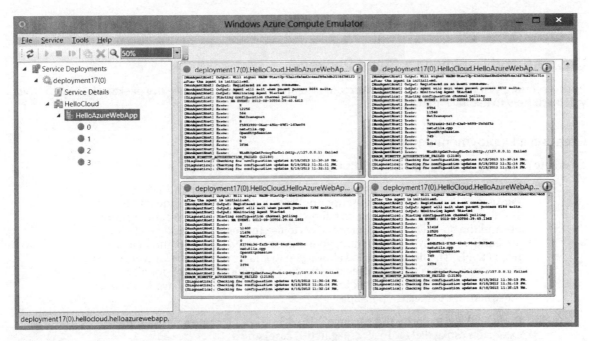

Figure 10-16. Compute Emulator running multiple instances of an application

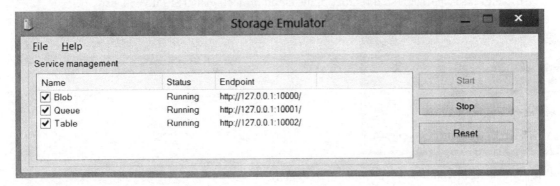

Figure 10-17. Storage Emulator

Deploying Your Cloud Service to Azure

Now that you've created a simple loud service, your next step would be to deploy it in an actual Azure datacenter. To do that, you need to first create a cloud service under your Windows Azure subscription. In order to create a cloud service, navigate to `http://manage.windowsazure.com` from your browser and create a cloud service similar to the way you created web sites in the previous section. Once you've created a cloud service in Azure, you can deploy your application in one of two ways:

- Create the deployment package from Visual Studio and upload it from the portal

- Publish the application directly from Visual Studio

Creating and Deploying a Cloud Package

In this section, you will first learn how to create a deployment package. Once the package is created, you will learn how to deploy it to the cloud.

Creating a Deployment Package

To create a deployment package, follow these steps:

1. Right-click the HelloCloud project from the Solution Explorer and select Package. A Package Windows Azure Application dialog box, as shown in Figure 10-18, is displayed. The dialog box allows you to pick the service configuration file and the build configuration you wish to use to create the package. If you are going to deploy to production, your choices would be Cloud and Release, respectively. The dialog box also allows you to enable remote desktop access to the instances you create by checking the Enable Remote Desktop for all roles check box and a Settings… link for further options. You do not have to alter these settings to create a package.

2. Press Package to create the package. Visual Studio will create a file with the extension cspkg (HelloCloud.cspkg in this case) and a ServiceConfiguration.Cloud.cscfg, and it will place this in the bin\Release\app.publish directory of the cloud project. Visual Studio will also open the location of the file in Windows Explorer for you to look at.

Figure 10-18. Package Windows Azure Application dialog box

■ **Tip** The cspkg file is nothing but a zip file. You can rename the file with a zip extension and unzip it to look at its contents. Be aware that the contents are encrypted, though. If you create a system variable called _CSPACK_FORCE_NOENCRYPT_ with the value set to true, the contents will not be encrypted. You wouldn't normally need to do this unless you hit an issue during deployment and want to check the contents manually on your machine.

Deploying the Package

To deploy this package, follow these steps:

1. Log in to http://manage.windowsazure.com and select Cloud Services on the left side pane. A list of cloud services that you have created as part of your Azure subscription will be displayed.

2. Click the name of the cloud service on which you wish to deploy your application. If you do not have any previously installed applications, you will see a screen similar to Figure 10-19.

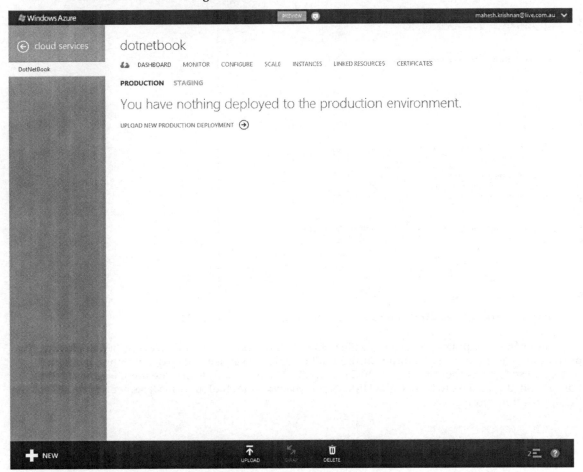

Figure 10-19. Cloud service with nothing deployed in production

3. Click the UPLOAD A NEW PRODUCTION DEPLOYMENT link. This will bring up in the Upload a package window as shown in Figure 10-20.

4. Set the DEPLOYMENT NAME to HelloCloud; then click the BROWSE YOUR COMPUTER button under PACKAGE. This opens up the File open dialog box. Browse to the directory where the Hellocloud.cspkg file was created and select it.

5. Next, click the BROWSE YOUR COMPUTER button under CONFIGURATION and choose the ServiceConfiguration.Cloud.cscfg file

6. Press the tick button to deploy the application.

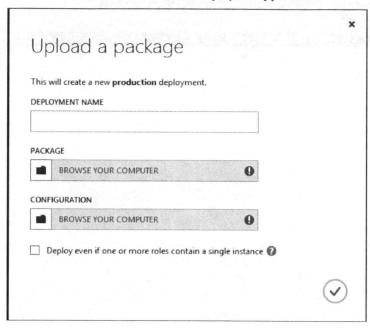

Figure 10-20. Upload a package dialog to deploy a package to Windows Azure

Deploying the application takes a while to finish. Once your application has finished deploying, the portal shows a whole load of information about the deployed service and tabs to monitor, configure, scale, and so forth as shown in Figure 10-21. You can click these tabs to explore these features further. You should also be able to browse the URL http://yourname-hellocloud.cloudapp.net and be able to see the application running.

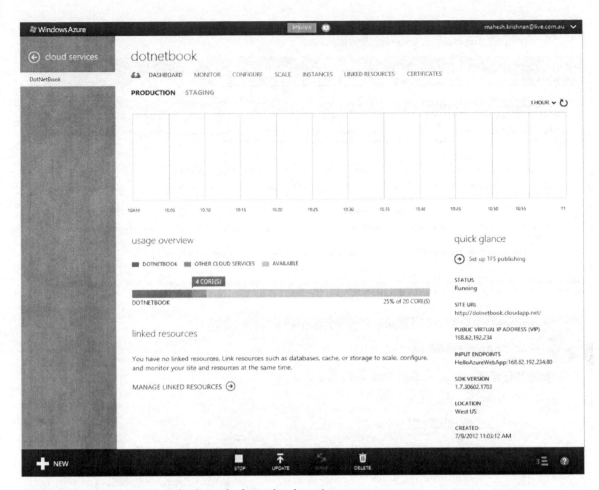

Figure 10-21. Dashboard and other tabs for a cloud service

Deploying the Cloud Application from Visual Studio

Deploying the application directly from within Visual Studio automates the multiple steps of creating a package, logging into the Azure Management Portal, and manually uploading the package with all the various options.

Deploying it for the first time involves a few extra steps, though. But let's do the same deployment that we did in the previous section from within Visual Studio by following these steps:

1. Right-click the cloud project and select Publish… from the menu. A Publish Windows Azure Application dialog box will be shown.

2. Click the link Sign in to download credentials. This will automatically open a browser and download a .publishsettings file that has all the details you need to deploy your application, as shown in Figure 10-22. (You may be prompted

to sign into to your Windows Azure account first.) Save the file into your project directory so you can find it easily.

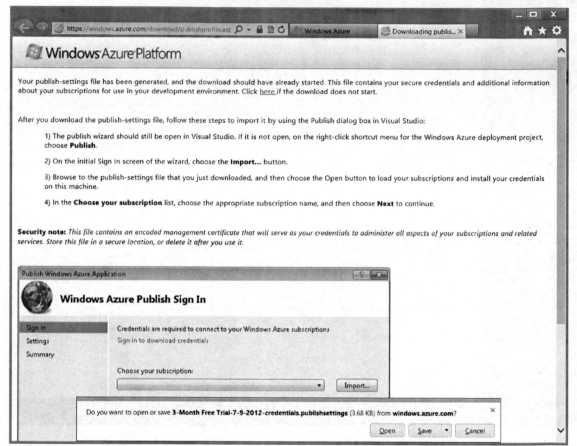

Figure 10-22. Downloading the .publishsettings file from Azure subscription

3. In the Publish Windows Azure Application dialog box, press the Import... button and pick the .publishsetttings file you just downloaded. The subscription name will then appear in the Choose your subscription field.

4. You can press the Next button to display options to change deployment settings, but instead press the Publish button. (If you already have instances running in your environment, you will be prompted to replace them.)

■ **Note** There is some pretty cool stuff in the Advanced tab. You can enable IntelliTrace and Profiling, which allows you to track problems and performance issues in your deployed application. There is also an option to delete deployment on failure, which is useful when an error occurs during deployment.

---

5. Visual Studio will display a Windows Azure activity log that shows the logs of the actual deployment as shown in Figure 10-23.

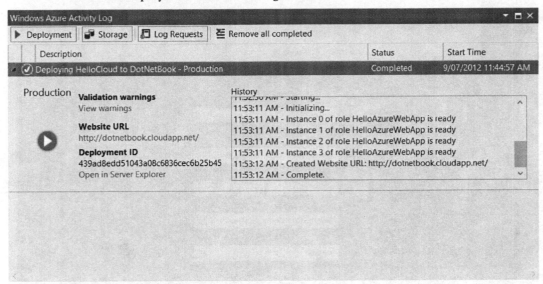

Figure 10-23. Windows Azure activity log in Visual Studio

Windows Azure Virtual Machines

As you saw in the cloud section earlier in this chapter, VMs in Windows Azure are the Infrastructure as a Service offering from Microsoft. These VMs can run an operating system of your choice (yes, even Linux if you wanted to) and there are some preconfigured VMs available for you to choose from. Strictly speaking, VMs should be considered an out-of-scope topic for this book as it has nothing to do with Visual Studio, but having covered so much on Windows Azure, it would be a shame not to touch on it.

To get it to work, follow these steps from the management portal:

1. Click on the NEW button at the bottom of the screen. This slides up the NEW panel.

2. Click on the VIRTUAL MACHINES option, and choose QUICK CREATE. You will be prompted to enter a DNS name and a few other fields as shown in Figure 10-24.

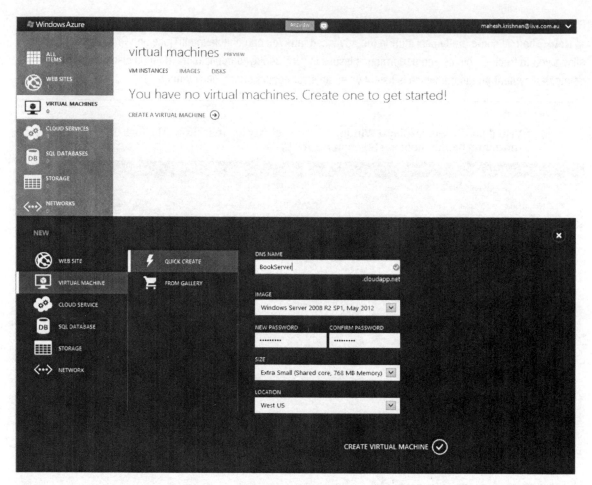

Figure 10-24. *Using the NEW panel to create a virtual machine*

3. Fill in the form and click CREATE VIRTUAL MACHINE. This creates a new VM image on Windows Azure and displays a screen as shown in figure 10-25.

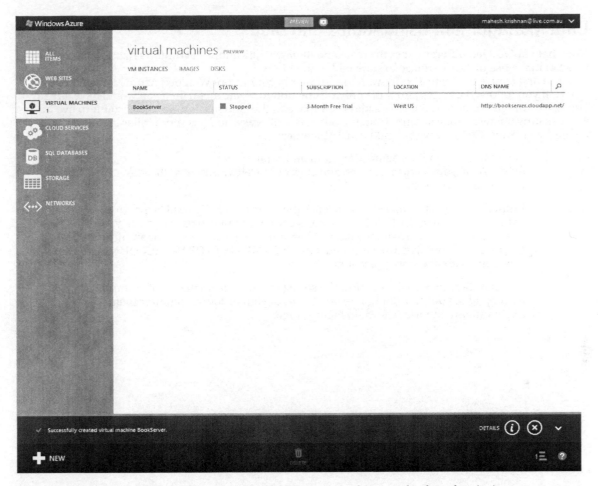

Figure 10-25. Virtual machines tab showing all the virtual machines under the subscription

Once you've created the server, you can plug a remote desktop into the machine and configure different server components or install server software.

■ **Note** At the time of writing, VMs were only available if you signed up to the preview program and will be grayed out if you haven't.

Data Management Using Tables and Blobs

Now that you've seen different ways to create and deploy applications in Windows Azure, let's see how you can make use of Azure storage to store tables and blobs.

The first step is to create a Windows Azure storage account from Windows Azure Management Portal. If you followed the steps from the previous section to create a VM, then you would have already created a storage account as the VM resides in a blob, and the blob needs a storage account to live in.

Creating a new storage account from the portal is quite easy, and it is very similar to the way you created Web Sites, Cloud Services, and Virtual Machines:

1. Log in to the Windows Azure Management Portal at http://manage.windowsazure.com and click on the NEW button at the left bottom of the screen.

2. From the NEW panel that slides up, click the Storage link. You will be provided with an option to QUICK CREATE a storage account. All you have to do is type in a unique URL where storage data will be stored, choose a region or affinity group where your data will be stored, and click CREATE STORAGE ACCOUNT. This will create the storage account for you.

3. You can then click on the name of the storage account from the list of accounts belonging to your subscription to see details of your accounts, monitor them, and configure them, as shown in Figure 10-26.

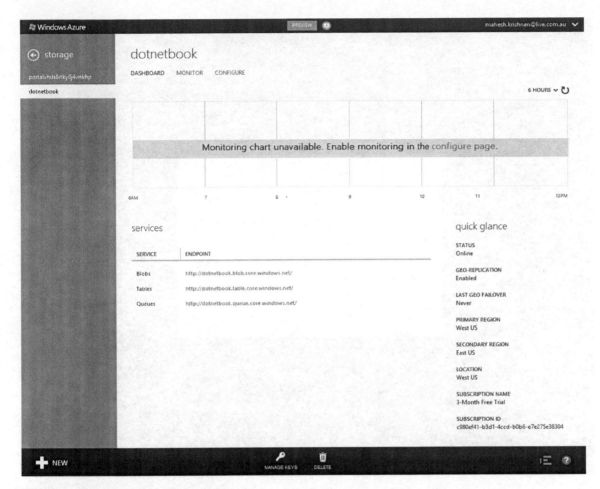

Figure 10-26. *Dashboard of a storage account*

If you look at the page, you will see that there are three separate endpoints (URLs) for the three services—blobs, tables, and queues—that are stored in Azure Storage. You are probably thinking, *What are queues doing in Azure storage? Aren't they used for messaging between applications?* Yes, but queues need to be stored somewhere too so that different applications can access them—what better place to put them than Azure storage, which is highly scalable, redundant, and available.

To access the storage account from your application, you need the name of the storage account (which is the name you typed into the URL field), followed by an access key. The access key can be obtained by clicking the MANAGE KEYS link at the bottom of the screen—this brings up the Manage Access Keys window as shown in Figure 10-27.

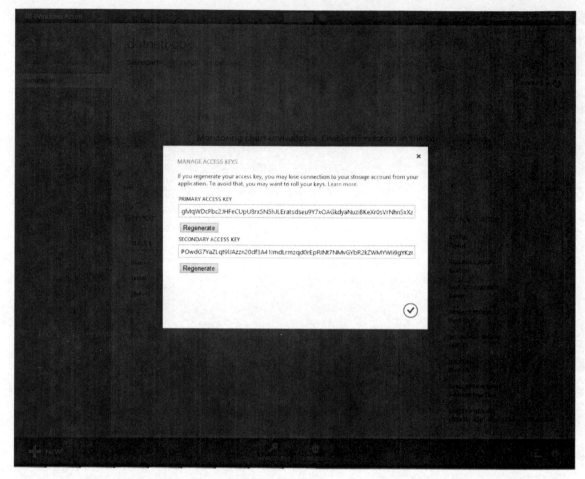

Figure 10-27. *Access keys needed to access storage accounts*

You can copy the primary access key from the text field present in the window. A connection string for a storage account will be in this format: `DefaultEndpointsProtocol=https;AccountName={storage name};AccountKey={primary access key}`

Accessing Entities Stored in Table Storage

Table storage stores data as entities. An entity is nothing but an object with a collection of properties. The best way of accessing these entities is by using WCF Data Services.

To create a simple entity class in C#, you need to extend the `TableServiceEntity` class that is present in the `Microsoft.WindowsAzure.StorageClient` namespace. A `Customer` class may look something like this:

```
public class Customer : TableServiceEntity
{
    public string FirstName { get; set; }
    public string LastName { get; set; }
    public string CompanyName { get; set; }
    public string PhoneNumber { get; set; }
    public string Email { get; set; }

}
```

An entity being stored in table storage also needs to have a Partition key, Row key, and a Timestamp field. These fields are already available in the TableServiceEntity class and do not have to be added to your Customer class.

Creating a Data Context Class

To use the WCF Data Service, you need to create a DataContext class. To create one for the Customer entity, you need to add code as follows:

```
public class CustomerServiceDataContext : TableServiceContext
{
    public CustomerServiceDataContext(CloudStorageAccount account)
        : base(account.TableEndpoint.AbsoluteUri, account.Credentials)
    {
        var tableStorage = new CloudTableClient(account.TableEndpoint.AbsoluteUri,
                                        account.Credentials);
        tableStorage.CreateTableIfNotExist("Customer");
    }
}
```

This code not only initializes the DataContext class, it also creates a table called Customer in Azure storage if it does not exist.

■ **Caution** Although this example shows the creation of the table if it doesn't exist during the creation of the class, this is generally not considered best practice, as you make a call to the service frequently. It is better to create it in your deployment script and just assume that the table exists in your code. The same logic applies when you are using the CreateIfNotExist call for queues and blobs, which is used in the following sections.

Querying Data from Table Storage

To run a LINQ query to get data from the Customer table in table storage, you can use the following code:

```
    public List<Customer> Load()
    {
        var context = new CustomerServiceDataContext(
CloudStorageAccount.FromConfigurationSetting("StorageAccount"));

        var customers = from customer in context.CreateQuery<Customer>("Customer")
                            select customer;

        return customers.ToList();

    }
```

■ **Note** You need to set up a configuration setting called StorageAccount for this to work. Select your web role from the cloud project in the Solution Explorer and press Alt+Enter to bring up the properties. Then go to the Settings tab and press the Add Setting button. In the settings list, add a property called StorageAccount, set the Type to Connection String, and press the ellipses button to bring up the Storage Account Connection String dialog box. If you are working with the storage emulator, you can just press the OK button. Alternatively, you can click the Enter Storage account credentials radio button and enter the account name and account key values from the management portal.

Updating and Inserting Data into Table Storage

Updating and inserting data also can be done using LINQ as seen in this example where the CompanyName for a whole bunch of entities are queried and updated:

```
    public void UpdateCompanyName(string oldCompanyName, string newCompanyName)
    {
        var context = new CustomerServiceDataContext(
                        CloudStorageAccount.FromConfigurationSetting("StorageAccount"));

        var customers = from customer in context.CreateQuery<Customer>("Customer")
                        where customer.CompanyName == oldCompanyName
                        select customer;

        foreach (var customer in customers)
        {
            customer.CompanyName = newCompanyName;
            context.UpdateObject(customer);
        }

        context.SaveChangesWithRetries();

        return customers.ToList();
    }
```

Accessing Blobs from Azure Storage

The `Microsoft.WindowsAzure.StorageClient` namespace contains a class called `CloudBlob` that contains all the methods you need to work with blobs in Azure Storage. You can get access to a `CloudBlob` object that represents the `photo.jpg` stored in a container called `images` by using the following code:

```
var account = CloudStorageAccount.FromConfigurationSetting("StorageAccount");

var client = account.CreateCloudBlobClient();
var cloudContainer = client.GetContainerReference("images");
cloudContainer.CreateIfNotExist();
var cloudBlob = cloudContainer.GetBlobReference("photo.jpg");
```

Once you've create a `CloudBlob` object, you can do a number of things using the methods in the class, a cross section of which is shown in Table 10-1.

Table 10-1. Methods available in CloudBlob object

Method	Description
DownloadText	Gets the content of the blob as a `String` object.
DownloadToFile	Downloads the contents of the blob into a file. `cloudBlob.DownloadToFile (@"c:\temp\photo.jpg")` will download the blob into a file called `photo.jpg` in the temp directory.
DownloadToStream	Downloads the content of the blog into a `Stream` object.
UploadText	Sets the content of the blob with a `String` object.
UploadFile	Uploads a file's content into the blob.
UploadFromStream	Uploads the content of a `Stream` object into the blob.
SetMetaData	Writes some metadata information into the blob. You need to set the metadata first, using calls such as `blob.Metadata["author"] = "Mahesh Krishnan";` before a call to `SetMetaData` can be made.
Delete	Deletes the blob from storage.

Working with Queues

Queues provide an asynchronous way for roles running in Windows Azure to communicate with each other. Each account can have any number of uniquely named queues and each queue can have any number of messages. Queues provide a reliable way of message delivery.

Messages get enqueued to the queue from one role, and another role dequeues the message from the same queue. Once the message is dequeued, the message becomes invisible for a specified amount of time. The role that dequeues the message needs to delete the message from the queue within this specified amount of time. If, for some reason, the role crashed before the message was processed, the item becomes visible again.

■ **Note** Although I said that each queue has to be uniquely named, each one needs to have a unique name only within the same account.

To start working with queues, you first need to get a CloudQueue object. You can do that by using the following code:

```
public CloudQueue GetQueue()
{
    var account =  CloudStorageAccount.FromConfigurationSetting("StorageAccount");

    var client = account.CreateCloudQueueClient();

    var queue = client.GetQueueReference("my-queue");

    queue.CreateIfNotExist();
    return queue;
}
```

Putting a Message into the Queue

Once you've obtained a CloudQueue object, you can add a message to it by using the AddMessage method. The message takes a CloudQueueMessage object as parameter, and the following code shows how to use the method:

```
public void PostToQueue(string message)
{
    var queue = GetQueue();
    queue.AddMessage(new CloudQueueMessage(message));
}
```

Reading the Message from the Queue

To read the message from the queue, you need to call the GetMessage method on the CloudQueue object. If no messages are present in the queue, the method returns a null value. Once you've processed the message, you need to call the DeleteMessage function to permanently remove the message from the queue as shown in the following code:

```
public string ReadFromQueue()
{
    var queue = GetQueue();
    var message = queue.GetMessage();
```

```
if (message != null)
{
    var returnValue = message.AsString;
    //remove the message from the queue once read
    queue.DeleteMessage(message);
    return returnValue;
}
else
{
    return null; //return null if no messages found
}
}
```

Accessing Azure Storage from within Visual Studio

You can access Azure storage table, blob, and queue data directly from Visual Studio via the Server Explorer panel. From the menu, select View ➤ Server Explorer to open the Server Explorer from within Visual Studio. The Server Explorer will look like the image shown in Figure 10-28.

You can add the various accounts that you want to work on directly from the Server Explorer.

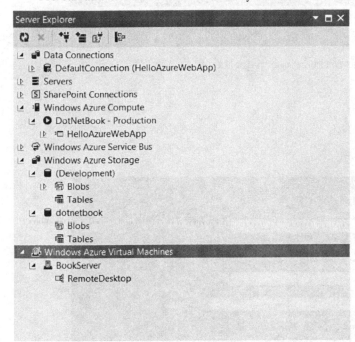

Figure 10-28. Server Explorer showing Windows Azure options

Working with the data from the Server Explorer is really easy. For instance, to look up the table data for Customer, all you need to do is double-click the table name and data will open up in a new window.

The Server Explorer also allows you to look at other Azure components such as virtual machines, service buses, and cloud services directly from within Visual Studio.

SQL Database

SQL Database, as mentioned earlier in this chapter, is the equivalent of SQL Server running in the cloud. To work with SQL Database in the cloud, all you have to change is the Connection string that you use to connect to the database. SQL Database has two components to it—the actual SQL Database instance and the server that this database lives on.

Quick Creating a New Database

To create a new SQL Database, you first need to log in to the management portal at http://manage.windowsazure.com. Once you've logged in, click the NEW button at the bottom left of the screen. This brings up the NEW panel.

Choose SQL Database and select QUICK CREATE from the options. You will be prompted to enter a few fields, as shown in Figure 10-29. Fill in the fields in the form and press the CREATE button. This creates a new SQL Database.

If you have a previously created server, the SERVER field shows the names of the servers for you to choose from.

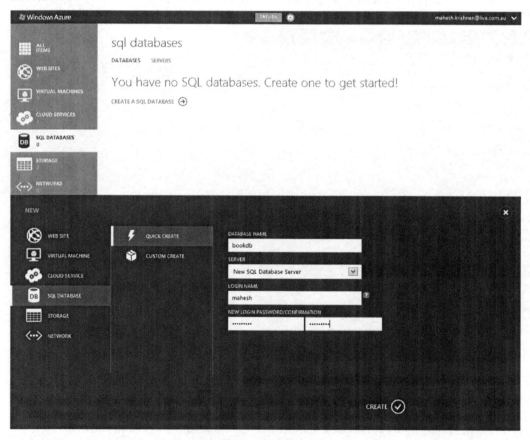

Figure 10-29. Creating a new SQL database in Azure

■ **Note** SQL Database restricts you from picking login names such as admin, sa, or administrator.

Custom Creating a SQL Database

Alternatively, if you choose the CUSTOM CREATE option, you will be shown a NEW SQL DATABASE CUSTOM CREATE window (as shown in Figure 10-30), which gives you more options while creating the database. As in the previous example, you can type in a name for the database, choose the database edition (Business or Web), the maximum size of the database, the type of collation to use, and the server to create the database in.

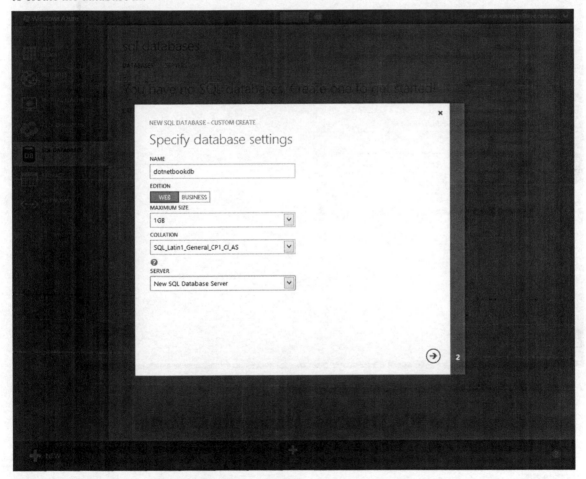

Figure 10-30. First step in custom creating a database

Click the right arrow icon (Next) to go to the next screen and fill in the remaining fields (as shown in Figure 10-31). Ensure that the Allow Windows Azure services to access the server check box is ticked. Applications running on Azure will not be able to connect to the database if this box is not ticked.

Click the check mark button to finish creating the database. Once the database is created, it will show up on the database list on the screen. You can click on the name of the database to take you to a detailed screen for the database.

Click the Show Connection strings link on the quick glance section in the dashboard—this brings up a pop-up dialog box showing the connection strings you can use to connect to the database.

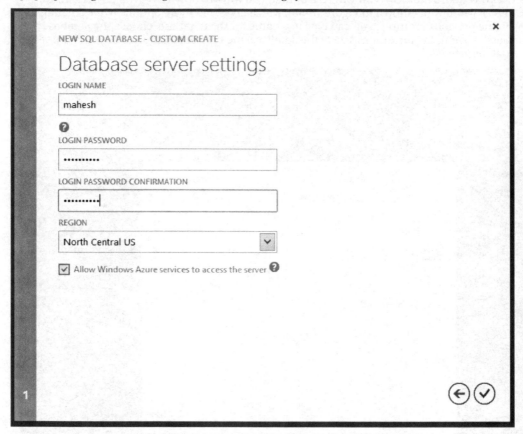

Figure 10-31. *Second step in custom creating a database*

Connecting to the SQL Database Management Portal

The SQL Database Management Portal allows you to manage the SQL Database and do things such as create tables, run queries, profile the database, and look at query plans. To connect to the portal, follow these steps:

1. Click the name of the database in the SQL Databases tab in the Windows Azure Management Portal. This takes you to the database's dashboard.

2. Click Manage in the application bar at the bottom of the screen. This should take you to the SQL Database Management Portal, but as your machine's IP may not be configured to access the database, you will be prompted with a message asking whether you would want to add your machine's IP address to allow access.

3. Once you are in the management portal, you will be prompted to enter username and password.

■ **Tip** You don't need to use the SQL Database Management Portal to create tables and manage the database—you can do that straight out of SQL Server Management Studio, which is a lot easier to use.

Conclusion

This chapter has given you an introduction to Windows Azure and taught you the basics of its various components—primarily Web Sites, Cloud Services, and Virtual Machines. In addition, we also looked at data storage options in Azure. The Windows Azure platform is not limited to just the components covered in this chapter. It has heaps of other offerings such as Caching, Service Bus, Content Delivery Network, Access Control Service, and many, many more. However, we hope this introduction to Azure has given you enough for you to start exploring some of these other offerings.

■ ■ ■

CHAPTER 11

Windows Workflow Foundation

Windows Workflow Foundation (WF) was one of the key features of the .NET 3.0 release along with WPF and WCF. Unlike WPF and WCF, Workflow Foundation never seemed to quite get wholehearted support from developers; however, WF has remained viable. A major overhaul in .NET 4.0 saw considerable improvements to the designer and overall performance as well as integration with WCF. The .NET 4.5 release builds on the 4.0 release by adding further functionality to the designer as well as the addition of new features, which stem from developers' feedback.

In this chapter, we will focus on the new features in WF rather than provide a how-to guide. If you haven't worked with WF before or haven't looked at it for a while, a comprehensive set of resources can be found at `http://msdn.microsoft.com/en-us/netframework/dd980559`.

New Designer Features and Changes

I suspect that among developers, there has always been a small amount of resistance to the use of visual designers to code. Over the years, we have seen tools that provide variations on UML to code round-tripping, such as the Class Diagram in Visual Studio, but they never seem to achieve a high level of adoption among developers. Even when developing UI, the desire and tendency to hack the HTML or XAML directly is a strong one. There are probably many reasons for this but, in part, I suspect there is a sense that designer gets in the way of what we are trying to achieve. On the other hand, visualization is a great way to handle complexity, especially when developing workflows. To this end, a number of new features have been added to workflow's visual designer to reduce the disconnect for developers.

C# Expressions

One of the frustrations that has existed for developers with WF has been the fact that no matter whether you created your workflow project in C# or VB.NET, expressions within the workflow could only be entered using VB. This use of VB for entering expressions was based on the idea that business users would be expected to modify workflows and that they would be coming from a Word/Excel background where the macro language is Visual Basic for Applications. Being limited to using VB has been a point of contention for developers, so with this release the WF team has now added C# expressions. In this version, a fully functional C# expression editor is provided including syntax highlighting, fully functional intellisense, and design-time validation. As a result, if you create a workflow project in VB, you will use VB expressions. On the other hand, if you create a C# project, you will use C# expressions. However, it is important to note that any C# workflow project created in Visual 2010 and opened in Visual Studio 2012 will still use VB expressions.

Something that is not obvious about the introduction of C# expressions, unless you look at the underlying XAML, is the introduction of two new classes: `CSharpReference<TRresult>` and

CSharpValue<TResult>. These two classes can be found under the new namespace Microsoft.CSharp.Activities in System.Activities. When using VB expressions in the XAML, an expression would be delineated using [ ]. For example, an Assign object would look like this:

```
<Assign sap:VirtualizedContainerService.HintSize="242,60">
  <Assign.To>
    <OutArgument x:TypeArguments="x:Int32">[r]</OutArgument>
  </Assign.To>
  <Assign.Value>
    <InArgument x:TypeArguments="x:Int32">[a + b + c]</InArgument>
  </Assign.Value>
</Assign>
```

Now if we implement the same Assign object using C# expressions, this is the resulting XAML:

```
<Assign>
  <Assign.To>
    <OutArgument x:TypeArguments="x:Int32">
      <mca:CSharpReference x:TypeArguments="x:Int32">r</mca:CSharpReference>
    </OutArgument>
  </Assign.To>
  <Assign.Value>
    <InArgument x:TypeArguments="x:Int32">
      <mca:CSharpValue x:TypeArguments="x:Int32">a + b + c</mca:CSharpValue>
    </InArgument>
  </Assign.Value>
  <sap2010:WorkflowViewState.IdRef>Assign_1</sap2010:WorkflowViewState.IdRef>
</Assign>
```

Given the introduction of these new classes, it would seem logical that if you are using imperative code to author activities and workflows, you could use the classes instead of the Visual Basic expression evaluators. For instance, in the code sample below, we have replaced all the instances of VisualBasicValue and VisualBasicReference with their C# equivalents. Unfortunately, if you run this code, it will fail.

```
static void Main(string[] args)
{
    Activity wf = new Sequence
  {
    Variables =
    {
        new Variable<int> { Name = "a", Default= 1 },
        new Variable<int> { Name = "b", Default = 2 },
        new Variable<int> { Name = "c", Default = 3 },
        new Variable<int> { Name = "r"}
    },
    Activities =
    {
      new Assign<int>
      {
        //Previously you would need to use the VB evaluators
        //To = new VisualBasicReference<int>("r"),
        //Value = new VisualBasicValue<int>(" a + b + c")
        To = new CSharpReference<int>("r"),
```

```
            Value = new CSharpValue<int>(" a + b + c")
        },
        new WriteLine
        {
         //Text = new VisualBasicValue<string>("\"The number is \"  + r.ToString()")
           Text = new CSharpValue<string>("\"The number is \"  + r.ToString()")
        }
      }
    }
  };

  WorkflowInvoker.Invoke(wf);
  Console.ReadKey();
}
```

This code would fail because, unlike the Visual Basic expression activities, the C# versions require compilation to run and, therefore, you need to compile your workflow.

At this point, we have two options—revert to using VisualBasicValue and VisualBasicReference or compile the Sequence into a DynamicActivity and pass that to the WorkFlowInvoker instead.

If you are interested in using the second option to get the previous code example to run, first add the following method.

■ **Note** You will also need to add using statements for System.Activities.XamlIntegration, System.IO, and System.Xaml.

```
static Activity CompileToDynamicActivity(Activity activity, string builderName)
{
  var builder = new ActivityBuilder();
  builder.Name = builderName;

  builder.Implementation = activity;
  Activity compiledActivity;
  using(var stream = new MemoryStream())
  {
    XamlWriter xw = ActivityXamlServices.CreateBuilderWriter(new XamlXmlWriter(stream, new
XamlSchemaContext()));
    XamlServices.Save(xw, builder);
    var settings = new ActivityXamlServicesSettings { CompileExpressions = true };
    stream.Position = 0;
    compiledActivity = ActivityXamlServices.Load(stream, settings);
  }
  return compiledActivity;
}
```

Once you have added this method, modify the line that invokes the workflow:

```
WorkflowInvoker.Invoke(CompileToDynamicActivity(wf, "CompiledActivity"));
```

All things being equal, the workflow should now successfully run. Whether there is any benefit to be gained from doing this or just sticking with Visual Basic implementation of the classes is really up to you.

Designer Search

Designer search is a small thing that makes working with complex workflows just that little bit easier. Both Quick Find (Ctrl +F or Edit ➤ Find and Replace ➤ Quick Find) and Find in Files (Ctrl + Shift + F or Edit ➤ Find and Replace ➤ Find in Files) will now search for keywords within the workflow designer. Search expressions will be matched against `Activity`, `FlowNode`, `State` and `Transition` objects, as well as custom flow-control items, variables, arguments, and expressions. With Find in Files, the search expression will match the content of the workflow files and if you double-click a result, you will be taken to the activity that contains the match in the workflow designer.

It should be noted that this functionality is only available within Visual Studio and not in a rehosted designer, nor is Replace supported.

Designer Annotations

To help you keep track of your thinking when working on a workflow, it is now possible to add annotations to activities, states, flowchart nodes, arguments, and variables. By right-clicking on any of these items and selecting Annotations in the context menu, you will be given a selection of annotation actions as shown in Figure 11-1.

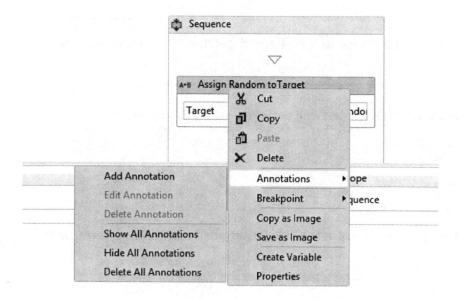

Figure 11-1. Annotations context menu

Clicking on Add Annotation will display an input window where you can type your annotation (see Figure 11-2). Once you have completed the annotation, an icon will be displayed in the right-hand side of the object's title bar indicating that there is an annotation associated with it (see Figure 11-3). Hovering the mouse over this icon will display the annotation.

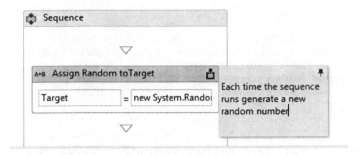

Figure 11-2. Adding an annotation

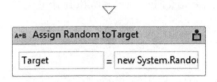

Figure 11-3. Assign object with Annotation icon

The same process applies for adding an annotation to a variable or argument with the icon being displayed to the far right of the name once the annotation is added (see Figure 11-4).

Name		Direction	Argument type
MaxNumber	📤	In	Int32
Turns		Out	Int32

Create Argument

Figure 11-4. Caption added to an argument

When you add an annotation by default, it is undocked. If you dock it, the annotation text will be displayed as greyed text within the object (see Figure 11-5). If you select Show All Annotations from the context menu, all annotations will be docked; Hide All Annotations does the reverse.

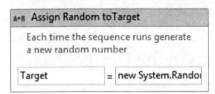

Figure 11-5. Docked annotation

Validation Changes

In previous versions, workflow validation was done as a foreground process, which could lead to the UI hanging during complex or time-consuming validations. With this version, validations now take place on a background thread so that UI is not blocked and is more responsive.

Another issue concerning validation was that validation errors, when building a workflow project, were not considered build errors. In .NET 4.5 validation errors will now cause the build to fail.

Pan Mode

Pan mode, a feature common in most graphic programs, has been implemented in the workflow designer. When enabled, this feature allows the developer to navigate a large workflow by clicking and dragging to move the visible portion. To activate pan mode, you can either click the button in the lower-right corner of the designer (Figure 11-6), or you can press and hold the space bar or the middle mouse button.

Figure 11-6. Pan mode button

Multi-select

The means by which you can select multiple activities in the designer has been extended so that not only can you select them one at a time by holding down the Ctrl key, but you can also select an activity by dragging a rectangle around it. More importantly, multiple activity selections can now be dragged and dropped around the design surface, and they can be interacted with via the context menu. Please keep in mind that multi-select is not available when you are using pan mode.

Auto-surround with Sequence

Workflows and certain other containers, such as NoPersistScope and InvokeDelegate, can only contain a single root activity. Previously, if you wanted to add a second activity, you had to delete or cut the existing activity, add a new Sequence activity, re-add the first activity, and then finally add the second activity. With WF 4.5, you can now add a second activity and a new Sequence will be automatically created to contain the two activities.

Define and Consume ActivityDelegate Objects in the Designer

ActivityDelegate objects are used by activities to expose execution points that allow other parts of the workflow to interact with a workflow's execution. Previously in WF4, utilizing these execution points required you to do a fair bit of coding, but with the newer version you can now define and consume activity delegates from within the designer. For a good example of this, see http://msdn.microsoft.com/en-us/library/hh305737(v=vs.110).aspx.

Working with the Rehosted Designer

If you are working with a rehosted designer in an application, this version of WF offers a couple of new features to manage what the user has access to in the designer.

Visibility of Shell Header Items

In .NET 4, you could only control what items were displayed in the shell bar at the bottom of the designer. Now you also have the ability to customize what items are displayed in the shell header. To modify what is displayed in the shell header, you need to access the DesignView and modify its WorkflowShellHeaderItemsVisibility property. The following method is a quick example of how to do it:

```
/// <summary>
/// Sets up the designer view for the workflow designer
/// </summary>
/// <param name="context">the work flow designer's editing Context</param>
private void SetDesignerView(EditingContext context)
{
  var designerView = context.Services.GetService<DesignerView>();
  if (designerView != null)
  {
      designerView.WorkflowShellHeaderItemsVisibility = ShellHeaderItemsVisibility.None;
  }
}
```

Then all you need to do is call this method, passing it the new workflow designer's editing context, as this example shows:

```
private void AddDesigner()
{
  this.wd = new WorkflowDesigner();
  Grid.SetColumn(this.wd.View, 1);
  this.wd.Load(new Sequence());
  SetDesignerView(wd.Context);
  Grid1.Children.Add(this.wd.View);
}
```

When modifying the design view, make sure you do it after you have loaded an activity into the designer. If you do it before loading the activity, it will fail since at that point the context does not have a reference to the DesignView class in its set of services.

Opt-in for WF4.5 Features

By default, some of the new features in 4.5 are not enabled in the rehost designer in order to preserve backward compatibility. This was done to ensure existing applications don't break when updating to the latest version and is the case even if you create a new application in .NET 4.5. For example, in Figure 11-7, you will see that there is no pan mode button in the shell bar and annotations are not listed in the context menu.

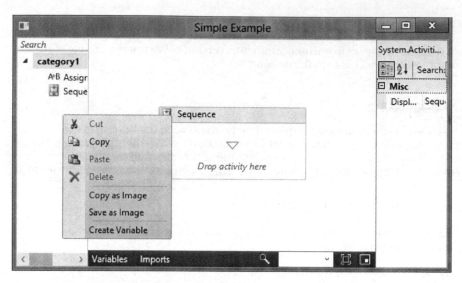

Figure 11-7. Default rehosted designer

To include the 4.5 features in the rehosted designer, you will need to access the
DesignerConfigurationService and either set its TargetFrameworkName property to the .NET 4.5
Framework, or, if you want more control, you can enable individual features. The following code snippet
shows how to opt-in for the 4.5 features, but it disables multi-select drag and drop.

```
/// <summary>
/// Sets the target framework to 4.5.
/// </summary>
/// <param name="context">The workflow designer's editing context.</param>
private void SetFrameWorkTarget(EditingContext context)
{
  var dcs = context.Services.GetService<DesignerConfigurationService>();
  if (dcs != null)
  {
    dcs.TargetFrameworkName = new System.Runtime.Versioning.FrameworkName(".NET Framework,
Version=4.5");
    dcs.MultipleItemsDragDropEnabled = false; //just because we can
  }
}
```

Then all you need to do is call this method after you have instantiated a new instance of the
workflow designer.

```
private void AddDesigner()
{
this.wd = new WorkflowDesigner();
SetFrameWorkTarget(wd.Context);
...
}
```

Now if we re-run the application, you will see that the pan mode button is now available and annotations are now in the context menu (see Figure 11-8).

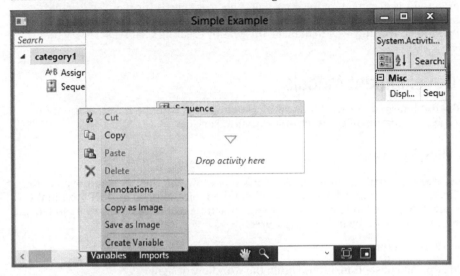

Figure 11-8. Rehosted designer with 4.5 features

One thing to be aware of is that if you are going to modify the target framework or enable any of the 4.5 features, you need to do it before you load an activity. Otherwise, your application will throw exception. Also a small quirk, at least at the time of writing, is that if you just try to enable annotations, your application will error. This doesn't appear to be the case when enabling any of the other features.

Additional Features

Here are a few other features that we won't cover in detail but might be of interest to you:

- View state information is now stored in a separate location in the XAML files, which should make it easier to remove if needed.

- Opening the Document Outline Window (Ctrl + Alt + T) will display the components of a workflow in a tree-style outline view. Clicking on a node in this view will navigate to the corresponding activity in the designer and vice versa.

- In the variable and argument designer, Delete is now a context menu item.

Activities

With the built-in activity library, little has changed or been added. In this release, some new capabilities have been added to Flowchart activities and a new container activity called NoPersistScope has been added.

The Flowchart activity now includes a new property called ValidateUnconnectedNodes. By default, this property is set to false. If set to true, any unconnected nodes will produce validation errors. The only other change is with the FlowSwitch and FlowDecision activities, which now have an editable

DisplayName property. Though a small change, this will at least allow the activity designer to show more information about the activity's purpose.

The NoPersistScope activity is designed to prevent a workflow from persisting if any of its child activities are executing. This is particularly useful when a workflow is accessing files or running a database transaction. Previously, the only way to manage this was by creating a NativeActivity that used a NoPersisthandle.

New Workflow Development Models

In this release, we see the full return of one workflow development model with the return of the state machine workflow and the introduction of contract-first workflow services.

State Machine Workflows

State machine workflows were originally included in Windows Workflow, but they were removed in the 4.0 release with the inclusion of flowchart workflows. They were then reintroduced in .NET 4.0.1 in the Microsoft .NET Framework 4 Platform Update1. With 4.5, state machine workflows are now included out of the box and have been updated with the following features:

- the ability to set breakpoints on states

- the ability to copy and paste transitions within the workflow designer

- designer support for shared trigger transition creation

Contract-First Workflow Development

The contract-first workflow development tool has been introduced to provide better integration between web services and workflows. Essentially what it allows you to do is to define your contract in code first, and then the tool will automatically generate an activity template in the toolbox for the operations in the contract.

Let's have a look at this in action:

1. With Visual Studio open, select File ➤ New Project, select the WCF or Workflow node in the templates tree, and select the WCF Workflow Service Application template.

2. Name the new project ProjectWorkflow and click OK.

3. Right-click on the project in the Solution Explorer and select Add ➤ Interface, name the interface IProjectService, and click OK.

4. If it is not open, open the IProjectService file, add using statements for System.ServiceModel and System.Runtime.Serialization, and then modify it as follows.

■ **Note** The Project class has been included in the same file for convenience.

```
[ServiceContract]
public interface IProjectService
{
  [OperationContract]
  Project AddNewProject(Project project);
  [OperationContract]
  int FindClient(string clientName);
}

[DataContract]
public class Project
{
  [DataMember]
  public int ProjectId { get; set; }
  [DataMember]
  public int ClientId { get; set; }
  [DataMember]
  public string ProjectName { get; set; }
  [DataMember]
  public DateTime StartDate { get; set; }
}
```

5. Once you have made the modifications, build the project.

6. Again right-click on the project in the Solution Explorer and this time select Import Service Contract… . This will bring up a dialog box that will list all of the available service contracts. Drill down into the <Current Project> node, select IProjectService, and click OK. A dialog box will display informing you that the operation was successful.

7. At this point, rebuild the project to get the generated activities to display in the toolbox (see Figure 11-9).

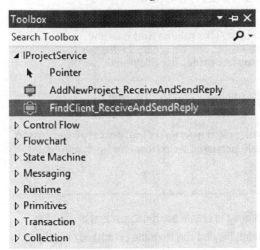

Figure 11-9. Toolbox with newly added activities

8. Next, open the file `Service1.xamlx` to display the workflow service in the designer.

9. In the Properties window for the `workflowservice`, click the "…" button in the `Implemented Contracts` property.

10. In the Type Collection Editor window that appears, click on Add new type. From the dropdown, select "Browse for Types…." Drill into the `<Current Project>` node, select `IProjectService`, and click OK.

11. Delete the existing activities in the Sequence activity. Then from the toolbox, drag a `FindClient_ReceiveAndSendReply` and an `AddNewProject_ReceiveAndSendReply` activity onto the Sequence Service.

If you modify the service contract at any point, the changes will not automatically be reflected in the designer or toolbox. To get the changes reflected in the designer, you will need to first open the Service Contracts folder in the project, right-click on the appropriate service, select Update Service Contract from the context menu, and then rebuild the project.

Workflow Versioning

In WF 4, there was no support for versioning workflows. If you wanted to version your workflows, you had to roll your own solution. Versioning becomes an issue when we start persisting long-running workflows. Say, for example, a workflow gets kicked off and then is persisted. If, before it gets reloaded, a new version of the activity is introduced, then when it is reloaded, it will more then likely fail.

To resolve this problem in 4.5, we have a new class to work with called `WorkflowIdentity`. This class provides the means within a workflow application to map a persisted workflow instance with its definition, and it is the basis for a number of new versioning features:

- `WorkflowApplication` hosting can use the WorkflowIdentity to enable multiple versions of a workflow side-by-side. By loading persisted instances with the new `WorkflowApplicationInstance` class, the `DefinitionIdentity` can be used to determine the correct workflow to use for instantiating the workflow application.

- The `WorkflowServiceHost` is now a multi-version host. This means that if a new version of a workflow service is deployed, new instances will be created with the new version while existing instances will run/complete under the previous version.

- It is now possible to dynamically update the definition of a persisted workflow instance.

To get a taste for how workflow versioning works, we will look at how `WorkflowIdentity` can be used to load the correct version of a workflow and how a previously persisted workflow can be dynamically updated.

■ **Note** To use the SQL workflow Instance Store feature, you will need to create the database that is used for persisting workflows. To do this, copy the following code into a batch file and run from the command console:

```
sqlcmd -S(local) -d Master -Q "Create Database Persistence"
sqlcmd -S(local) -d Persistance -i
"C:\Windows\Microsoft.NET\Framework\v4.0.30319\SQL\en\SqlWorkflowInstanceStoreSchema.sql"
sqlcmd -S(local) -d Persistance -i
"C:\Windows\Microsoft.NET\Framework\v4.0.30319\SQL\en\SqlWorkflowInstanceStoreLogic.sql"
```

Side-by-Side Versioning

In this example, we are going to look at how versioning can be used to load the correct definition for a persisted workflow. The example is reasonably trivial and the activities are created completely in code purely for expediency and not as a requirement for versioning.

1. To get started, create a new workflow console application, add references to System.Activities.DurableInstancing and System.Runtime.DurableInstancing, and delete the file workflow1.xaml.

2. Add a new class and name it GetInput, add a using statement for System.Activities, and then implement the following code:

```
public class GetInput<T> : NativeActivity<T>
{
  [DefaultValue(null)]
  public string BookmarkName { get; set; }

  protected override bool CanInduceIdle
  {
    get { return true; }
  }

  protected override void Execute(NativeActivityContext context)
  {
    context.CreateBookmark(this.BookmarkName, Continue);
  }

  void Continue(NativeActivityContext context, Bookmark bookmark, object state)
  {
    Result.Set(context, state);
  }
}
```

3. Next, create some preliminary code in order to enable persistence and to create our test activities. Open the Program.cs file and add the following code:

```
static void Main(string[] args)
{
 //[Setup]

  var connectionString = @"Data Source=(local);Initial Catalog=Persistence;Integrated
Security=True";
```

```
    var instanceStore = new SqlWorkflowInstanceStore(connectionString);
    var bookmarkId = "ReadLine";

    //[Step 1] start up version 1 of the activity and persist it.
    var application = new WorkflowApplication(CreateActivityV1( bookmarkId));
    application.InstanceStore = instanceStore;
    var instanceId = ForcePersistance(application);

    //[Step 2]

   // [Step 3] Finish
    Console.WriteLine("\nPress any key to exit");
    Console.ReadKey();

}

/// <summary>
/// Runs the application so that the workflow is persist.
/// </summary>
/// <param name="application">The workflow application.</param>
/// <returns>The instance id. </returns>
private static Guid ForcePersistance(WorkflowApplication application)
{
  var syncEvent = new AutoResetEvent(false);
  application.PersistableIdle = (e) => PersistableIdleAction.Unload;
  application.Unloaded = (e) =>
    {
      syncEvent.Set();
      Console.WriteLine("[Application unloaded]");
    };

  application.Run();
  syncEvent.WaitOne();

  return application.Id;
}

/// <summary>
/// Creates version 1 of the test activity
/// </summary>
/// <param name="bookmarkId">the bookmark name used by GetInput</param>
/// <returns>A Sequence activity</returns>
private static Activity CreateActivityV1(string bookmarkId)
{
  var activity = new Sequence
  {
    DisplayName = "Activity 1",
    Variables = { new Variable<string>("Name"),
                  new Variable<string>("Message","Hi {0} from activity 1")
                },
    Activities =
      {
```

```
          new WriteLine{Text="Please enter your name"},
          new GetInput<string>
          {
            BookmarkName = bookmarkId,
            DisplayName = "ReadLine",
            Result = new OutArgument<string>( new VisualBasicReference<string>("Name"))
          },
          new WriteLine
          {
            Text = new InArgument<string>(new
VisualBasicValue<string>("string.Format(Message,Name)"))
          }
      }
  };

  return activity;
}

/// <summary>
/// Creates version 2 of the test activity
/// </summary>
/// <param name="bookmarkId">The bookname for GetInput</param>
/// <returns>A Sequence activity</returns>
private static Activity CreateActivityV2(string bookmarkId)
{
  var activity = new Sequence
  {
    DisplayName = "Activity 2",
    Variables = { new Variable<string>("Name"),
                  new Variable<string>("Message","Hi {0} from activity 2")
                },
    Activities =
    {
      new WriteLine{Text="Please enter your name"},
      new GetInput<string>
      {
        BookmarkName = bookmarkId,
        DisplayName = "ReadLine",
        Result = new OutArgument<string>( new VisualBasicReference<string>("Name"))
      },
      new If
      {
        Condition = new InArgument<bool>(new
VisualBasicValue<bool>("String.IsNullOrEmpty(Name)")),
        Then = new WriteLine{Text="You have no name."},
        Else = new WriteLine
            {
              Text = new InArgument<string>(new
VisualBasicValue<string>("string.Format(Message,Name)"))
            }
      }
    }
```

```
  };

return activity;
}
```

4. To make sure that everything is working, add some code that will load the persisted activity and complete it. Immediately after [Step 2], add this code:

```
var instance = WorkflowApplication.GetInstance(instanceId, instanceStore);
application = new WorkflowApplication(CreateActivityV1(bookmarkId));
application.InstanceStore = instanceStore;
var workflowCompleted = new AutoResetEvent(false);
application.Completed = e => workflowCompleted.Set();

try
{
  application.Load(instance);
  string input = Console.ReadLine();
  var result = application.ResumeBookmark(bookmarkId, input);

  workflowCompleted.WaitOne();
  application.Unload();
}
catch (Exception ex)
{
  Console.WriteLine(ex.Message);
}
```

5. Run the application at this point, and you should get something similar to Figure 11-10.

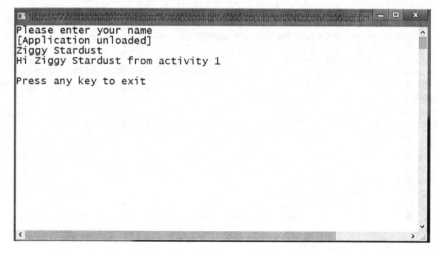

Figure 11-10. Output after running activity

At this point, if you are curious to see what happens when you load a persisted workflow into an updated activity, modify the instantiation of the workflow application in the previous step to the following:

```
application = new WorkflowApplication(CreateActivityV2(bookmarkId));
```

Up to this point, the code we have written basically reflects the state of play in WF 4. Now we will introduce the WorkflowIdentity and see how it allows us to manage multiple workflow versions.

1. First, we need to version the workflow that is being persisted. To do this, we will create an instance of WorkflowIdentity and add it the constructor of the workflow application by adding and modifying the code at [Step 1] as follows:

```
var identityV1 = new WorkflowIdentity("SampleActivity", new Version(1, 0, 0, 0), null);
var application = new WorkflowApplication(CreateActivityV1( bookmarkId),identityV1);
```

2. For convenience, we add a collection of workflows using a Dictionary<> object. Just before [Step 2], add the following code:

```
var workflows = new Dictionary<WorkflowIdentity, Activity>
  {
    {new WorkflowIdentity("SampleActivity", new Version(1, 0, 0, 0), null),
     CreateActivityV1(bookmarkId)
    },
    {new WorkflowIdentity("SampleActivity", new Version(2, 0, 0, 0), null),
     CreateActivityV2(bookmarkId)
    }
  };
```

3. Finally, we will get the identity of the persisted activity from the WorkflowApplicationInstance and use it to select the activity we need to use from our workflow collection. In [Step 2], modify the first two lines as follows:

```
var instance = WorkflowApplication.GetInstance(instanceId, instanceStore);
var definitionIdentity = instance.DefinitionIdentity;
var activityToLoad = workflows[definitionIdentity];
application = new WorkflowApplication(activityToLoad,definitionIdentity);
```

Now if you run the application, it should all work as advertised.

Dynamically Updating a Workflow

There are cases when you need to update the workflow definition of a persisted workflow. This can be achieved by using the new DynamicUpdateServices class to create a DynamicUpdateMap, which can then be applied to a persistence instance when it is loaded. Following are the four steps involved in creating and applying an update map:

1. **Prepare the workflow definition for update**. This is done by calling DynamicUpdateServices.PrepareForUpdate() with the current workflow. This method validates the workflow and then processes the workflow tree, identifying all the objects that need to be tagged for comparison with the updated workflow definition. Once this is done, the tree is cloned and attached to the original workflow definition.

2. **Modify the workflow definition with the changes required**. You cannot apply a new workflow definition, so you need to actually modify the existing workflow definition. Given that restriction, you can add or remove activities; add, move, or delete public variables; remove arguments; and change the signatures of activity delegates.

3. **Create the update map**. To create a dynamic update map, you invoke the method DynamicUpdateServices.CreateUpdateMap() passing it the modified workflow definition. This will return a DynamicUpdateMap that will contain the information the runtime needs to modify a persisted workflow instance.

4. **Apply the update map to the desired persisted workflow instance**. This is done by passing in the dynamic update map to the WorkflowApplication. Load() method along with the instance you want to run. If you don't want to run the workflow immediately, you can just update the persisted instance by calling WorkflowApplication.Unload() immediately after loading the instance.

The code example below will cover each of these steps. As with the previous example, you will need to ensure that your database has been configured for persisting workflows for the code to work.

5. First, create a workflow console application project, delete the workflow1.xaml file since we won't be using it, and add references to System.Runtime.DurableInstancing and System.Activities.DurableInstancing.

6. As with the previous example, we have some preliminary code we need to put in place. Open the file Program.cs, add using statements for System.Threading, System.Activities.DurableInstancing, and System.Activities.DynamicUpdate, and then update the code to correspond to the following:

```
class Program
{
  static void Main(string[] args)
  {
    //Modify this connection string to match your data source
    var connectionString = @"Data Source=(local);Initial Catalog=Persistence;Integrated Security=True";
    var instanceStore = new SqlWorkflowInstanceStore(connectionString);

    //[Step 1] We will add the code for creating a dynamic update map here

    //[Step 2] start up version 1 of the activity and persist it.
    var identityV1 = new WorkflowIdentity("SampleActivity", new Version(1, 0, 0, 0), null);
    var application = new WorkflowApplication(CreateSequence(1), identityV1);
    application.InstanceStore = instanceStore;
    var instanceId = ForcePersistance(application);

    //[Step 3] Get  Persisted instance and create new WorkflowApplication
    var instance = WorkflowApplication.GetInstance(instanceId, instanceStore);
    var definitionIdentity = instance.DefinitionIdentity;
```

```csharp
application = new WorkflowApplication(CreateSequence(1), identityV1);
application.InstanceStore = instanceStore;
var workflowCompleted = new AutoResetEvent(false);
application.Completed = e => workflowCompleted.Set();

//[Step 4] Run and complete workflow.
try
{
  application.Load(instance);
  Console.WriteLine("Completing {0}", application.WorkflowDefinition.DisplayName);
  application.Run();
  workflowCompleted.WaitOne();
  application.Unload();
}
catch (Exception ex)
{
  Console.WriteLine(ex.Message);
}

Console.ReadKey();
}

/// <summary>
/// Runs the application so that the workflow is persist.
/// </summary>
/// <param name="application">The workflow application.</param>
/// <returns>The instance id. </returns>
private static Guid ForcePersistance(WorkflowApplication application)
{
  var syncEvent = new AutoResetEvent(false);
  application.PersistableIdle = (e) => PersistableIdleAction.Unload;
  application.Unloaded = (e) =>
  {
  syncEvent.Set();
  Console.WriteLine("[Application unloaded]");
  };

  application.Run();

  syncEvent.WaitOne();

  return application.Id;
}

private static Sequence CreateSequence(int version)
{
  var activity = new Sequence
  {
  DisplayName = version == 1?"Sequence 1": "Sequence 2",
  Activities =
  {
    new WriteLine{Text = "Run Process A"},
```

```
          new Persist(),
          new Delay{ Duration =  new TimeSpan(0,0,3)},
          new WriteLine{Text = "Run Process B"}
      }
    };

    if (version == 1)
    {
      activity.Activities.Add(new WriteLine { Text = "Run Process C" });
      activity.Activities.Add(new WriteLine { Text = "Run Process D" });
    }
    else
    {
      activity.Activities.Add(new WriteLine { Text = "Run Process E" });
      activity.Activities.Add(new WriteLine { Text = "Run Process F" });
      activity.Activities.Add(new WriteLine { Text = "Run Process Z" });

    }
    return activity;
  }
}
```

7. If you build and run this code, it will persist and then reload and complete version 1 of the workflow definition resulting in output similar to Figure 11-11.

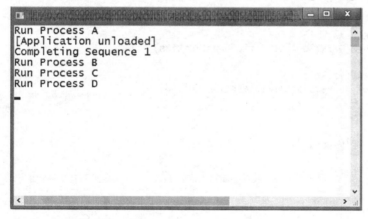

Figure 11-11. Pre-update output

8. Next, you need to add a method that will modify an instance of the version 1 sequence so that its set of activities corresponds to that in the version 2 sequence. Add the following method in the Program class:

```
private static Sequence ModifyWorkflow(Sequence workflowToUpdate)
{
  workflowToUpdate.DisplayName = "Activity 2";
  workflowToUpdate.Activities[3] = new WriteLine { Text = "Run Process E" };
  workflowToUpdate.Activities[4] = new WriteLine { Text = "Run Process F" };
```

```
workflowToUpdate.Activities.Add(new WriteLine { Text = "Run Process Z" });

 return workflowToUpdate;
}
```

9. Now you can create our dynamic update map. At this point, you will create an instance of the version 1 workflow, prepare it for updating, pass the instance to your ModifyWorkflow() method to get an updated version, and then use that create the update map. In the Main() method at [Step 1], add these four lines of code:

```
var workflowToUpdate = CreateSequence(1);
DynamicUpdateServices.PrepareForUpdate(workflowToUpdate);

var updatedWorkflow = ModifyWorkflow(workflowToUpdate);
var duMap = DynamicUpdateServices.CreateUpdateMap(updatedWorkflow);
```

10. To use the map, you will first modify the workflow application in [Step 3] to use version 2 of the workflow as well as to update the version. To do this, update the code for creating the workflow application so it matches the following:

```
var identityV2 = new WorkflowIdentity("SampleActivity", new Version(2, 0, 0, 0), null);
application = new WorkflowApplication(CreateSequence(2),identityV2);
```

11. Now in [Step 4], replace the application.Load(instance) with this code:

```
if (definitionIdentity.Equals(identityV1))
  application.Load(instance, duMap);
else
 application.Load(instance);
```

If you now run this code, you will see that the persisted instance will now complete using version 2 of the workflow (see Figure 11-12).

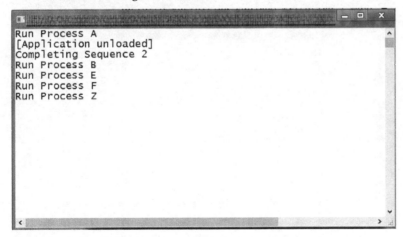

Figure 11-12. Result after applying the update map

Even though in this example we created the dynamic update map at runtime, a better option would be to create and save the map ahead of time and then apply it later. One way to do this is to serialize the update map to a file and then load when required.

```
//Save the map
var serializer = new DataContractSerializer(typeof(DynamicUpdateMap));
using (FileStream fs = System.IO.File.Open(@"C:\temp\Workflow_v2.map", FileMode.Create))
{
    serializer.WriteObject(fs, duMap);
}

//And at some point in the future...
DynamicUpdateMap loadedMap;
using (FileStream fs = File.Open(@"C:\temp\Workflow_v2.map", FileMode.Open))
{
    var dcSerializer = new DataContractSerializer(typeof(DynamicUpdateMap));
    loadedMap = dcSerializer.ReadObject(fs) as DynamicUpdateMap;
    if (loadedMap == null)
    {
        throw new ApplicationException("DynamicUpdateMap is null.");
    }
}
```

Conclusion

This release of Workflow Foundation is very much about consolidating the changes that were made in 4.0 and responding to the feedback the team has received from users, with the big-ticket items being the introduction of C# expressions in the designer and versioning. It is clear that WF is in for the long haul, so if you haven't really given much thought to WF since it was first released, now would be a good time to revisit it.

CHAPTER 12

WPF

.NET 4.0 introduced a number of nice changes to WPF—a lot of them inspired by Silverlight, such as the Visual State Manager and Easing functions. In addition, there were several controls, such as DataGrid, Calendar, and Datepicker, which were introduced. In contrast, .NET 4.5 brings only one new control of significance to WPF—the Ribbon control—but it is a pretty important one. We start this chapter by introducing you to the Ribbon control. We then discuss some of the changes that have been introduced in WPF 4.5 around databinding—things like the Delay property. We also explore new features for VirtualizingPanel and how to access collections on the non-UI thread. We finish the chapter by talking about some of the changes that have been introduced around events and the new methods that have been added for the Dispatcher class.

Ribbon Control

The Ribbon was introduced with the Office suite of products a while back and has become a standard feature for a number of applications. Support for the Ribbon control is now built into WPF 4.5. (The Ribbon control is available as a separate download for WPF 4.) Although I refer to it like a single control, it is, in fact, made up of a number of controls and these controls are available from the System.Windows.Controls.Ribbons library. A typical Ribbon consists of an application menu, a quick access toolbar, tabs, groups, and controls within the group. Some of the Ribbon's controls are shown in Figure 12-1.

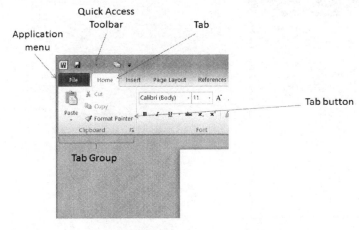

Figure 12-1. Some of the components of a Ribbon

To start using the Ribbon control, you first need to add a reference to this assembly in your project. After you've added the reference, you may want to create a number of tabs in the Ribbon. To add tabs to the Ribbon, all you need to do is add a bunch of RibbonTab controls to your Ribbon in XAML as shown in the following code snippet:

```
<Window x:Class="WpfRibbonSample.MainWindow"
        xmlns="http://schemas.microsoft.com/winfx/2006/xaml/presentation"
        xmlns:x="http://schemas.microsoft.com/winfx/2006/xaml"
        Title="MainWindow" Height="350" Width="525">
    <Grid>
        <Ribbon>
            <RibbonTab Header="Home" />
            <RibbonTab Header="Insert" />
        </Ribbon>
    </Grid>
</Window>
```

To add buttons and group them together, you can create a RibbonGroup and add RibbonButtons to them as shown in the following markup snippet:

```
<RibbonTab Header="Home" >
    <RibbonGroup Header="Clipboard">
        <RibbonButton Label="Paste"
LargeImageSource="Images/Paste.png"></RibbonButton>
        <RibbonButton Label="Cut"
SmallImageSource="Images/Cut.png"></RibbonButton>
        <RibbonButton Label="Copy"
SmallImageSource="Images/Copy.png"></RibbonButton>
    </RibbonGroup>
</RibbonTab>
```

As their names suggest, LargeImageSource and SmallImageSource are used to display the image either in a large size or small size, and the Label property displays the label for the button in the Ribbon. The XAML snippet will display tabs as shown in Figure 12-2.

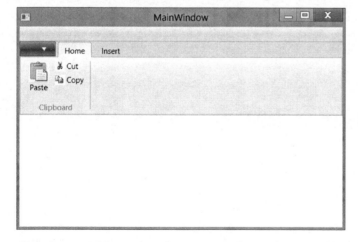

Figure 12-2. Ribbon tab with a group and some buttons

To add items to the quick access toolbar, you can use the RibbonQuickAccessToolbar control as shown in the following code snippet:

```
<Ribbon>
        <Ribbon.QuickAccessToolBar>
                <RibbonQuickAccessToolBar >
                        <RibbonButton x:Name="SaveButton" SmallImageSource="Images/Save.png" />
                </RibbonQuickAccessToolBar>
        </Ribbon.QuickAccessToolBar>
...
```

To add items to the application menu bar, you use RibbonApplicationMenu control and RibbonApplicationMenuItem controls as shown in the following markup:

```
<Ribbon>
        <Ribbon.ApplicationMenu>
                <RibbonApplicationMenu Label="File" >
                        <RibbonApplicationMenuItem Header="New"  ImageSource="Images\New.png"/>
                        <RibbonApplicationMenuItem Header="Open" ImageSource="Images\Open.png"/>
                        <RibbonApplicationMenuItem Header="Exit" ImageSource="Images\Exit.png"/>
                </RibbonApplicationMenu>
        </Ribbon.ApplicationMenu>
...
```

Figure 12-3 shows both the quick access toolbar and the application menu control in use.

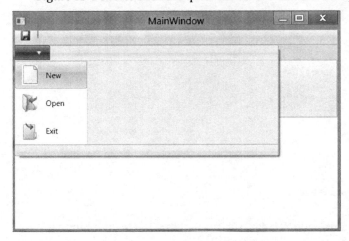

Figure 12-3. Quick access toolbar and the application menu control of a Ribbon

Synchronously and Asynchronously Validating Data

If you wanted to do validation of UI controls in .NET 4, you had to use the IDataErrorInfo interface, which validates your fields synchronously. To implement it, you first needed to implement the IDataErrorInfo on the object that your control was bound to as shown in the following code snippet:

```
public class Person : INotifyPropertyChanged, IDataErrorInfo
{
    public event PropertyChangedEventHandler PropertyChanged;

    protected virtual void OnPropertyChanged(string propertyName)
    {
        var handler = PropertyChanged;
        if (handler != null) handler(this, new PropertyChangedEventArgs(propertyName));
    }

    private string _name;
    public string Name
    {
        get { return _name; }
        set
        {
            _name = value;
            OnPropertyChanged("Name");
        }

    }

    public string this[string columnName]
    {
        get
        {
            if (columnName == "Name")
            {
                if (string.IsNullOrEmpty(Name))
                {
                    return "Name cannot be empty";
                }
            }
            return String.Empty;
        }
    }

    public string Error { get { return string.Empty; } }
}
```

In your XAML markup, all you had to do was add ValidatesOnDataErrors=True to your binding:

```
<TextBox Text="{Binding Name, Mode=TwoWay, ValidatesOnDataErrors= True}" />
```

This allowed you to synchronously validate your data. However, if your validation routine took time, it would freeze up the user interface, which you did not want. To fix this problem, WPF borrowed the INotifyDataErrorInfo interface from Silverlight to asynchronously validate controls. So, rather than implement the IDataErrorInfo, you needed to implement the INotifyDataErrorInfo interface:

```
public class Person : INotifyPropertyChanged, INotifyDataErrorInfo
{
    ...

    public IEnumerable GetErrors(string propertyName)
```

```
    {
        //A very simple implementation...
        if (propertyName == "Name")
        {
            if (string.IsNullOrEmpty(Name))
            {
                Thread.Sleep(5000); //Simulate a long running validation
                HasErrors = true;
                OnErrorsChanged(propertyName);
                return "Name cannot be empty";
            }
        }
        OnErrorsChanged(propertyName);
        HasErrors = false;
        return String.Empty;
    }

    public bool HasErrors { get; private set; }
    public event EventHandler<DataErrorsChangedEventArgs> ErrorsChanged;

    public void OnErrorsChanged(string propertyName)
    {
        var handler = ErrorsChanged;
        if (handler != null) handler(this, new DataErrorsChangedEventArgs(propertyName));

    }
}
```

You would also have to change the ValidatesOnDataErrors=True binding in your XAML file to ValidatesOnNotifyDataErrors=True.

Databinding Changes

WPF 4.5 introduces a number of databinding-related changes—a new Delay property, the ability to bind to static properties, the ability to retrieve databinding information at runtime, and the ability to check if the DataContext used in binding is still valid. This section covers these changes.

Delay Property

Starting from WPF 4.5, a new Delay property has been added to databinding. This introduces a time delay before the property of the Source object used in databinding is updated. This can be particularly useful when you don't want frequent changes on the UI modifying the value of the property on the source it is bound to.

To see how this works, create a simple class for databinding as shown in the following code snippet:

```
public class Person : INotifyPropertyChanged
{
    public event PropertyChangedEventHandler PropertyChanged;

    protected virtual void OnPropertyChanged(string propertyName)
    {
```

```
            var handler = PropertyChanged;
            if (handler != null) handler(this, new PropertyChangedEventArgs(propertyName));
        }

        private string _name;
        public string Name
        {
            get  { return _name; }
            set
            {
                _name = value;
                OnPropertyChanged("Name");
            }
        }

    }
}
```

To create a person object and databind this in XAML, you typically would do something like the following:

```
<Window x:Class="WpfDataBindingWait.MainWindow"
        xmlns="http://schemas.microsoft.com/winfx/2006/xaml/presentation"
        xmlns:x="http://schemas.microsoft.com/winfx/2006/xaml"
        Title="MainWindow" Height="350" Width="525">
    <Window.Resources>
        <WpfDataBindingWait:Person x:Key="PersonObject" Name="John Doe" />
    </Window.Resources>
    <StackPanel DataContext="{StaticResource PersonObject}">
        <TextBox Text="{Binding Name" />
        <TextBlock Text="{Binding Name}" />
</StackPanel>
</Window>
```

In this example, if you update the text in the TextBox, the text in the TextBlock will automatically be updated as they are both bound to the same property—Name. To introduce a delay of, say, five seconds, all you need to do is change the XAML as shown in bold:

```
...
<StackPanel>
        <TextBox x:Name="BoundTextBox" Text="{Binding Name,
UpdateSourceTrigger=PropertyChanged, Delay=5000}" />
        <TextBlock Text="{Binding Name}" />
...
```

Binding to Static Properties

Typically, when a class is used in databinding, it implements the INotifyPropertyChanged interface, which has a PropertyChanged event that the databinding engine uses to recognize any change that occurs on databound properties. This obviously does not work if the property being used is a static property. To cater for static properties, WPF 4.5 introduces static event handlers that can be implemented as shown in the following code snippet:

```
public class MyClass
{
    private static string _myProperty;
    public static string MyProperty
    {
        get { return _myProperty; }
        set
        {
            _myProperty = value;
            OnMyPropertyChanged();
        }
    }

    public static event EventHandler MyPropertyChanged;

    public static void OnMyPropertyChanged()
    {
        var handler = MyPropertyChanged;
        if (handler != null) handler(null, EventArgs.Empty);
    }
}
```

Alternatively, the event handlers can also be implemented:

```
public class MyClass
{
    private static string _myProperty;
    public static string MyProperty
    {
        get { return _myProperty; }
        set
        {
            _myProperty = value;
            OnStaticPropertyChanged("MyProperty");
        }
    }

    private static EventHandler<PropertyChangedEventArgs> StaticPropertyChanged;
    public static void OnStaticPropertyChanged(string propertyName)
    {
        var handler = StaticPropertyChanged;
        if (handler != null) handler(null, new PropertyChangedEventArgs(propertyName));
    }
}
```

Checking for a Valid DataContext Object

When you use an ItemControl in your WPF application, an item container is generated for each item of the collection the ItemControl is bound to. Each item container will then be associated with a DataContext. This DataContext could become invalid if an item from the collection is removed or if the user starts scrolling and virtualization is enabled for the ItemControl. WPF 4.5 provides a way of testing whether the DataContext is still valid in these scenarios—all you need to do is ensure that the DataContext is not equal to BindingOperations.DisconnectedSource before you use it.

Retrieving Databinding Information from a Binding Expression

In .NET 4.5, new APIs have been added to retrieve information about a databinding expression. To retrieve a databinding expression, all you need to do is call the static method GetBindingExpression in the BindingExpression class and make use of the newly added methods:

```
BindingExpression bindingExpression =
    BindingOperations.GetBindingExpression(MyTextBox, TextBlock.TextProperty);

var target = bindingExpression.Target;
target.SetValue("abcd");

var targetProperty = bindingExpression.TargetProperty;
var name = targetProperty.Name;
```

The new methods that have been added are shown in Table 12-1.

Table 12-1. Properties available to inspect binding information

Properties	Description
Target	Gets the target object
TargetProperty	Gets the dependency property of the target
ResolvedSource	Gets the source object
ResolvedSourcePropertyName	Gets the dependency property of the source
BindingGroup	Gets the binding group that the binding belongs to
Owner	Gets the dependency object of the assigned binding group

New Features for the VirtualizingPanel

When you have a large number of items to be displayed in controls such as the DataGrid, you do not want all the data to be loaded at once. Virtualizing panels such as the VirtualizingStackPanel allow you to load only a certain amount of data and load other data on demand when you start scrolling.

In WPF 4.5, some new properties have been defined for the VirtualizingPanel. For starters, you can now set the ScrollUnit property to Pixel to display partial items during scrolling. The default value of Item will always display the whole item when you scroll.

You can also now set the cache size by using the CacheLength attached property. The CacheLength is used to specify the number of items, pixels, or pages below or above the viewport that is not virtualized. The CacheLengthUnit property is used to specify the CacheLength's unit—in other words, whether to use number of items, pixels, or pages (a single page is the equivalent of the size of the viewport).

In addition to these properties, a new attached property called IsVirtualizingWhenGrouping has also been added to the VirtualizingPanel to enable virtualization for grouped data.

Accessing Collections on Non-UI Threads

Previously in WPF, if you tried to access or modify a collection that was bound to a control on a thread other than the UI thread, an exception would be thrown. To understand the problem, let's create a simple application.

1. First, create the view model that has an ObservableCollection of the type Person and method that modifies the collection on another thread:

```
public class PeopleViewModel
{
  private object _lock = new object();
  public ObservableCollection<Person> People { get; private set; }

  public PeopleViewModel()
  {
    People = new ObservableCollection<Person>();
  }

  public void LoadPeople()
  {
    var seedNames = new string[] { "bob", "ted", "alice", "fred", "anne", "Larry", "Helen",
"Cathy", "joe", "Brett" };

    Task.Factory.StartNew(() =>
    {
      foreach (var name in seedNames)
      {
      People.Add(new Person { Name = name });
      Thread.Sleep(1000);
      }
    });
  }
}
public class Person
{
  public string Name { get; set; }
}
```

2. Next, create a form with a button and list box:

```
<Window
  xmlns="http://schemas.microsoft.com/winfx/2006/xaml/presentation"
  xmlns:x="http://schemas.microsoft.com/winfx/2006/xaml"
  xmlns:d="http://schemas.microsoft.com/expression/blend/2008"
  xmlns:mc="http://schemas.openxmlformats.org/markup-compatibility/2006"
  mc:Ignorable="d"
  x:Class="CollectionsAccessThreadsExample.MainWindow"
  Title="MainWindow" Height="350" Width="525">
```

```
<Grid>
  <Button
  x:Name="AddPeopleBtn"
  Content="Add People"
  HorizontalAlignment="Left"
  Margin="83,264,0,0"
  VerticalAlignment="Top"
  Width="115"
  Click="PopulateNameBtn_Click"/>
  <ListBox
  HorizontalAlignment="Left"
  Height="274"
  Margin="233,10,0,0"
  VerticalAlignment="Top"
  Width="236"
  ItemsSource="{Binding People}"
  DisplayMemberPath="Name"/>
  </Grid>
</Window>
```

3.   Finally, in the code behind add the following:

```
public partial class MainWindow : Window
{
  private PeopleViewModel peopleViewModel = new PeopleViewModel();

  public MainWindow()
  {
    InitializeComponent();
    DataContext = peopleViewModel;
  }

  private void AddPeopleBtn_Click(object sender, RoutedEventArgs e)
  {
    peopleViewModel.LoadPeople();
  }
}
```

4.   At this point, if you run the application and click the Add People button, you
will get the following exception:

"This type of CollectionView does not support changes to its SourceCollection from a thread
different from the Dispatcher thread"

There are, of course, workarounds to get this to work, but in 4.5 these aren't necessary since we can
instead use the BindingOerations.EnableCollectionSynchronization() method to enable a collection to
be accessed across multiple threads.

There are two overloads of this method—one that leaves it up to the system to lock the collection
when you access it, and another that allows you to specify a callback to handle locking the collection
yourself. We will modify the view model to use the first option in order to get the example to work as
expected.

In the view model code, we will add a lock object and modify the constructor to call the
EnableCollectionSynchronization() method. The following code extract shows you the changes:

```
private object _lock = new object();
public PeopleViewModel()
{
  People = new ObservableCollection<Person>();
  BindingOperations.EnableCollectionSynchronization(People, _lock);
}
```

Now run the application and click the Add People button—everything should work as expected.

Binding to Types That Implement ICustomTypeProvider

The ICustomTypeProvider was part of the Silverlight 5.0 release and has now been included in this release of WPF. Similar to ICustomTypeDescriptor, it provides a more lightweight means for dynamically adding properties to a class at runtime and binding them to a control or controls. The databinding now checks whether an object has implemented this interface and the binding engine uses your custom type rather than System.Type.

The ICustomTypeDescriptor interface is in itself pretty simple, defining only one method, GetCustomType(), which returns an instance of Type, but implementing it requires a bit of work. As outlined by Alexandra Rusina in her blog post on implementing it in Silverlight 5 (http://bit.ly/MkV2Vb), you will need to do the following:

- Create your type by deriving from System.Type.

- Your new type needs to store its properties somewhere; this requires you to create your own PropertyInfo by deriving from System.Reflection.PropertyInfo.

- So that your properties work properly with databinding, you will need to implement the INotifyPropertyChanged interface.

Though you don't need to, a common solution is to write a reusable helper class to pull all of the bits together. (See Jonathan Antione's blog post at http://bit.ly/RBFKxD for a WPF implementation of Rusina's Silverlight helper class.) With the helper class, you can then create a base class that provides wrapper methods to call into the helper class. The following code is an example of how this can be done:

```
public class CustomType :ICustomTypeProvider
{
  CustomTypeHelper<CustomType> helper = new CustomTypcHelper<CustomType>();

  public static void AddProperty(String name)
  {
    CustomTypeHelper<CustomType>.AddProperty(name);
  }

  public static void AddProperty(String name, Type propertyType)
  {
    CustomTypeHelper<CustomType>.AddProperty(name, propertyType);
  }

  public static void AddProperty(String name, Type propertyType, List<Attribute> attributes)
  {
    CustomTypeHelper<CustomType>.AddProperty(name, propertyType, attributes);
  }
```

```
public void SetPropertyValue(string propertyName, object value)
{
  helper.SetPropertyValue(propertyName, value);
}

public object GetPropertyValue(string propertyName)
{
  return helper.GetPropertyValue(propertyName);
}

public PropertyInfo[] GetProperties()
{
  return helper.GetProperties();
}

public Type GetCustomType()
{
  return helper.GetCustomType();
}
}
```

Once this is done, at runtime all you need to do is define the properties that you want by calling one of the overloads of the static method AddProperty() and then for each instance of the class, call SetPropertyValue() to set the property:

```
CustomType.AddProperty("FirstName", typeof(string));
CustomType.AddProperty("LastName", typeof(string));

var person = new CustomType();
person.SetPropertyValue("FirstName", "Bob");
person.SetPropertyValue("LastName", "Roberts");
```

To give you a better idea of how this works and to provide an example of a case where this could be used, you can download the example from http://sdrv.ms/PvKh2J. In this example, we take some JSON data, which is an array of a simple object graph, and generate a list of CustomTypes with the properties and property values generated at runtime and displayed in a GridView.

Repositioning Data as the Data's Values Change (Live Shaping)

There are controls in WPF, such as a DataGrid, that bind to a collection of objects. WPF also allows the data in these controls to be grouped, sorted, or filtered. When the data changes in this collection, then the grouping, sorting, and filtering should automatically update the UI based on these changes. To help with this, WPF 4.5 introduces a new interface called ICollectionViewLiveShaping. This interface has the properties shown in Table 12-2.

Table 12-2. Properties that can be used for live shaping of data

Property Names	Description
CanChangeLiveFiltering, CanChangeLiveGrouping, CanChangeLiveSorting	Readonly boolean value indicating whether live filtering, grouping, or sorting can be activated in the collection.
IsLiveFiltering, IsLiveGrouping, IsLiveSorting	Boolean property indicating whether filtering, grouping, and sorting are turned on.
LiveFilteringProperties, LiveGroupingProperties, LiveSortingProperties	An observable collection of strings with names of the properties that participate in filtering, grouping, and sorting.

The classes ListCollectionView, BindingListCollectionView, and ItemCollection in WPF already implement this interface, but you can implement a custom collection for your own purposes.

New Methods for the Dispatcher Class

If you've been writing applications in WPF for a while, then you know that you can't update the UI from another thread. To update the UI from a thread that doesn't own the control, you need to use the Dispatcher class. Some new methods have been added to the Dispatcher class in WPF 4.5.

Previously in WPF, the Dispatcher had a number of Invoke methods that took a Delegate as a parameter. In WPF 4.5, you can now pass either an Action or Func<TResult> as parameters instead of a Delegate. In addition, InvokeAsync methods have been added that let you call the same methods asynchronously.

Event-related Changes

One of my favorite features in WPF 4.5 is the introduction of the long-due markup extensions for events. This feature allows you to extend the markup to use methods that are present in the databound object instead of event handlers present in the code behind files. In addition, the introduction of the WeakEventManager in WPF 4.5 also makes it easier to avoid memory leaks that arise out of event handlers that aren't properly unsubscribed. These two features of WPF 4.5 are covered in this section.

Markup Extensions for Events

WPF 4.5 now supports markup extensions that allow you to specify custom events in your markup. This is particularly useful when you want to use the Model View View-Model (MVVM) pattern. In the MVVM pattern, your UI is split up into a view (which is represented in your XAML), a model (which is a representation of your data class—typically these are POCOs, or Plain Old CLR Objects), and a view model, which is a representation of the model that is used by the view for databinding purposes.

In the past, although you could easily bind data to the view, binding events through the view model was not a trivial exercise. By using markup extensions for events, this can now be achieved easily.

To create a markup extension for an event, you need to extend the abstract class MarkupExtension and implement the method ProvideValue. Following is a sample implementation of a markup extension:

```
public class EventExtension : MarkupExtension
{
    private readonly string _methodToInvoke;

    public EventExtension(string methodToInvoke)
    {
        _methodToInvoke = methodToInvoke;
    }

    public override object ProvideValue(IServiceProvider serviceProvider)
    {
        var targetProvider = serviceProvider.GetService(typeof (IProvideValueTarget))
                                as IProvideValueTarget;

        if (targetProvider != null)
        {
            var methodInfo = GetType().GetMethod("CallExtensionMethod",
                                            BindingFlags.NonPublic |
BindingFlags.Instance);
            var eventInfo = targetProvider.TargetProperty as EventInfo;

            if (eventInfo != null)
            {
                var eventType = eventInfo.EventHandlerType;
                return Delegate.CreateDelegate(eventType, this, methodInfo);
            }

            //If it is not a event, then it is a method
            var targetPropertyMethodInfo = targetProvider.TargetProperty as MethodInfo;
            if (targetPropertyMethodInfo != null)
            {
                var parameterType = targetPropertyMethodInfo.GetParameters()[1].ParameterType;
                return Delegate.CreateDelegate(parameterType, this, methodInfo);
            }
        }

        return null;
    }

    private void CallExtensionMethod(object sender, EventArgs e)
    {
        var target = sender as FrameworkElement;
        if (target != null)
        {
            var dataContext = target.DataContext;
            if (dataContext != null)
            {
                var methodInfo = dataContext.GetType()
                    .GetMethod(_methodToInvoke, BindingFlags.Public | BindingFlags.Instance);
                methodInfo.Invoke(dataContext, new object[] {e});
            }
        }
    }
```

```
    }
}
```

The EventExtension class takes the name of the method on the ViewModel to invoke as a parameter in the constructor. And this method is invoked in the CallExtensionMethod implementation. The ProvideValue method returns a delegate that is created using the target provider's TargetProperty. The TargetProperty can either be an EventInfo or a MethodInfo.

The usage of this extension in your markup will look something like the following (the actual use of the EventExtension is shown in bold):

```
<Window x:Class="EventBinding.MainWindow"
        xmlns="http://schemas.microsoft.com/winfx/2006/xaml/presentation"
        xmlns:x="http://schemas.microsoft.com/winfx/2006/xaml"
        xmlns:EventBinding="clr-namespace:EventBinding"
        Title="MainWindow" Height="350" Width="525">
    <Window.Resources>
        <EventBinding:MainWindowViewModel x:Key="ViewModel"/>
    </Window.Resources>
    <StackPanel DataContext="{StaticResource ViewModel}">
        <Rectangle Fill="Azure" Height="50" Width="250"
                MouseDown="{EventBinding:EventExtension MouseDownMethod}" />
        <Button Content="Button" Width="250" Height="50"
                MouseDoubleClick="{EventBinding:EventExtension MouseDoubleClickMethod}"/>

    </StackPanel>
</Window>
```

The ViewModel class, which is used in the event binding, will look like the following code snippet:

```
public class MainWindowViewModel
{
    …
    public void MouseDoubleClickMethod(EventArgs e)
    {
        //Do Something
    }

    public void MouseDownMethod(EventArgs e)
    {
        //Do Something else
    }
}
```

Improved Support for Establishing a Weak Reference to an Event

When you do not unhook an event handler, you end up with memory leaks. This issue led to the introduction of the Weak Event Pattern (http://msdn.microsoft.com/en-us/library/aa970850.aspx) in WPF. The problem with this pattern is that it required creating a custom subclass of WeakEventManager for each event type and the listener needed to implement the corresponding IWeakEventListener interface. With this release, implementing this pattern has been made easier with the inclusion of a generic version of WeakEventManager.

By using WeakEventManager<TEventSource, TEventArgs> it is no longer necessary to create a custom WeakEventManager or implement IWeakEventListener. Instead, you just need to pass the event to subscribe to, the source of the event, and the event handler to the AddHandler() method.

The following code snippet is an example of how the WeakEventManager can be used to wire up the CollectionChanged event on a view model:

```
public partial class MainWindow : Window
{
  private PeopleViewModel peopleViewModel = new PeopleViewModel();

  public MainWindow()
  {
    InitializeComponent();
    WeakEventManager<ObservableCollection<Person>, NotifyCollectionChangedEventArgs>
      .AddHandler(peopleViewModel.People, "CollectionChanged", People_CollectionChanged);

  DataContext = peopleViewModel;
  }

  void People_CollectionChanged(object sender, NotifyCollectionChangedEventArgs e)
  {
    Debug.WriteLine(string.Format("Collection changed. Count = {0}",
peopleViewModel.People.Count));
  }
}
```

Though flexible, there are a couple of limitations with this new class. First, the event is identified by name, which could lead to subtle bugs being introduced. Second, under the covers it uses reflection to wire up the event so there is a slight performance hit as compared with the alternatives.

Summary

.NET 4.5 does not bring any radical changes to WPF, and the most important addition is the introduction of the Ribbon control that comes out of the box. There are several other changes that have been introduced to the framework, some of which have had their origin in Silverlight. The INotifyDataErrorInfo is one such change and it lets you validate your data asynchronously. Several changes have also been made in WPF around databinding—the most important of them being the introduction of a Delay property. This chapter has covered each one of these changes in detail, and it finishes up with another one of the most important changes—markup extensions for events. If you are writing applications in WPF and you use the MVVM pattern, you will be very happy with the change as you can write all your event handler code in your View Model and databind them in the view quite easily.

CHAPTER 13

■ ■ ■

Silverlight 5

Silverlight's release cycle is separate from the release cycle of Visual Studio, but it occupies an important place in Microsoft's line of products that depend on Visual Studio—so important that it warrants a chapter on its own. This chapter covers all the changes that have been added to Silverlight 5. We start by walking you through a brief history of Silverlight itself followed by each of the changes. These changes range from the addition of new controls (`PivotViewer` and `RichTextBlockOverFlow` controls) to changes made to databinding and improvements to graphics (3D and independent animations). We finish the chapter talking about how you can call native code from Silverlight.

A Brief History of Silverlight

Silverlight is currently up to version 5, and looking back, the first version was released sometime in 2007. So, in about five years, we've had about five releases, which speaks volumes about Microsoft's initial push into the Rich Internet Application (RIA) space—a space that was dominated by companies such as Adobe with its Adobe Flash product and now strongly challenged by the emergence of HTML5.

When Silverlight was first introduced, it was primarily used for playing media files. You could do a bit more than just play audios and videos, but that involved working with JavaScript, and it did not necessarily provide the best developer experience.

With Silverlight 2, you could develop with languages such as C# and VB.NET and the screens could be designed in XAML, which was what WPF used. In fact, Silverlight was based out of WPF and was initially even code named WPF/e (or WPF everywhere). Silverlight 2 provided a subset of the .NET Framework, a number of controls that you could use out of the box, and even nice features such as data access over WCF, ADO.NET Data Services.

Silverlight 3 added features such as Out-of-Browser (OOB) mode, more controls, better databinding, and so on.

Silverlight 4 went further with these changes and enabled better support for running the application in elevated trust mode, support for webcams and microphones, a RichTextBox control, printing support, ability to connect to COM components, drag-drop support, RIA services, and so forth.

The big changes in Silverlight 5 include improvements to databinding, changes to text controls, support for 3D API, and an ability to call low-level OS calls using P/Invoke.

In spite of all these nice features in Silverlight, specific versions of Silverlight are not packaged with Visual Studio. It usually has its own release cycle and like some other products (such as Windows Azure and MEF), it is released as a separate download. Once you've installed the tools, the integration in Visual Studio is quite seamless.

Improvements to Text

Silverlight 5 introduces a number of improvements to text and text-related controls. For starters, several new properties have been added to text controls, such as TextBox, that control character spacing, line spacing, and so on. Apart from new properties to existing controls, a new control (RichTextBoxOverflow) has also been added to Silverlight to allow displaying text in columns. Improvements to printing and support for OpenType fonts caps off text-related improvements in Silverlight 5.

Silverlight 5 introduces some new properties to control how text is displayed. These properties include the following:

- CharacterSpacing: This property lets you set the spacing between two successive characters in a word. The XAML snippet below shows an example of how to set the character spacing, and Figure 13-1 shows how it gets displayed on screen:

```
<StackPanel x:Name="LayoutRoot" Background="White">
    <TextBlock FontSize="24">Hello, World!</TextBlock>
    <TextBlock FontSize="24" CharacterSpacing="0">Hello, World!</TextBlock>
    <TextBlock FontSize="24" CharacterSpacing="250">Hello, World!</TextBlock>
    <TextBlock FontSize="24" CharacterSpacing="-125">Hello, World!</TextBlock>
</StackPanel>
```

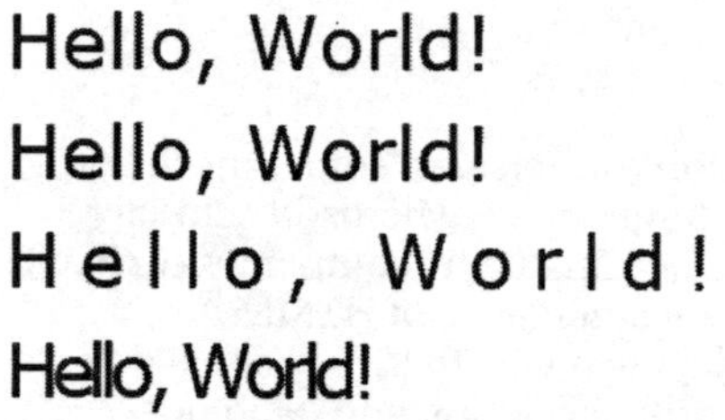

Hello, World!

Hello, World!

H e l l o ,   W o r l d !

Hello, World!

Figure 13-1. Different character spacings in text

By looking at the sample XAML snippet and the resulting output, you would have realized that a value of 0 for the character spacing is the default value, it can take negative values, and that the unit for it is not in pixels. *So, what is the unit on which* CharacterSpacing *is based on?* This is the distance between characters measured in one-thousandths of the font size. So, in our example, a character spacing of 250 for font size 24 results in 250/1000*24 = 6 pixels. This property is available in the Control class, and any control that inherits from this class can also make use of this property.

- LineHeight: This sets the height between two successive lines in a text control (TextBox and all its inherited controls). This value is set in pixels and an example of its use is shown in the following XAML snippet. Its output is shown in Figure 13-2, along with an output for normal line height.

```
<TextBlock FontSize="20" LineHeight="50">
    Lorem ipsum dolor sit amet, consectetur adipiscing elit.
    <LineBreak />
    Integer cursus tincidunt ligula, ut placerat sem mollis non.
    <LineBreak />
```

```
    Fusce non placerat enim.
</TextBlock>
```

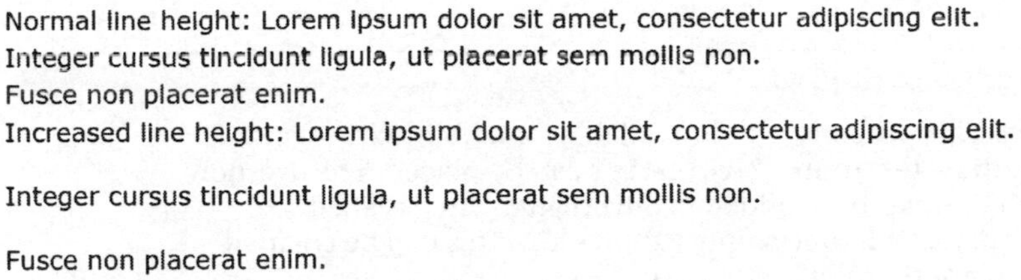

Normal line height: Lorem ipsum dolor sit amet, consectetur adipiscing elit.
Integer cursus tincidunt ligula, ut placerat sem mollis non.
Fusce non placerat enim.
Increased line height: Lorem ipsum dolor sit amet, consectetur adipiscing elit.

Integer cursus tincidunt ligula, ut placerat sem mollis non.

Fusce non placerat enim.

Figure 13-2. Normal line height and increased line height in text

- LineStackingStrategy: This property is used to specify how each line in a TextBox is stacked. It is particularly useful if the font height in some of these lines varies. This property can take three values. Figure 13-3 shows how text is displayed when these values are used:

    - MaxHeight: This is the default value and each line height is calculated based on the maximum height of the text present in it.

    - BlockLineHeight: This adds the LineHeight property to set the height of each line. If this property is not specified, then it behaves like a MaxHeight.

    - BaselineToBaseline: This behaves the same as a BlockLineHeight, but if the LineHeight property is not set, each line has the same height.

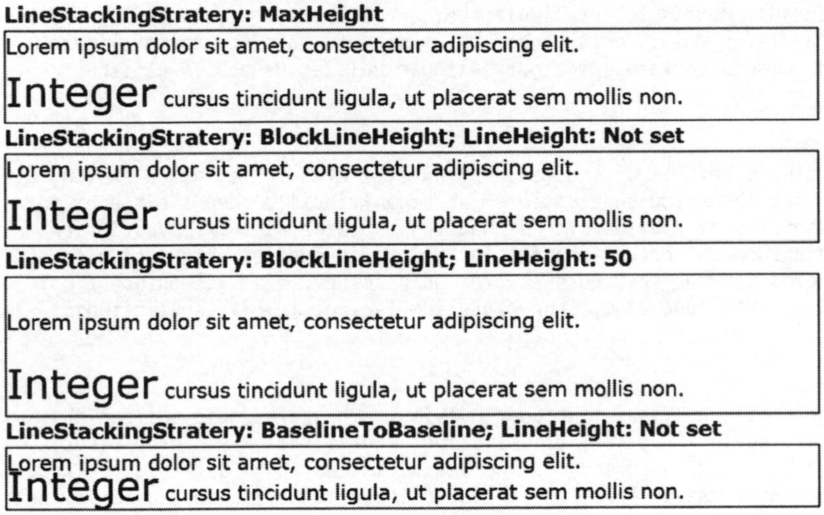

LineStackingStratery: MaxHeight

Lorem ipsum dolor sit amet, consectetur adipiscing elit.

Integer cursus tincidunt ligula, ut placerat sem mollis non.

LineStackingStratery: BlockLineHeight; LineHeight: Not set

Lorem ipsum dolor sit amet, consectetur adipiscing elit.

Integer cursus tincidunt ligula, ut placerat sem mollis non.

LineStackingStratery: BlockLineHeight; LineHeight: 50

Lorem ipsum dolor sit amet, consectetur adipiscing elit.

Integer cursus tincidunt ligula, ut placerat sem mollis non.

LineStackingStratery: BaselineToBaseline; LineHeight: Not set

Lorem ipsum dolor sit amet, consectetur adipiscing elit.
Integer cursus tincidunt ligula, ut placerat sem mollis non.

Figure 13-3. Figure showing different LineStackingStrategy values

---

▪ **Note** The LineStackingStrategy used to exist in Silverlight 4, but it could only take the values MaxHeight and BlockLineHeight.

- OverflowContentTarget: This property is only available for a RichTextBox and specifies where the overflow text from a RichTextBox can be placed. The overflow control is a new control that has been added to Silverlight 5 and is called RichTextBoxOverflow. This XAML code snippet shows how this can be chained from one RichTextBox to another:

```xaml
<UserControl x:Class="SilverlightApplication5.MainPage"
    xmlns="http://schemas.microsoft.com/winfx/2006/xaml/presentation"
    xmlns:x="http://schemas.microsoft.com/winfx/2006/xaml"
    xmlns:d="http://schemas.microsoft.com/expression/blend/2008"
    xmlns:mc="http://schemas.openxmlformats.org/markup-compatibility/2006"
    mc:Ignorable="d"
    d:DesignHeight="1024" d:DesignWidth="800">

    <StackPanel x:Name="LayoutRoot" Background="White" Margin="10, 10, 10, 10"
Orientation="Horizontal" >
        <RichTextBlock Width="200" Margin="10 10 10 10" OverflowContentTarget="{Binding
ElementName=Overflow1}">
            <Paragraph>
                Lorem ipsum dolor sit amet, consectetur adipiscing elit. Curabitur justo
lorem, rhoncus eget iaculis sit amet, rhoncus non turpis. Vivamus scelerisque est nec nisi
sodales ac euismod tortor luctus. Mauris tellus ligula, porta vel laoreet at, venenatis sed
orci. Etiam dapibus sem vitae felis mollis quis ornare metus dictum. Duis non tortor libero,
et sagittis mauris. Vivamus commodo porta ullamcorper. Aliquam vel lectus ac leo ultrices
hendrerit.
            </Paragraph>
            <Paragraph>
                Curabitur euismod, eros sed condimentum ornare, lectus felis cursus sapien,
vel luctus orci ligula sit amet lacus. Quisque ut lorem ac urna fringilla semper sit amet ac
diam. Fusce accumsan accumsan arcu at gravida. In hac habitasse platea dictumst. Vestibulum
pharetra, dui in sollicitudin rhoncus, metus arcu feugiat dolor, id sodales ante nisi a eros.
Quisque vehicula risus sed eros commodo eget cursus lorem adipiscing. Etiam vel purus et est
egestas consequat ut ac justo. Cras nunc diam, congue pretium laoreet tempus, sollicitudin
ultricies velit.
            </Paragraph>
            <Paragraph>
                Curabitur ac sapien et risus tincidunt pulvinar. Phasellus quis velit nibh.
Cras est leo, sollicitudin sed scelerisque sed, tristique vel mauris. Etiam at lorem risus,
vel mollis neque. Maecenas iaculis, nibh eu sodales facilisis, lectus ipsum ultricies tellus,
aliquam lobortis purus ante tempor massa. Phasellus molestie scelerisque libero, id tempor est
sollicitudin nec. Sed sit amet dui vitae arcu convallis ullamcorper. Nunc quis mi purus.
Vivamus elementum, mauris non dignissim cursus, lorem massa tincidunt leo, dignissim convallis
enim tellus quis dui. Aliquam elementum dapibus sollicitudin. Ut pulvinar, odio sed auctor
facilisis, sapien erat bibendum ante, vitae placerat turpis urna a nisi. Duis tempus, eros nec
```

semper pulvinar, eros diam fermentum velit, eu varius felis enim quis augue. Nulla malesuada bibendum erat, id semper nulla pulvinar eu. Suspendisse faucibus blandit magna non vehicula.

```
        </Paragraph>
    </RichTextBlock>

    <RichTextBlockOverflow x:Name="Overflow1" Width="200" Margin="10 10 10 10"
OverflowContentTarget="{Binding ElementName=Overflow2}" />

    <RichTextBlockOverflow  x:Name="Overflow2" Width="200" Margin="10 10 10 10" />

    </StackPanel>
</UserControl>
```

This feature is really useful to create a multicolumn layout for free-flowing text in your application. Figure 13-4 shows how the text overflows to the other `RichEditBlock` controls.

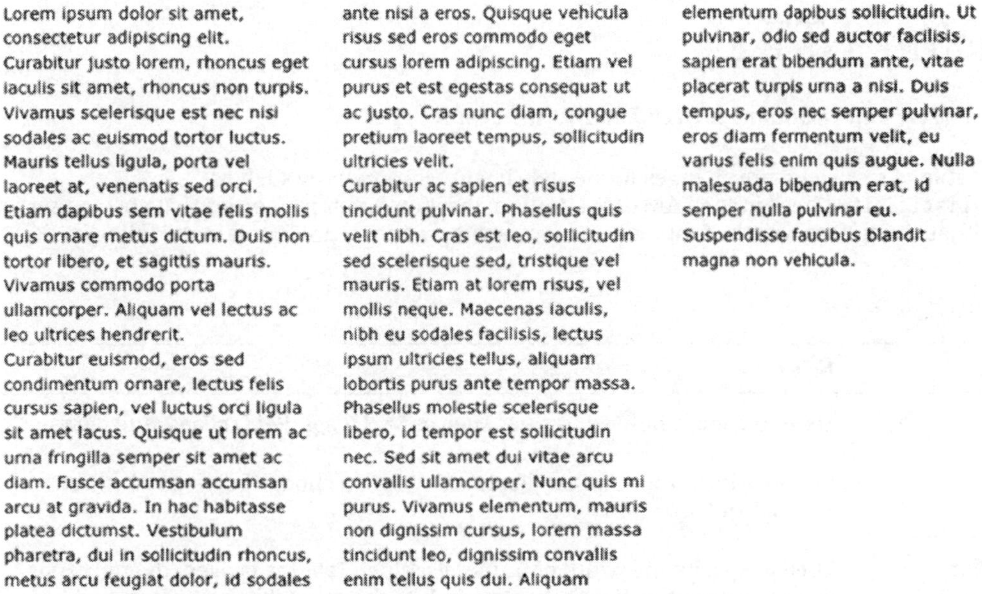

Lorem ipsum dolor sit amet, consectetur adipiscing elit. Curabitur justo lorem, rhoncus eget iaculis sit amet, rhoncus non turpis. Vivamus scelerisque est nec nisi sodales ac euismod tortor luctus. Mauris tellus ligula, porta vel laoreet at, venenatis sed orci. Etiam dapibus sem vitae felis mollis quis ornare metus dictum. Duis non tortor libero, et sagittis mauris. Vivamus commodo porta ullamcorper. Aliquam vel lectus ac leo ultrices hendrerit. Curabitur euismod, eros sed condimentum ornare, lectus felis cursus sapien, vel luctus orci ligula sit amet lacus. Quisque ut lorem ac urna fringilla semper sit amet ac diam. Fusce accumsan accumsan arcu at gravida. In hac habitasse platea dictumst. Vestibulum pharetra, dui in sollicitudin rhoncus, metus arcu feugiat dolor, id sodales ante nisi a eros. Quisque vehicula risus sed eros commodo eget cursus lorem adipiscing. Etiam vel purus et est egestas consequat ut ac justo. Cras nunc diam, congue pretium laoreet tempus, sollicitudin ultricies velit. Curabitur ac sapien et risus tincidunt pulvinar. Phasellus quis velit nibh. Cras est leo, sollicitudin sed scelerisque sed, tristique vel mauris. Etiam at lorem risus, vel mollis neque. Maecenas iaculis, nibh eu sodales facilisis, lectus ipsum ultricies tellus, aliquam lobortis purus ante tempor massa. Phasellus molestie scelerisque libero, id tempor est sollicitudin nec. Sed sit amet dui vitae arcu convallis ullamcorper. Nunc quis mi purus. Vivamus elementum, mauris non dignissim cursus, lorem massa tincidunt leo, dignissim convallis enim tellus quis dui. Aliquam elementum dapibus sollicitudin. Ut pulvinar, odio sed auctor facilisis, sapien erat bibendum ante, vitae placerat turpis urna a nisi. Duis tempus, eros nec semper pulvinar, eros diam fermentum velit, eu varius felis enim quis augue. Nulla malesuada bibendum erat, id semper nulla pulvinar eu. Suspendisse faucibus blandit magna non vehicula.

Figure 13-4. Use of Overflow Text controls to display text in columns

OpenType Font Support

OpenType is a cross-platform font file format that was jointly developed by Adobe and Microsoft. It is already supported in WPF, and you can do some really fancy things with the font such as using ligatures, expressing fractions in a nice way, using property subscripting and superscripting, and applying different stylistic sets in the same font.

Silverlight now supports OpenType fonts, and you can set the FontFamily to one of the OpenText fonts available in Windows. Once you do that, you can set a number of Typography settings for it. In the following code snippet, the font family is set to Gabriola and the text `Introducing .NET 4.5`, which is the output of the XAML as shown in Figure 13-5.

```
<TextBlock FontSize="80" FontFamily="Gabriola" >
    Introducing .NET 4.5
</TextBlock>
```

Introducing .NET 4.5

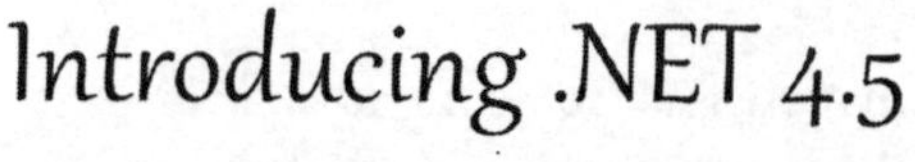

Figure 13-5. *OpenText font Gabriola in use*

If you add the property Typography.StylisticSet1="True" to the TextBlock as shown in the following code snippet, you will notice the style of the font changes. (Notice the change to the character *g* in Figure 13-6.)

```
<TextBlock FontSize="80" FontFamily="Gabriola" Typography.StylisticSet1="True">
    Introducing .NET 4.5
</TextBlock>
```

Introducing .NET 4.5

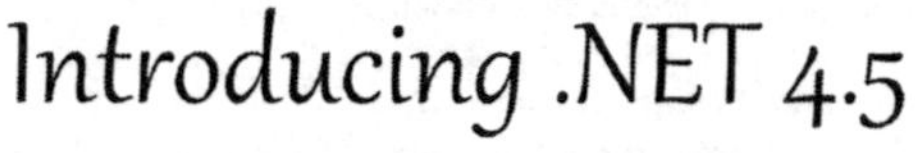

Figure 13-6. *OpenText font Gabriola with a different stylistic set*

You will be able to see a lot more changes to the style if you set something such as Typography.StylisticSet6="True" in the XAML. In addition, there are other properties that you can set for typography that change the way the font looks. Some useful properties are found in the following table.

Table 13-1. *Table Caption*

Property	Notes
Capitals	Used to choose between values such as SmallCaps, PetiteCaps, and Normal.
Fraction	Specifies how fractions are displayed. You can choose between Slashed, Stacked, or Normal.
NumeralAlignment	Used to specify the width of numerals. When Tabular is used, the numerals have equal widths. With Proportional, each numeral has a different width.
SlashedZero	Used to specify whether the zero requires a slash. This is useful in fonts in which zero and the letter *O are difficult to differentiate.*
StandardLigatures	Used to combine the glyphs of two separate letters (such as *ff*, *ft*, and *fi*). When this is set to false, each character will be displayed as two separate glyphs.
StandardSwashes	Used as embellishments to letters. Swashes can be enabled using values greater than zero.

Printing Enhancements

With Silverlight 4, printing was a slow operation, particularly when it involved a lot of pages. This slow speed was mainly because the output to the printer was sent as a bitmap for each page to be printed, and these bitmaps weren't small. You can still do this in Silverlight 5, but in addition, you can also send vector-based graphics that your Postscript printer can pick up and print.

To enable this feature, rather than call the method void Print(string documentName) in the PrintDocument class, you call the overloaded method that takes a PrinterFallBackSettings object as a parameter. The PrinterFallBackSettings class contains two properties—ForceVector and OpacityThreshold. These properties can be used to force the PrintDocument class to send postscript vector data to the printer as shown in the following code snippet:

```
void Print()
{
    var doc = new PrintDocument();
    doc.PrintPage += (s, ea) =>
    {
        ea.PageVisual = LayoutRoot;
        ea.HasMorePages = false;
    };
    var settings = new PrinterFallbackSettings
    {
        ForceVector = true,
        OpacityThreshold = 0.5
    };
    doc.Print("Silverlight 5 doc", settings);
}
```

Changes to Other Controls

Apart from changes to Text controls, Silverlight also introduces some useful changes to other existing controls. Type-ahead text searching in list boxes, where you can select an item by typing its value using a keyboard, is one such change. Multi-click support, which allows you do figure out double-clicks (or even multiple-clicks), is another useful change. In addition to these changes, a new control, PivotViewer, has also been introduced.

Type-Ahead Text Searching in List Box

One frustrating thing with list boxes and combo boxes is that it is very hard to select an item down the list using the keyboard. Silverlight 5 addresses this issue by providing a type-ahead, text-searching facility. This is available to the whole family of list box classes and includes combo boxes as well.

In Silverlight, each item in a list box can contain multiple properties. For example, *if we bind our list box to a* Book *class,* then *what property within the* Book *class should we be using for our type-ahead text search?* The answer is quite simple—you need to set the name of the property in the list box's DisplayMemberPath property.

■ **Note** Type-ahead works well when you type fast. If you leave sufficient gaps between each character you type, the type-ahead feature resets, and you end up selecting the next item that starts with the letter you are typing.

Multiple-click Support

If you wanted to find out if a user double-clicked in previous versions of Silverlight, it involved juggling chainsaws blindfolded while riding a one-wheel cycle. Okay, I exaggerate, but it was not a trivial task. With Silverlight 5, there is now built-in support in the framework for detecting double-clicks, or triple-clicks (if there is such a thing), or even multiple-clicks.

The MouseButtonEventArgs object that gets passed over to mouse event handlers now has a property called ClickCount that can be used to determine double-clicks (and multiple-clicks). To check for a double-click, all you need to do is check if the event's ClickCount property equals 2, as shown in the following code snippet:

```
private void TextBlock_MouseLeftButtonDown(object sender, MouseButtonEventArgs e)
{

    if (e.ClickCount == 2)
    {
        //Double click
    }
}
```

One of the things you need to remember is that a mouse-click event will be generated each time the mouse is clicked, and although you may only be interested in a double-click event, the event handler will be called twice—once during the first click and the second time during the double-click. To see how this works, set up a XAML using the following code snippet:

```
<Grid x:Name="LayoutRoot" Background="White">
    <Grid.RowDefinitions>
        <RowDefinition Height="31*" />
        <RowDefinition Height="269*" />
    </Grid.RowDefinitions>
    <TextBlock Text="Click me!" MouseLeftButtonDown="TextBlock_MouseLeftButtonDown"
            HorizontalAlignment="Center" VerticalAlignment="Center" />
    <ScrollViewer Grid.Row="1" >
        <TextBlock x:Name="ClickCount" />
    </ScrollViewer>
</Grid>
```

Set the event handler for the text block to handle left button down events as shown below:

```
private void TextBlock_MouseLeftButtonDown(object sender, MouseButtonEventArgs e)
{
    if (e.ClickCount == 2)
    {
        //Double click
    }
}
```

When you run the program, you will notice that when you click, double- click, or multiple-click Click me!, then the click count is shown below. You will notice that when you double-click, then a mouse-down event with ClickCount set to 1 is called first, followed by another event with the ClickCount set to 2.

■ **Caution** Although the MouseButtonEventArgs object is also sent on mouse-up events, the ClickCount property on these events is always 1. You should never use these events to determine multiple-clicks.

PivotViewer Control

The PivotViewer control allows users to interactively visualize large amounts of data in an intuitive fashion—such as applying filters on items, sorting -on properties, or viewing data in a chartlike fashion.

To see how the PivotViewer control works, let's first define the class we are going to use in our sample:

```
public class Book
{
    string Title { get; set; }
    string Isbn { get; set; }
    string Publisher { get; set; }
    string Authors { get; set; }
    int YearPublished { get; set; }
    string Genre { get; set; }
}
```

To get the control to work, follow these steps:

1. Add the System.Windows.Controls.Pivot assembly to your Silverlight project. This assembly contains the PivotViewer control.

2. Replace the XAML in your MainPage.xaml to markup:

```
<UserControl x:Class="PivotApp.MainPage"
    xmlns="http://schemas.microsoft.com/winfx/2006/xaml/presentation"
    xmlns:x="http://schemas.microsoft.com/winfx/2006/xaml"
    xmlns:d="http://schemas.microsoft.com/expression/blend/2008"
    xmlns:mc="http://schemas.openxmlformats.org/markup-compatibility/2006"
    xmlns:pivot="clr-
namespace:System.Windows.Controls.Pivot;assembly=System.Windows.Controls.Pivot"
    mc:Ignorable="d"
    d:DesignHeight="300" d:DesignWidth="400">

    <Grid x:Name="LayoutRoot" Background="White" DataContext="{Binding Source={StaticResource
SampleDataSource}}">
        <pivot:PivotViewer x:Name="Pivot" ItemsSource="{Binding Collection}" >

            <pivot:PivotViewer.PivotProperties>
                <pivot:PivotViewerStringProperty                    Id="Title" Options="CanFilter"
DisplayName="Title" Binding="{Binding Title}" />
```

```xml
                <pivot:PivotViewerStringProperty              Id="Genre" Options="CanFilter"
DisplayName="Genre" Binding="{Binding Genre}" />
                <pivot:PivotViewerStringProperty              Id="Author" Options="CanFilter"
DisplayName="Author" Binding="{Binding Authors}" />
                <pivot:PivotViewerStringProperty              Id="Publisher" Options="CanFilter"
DisplayName="Publisher" Binding="{Binding Publisher}" />
                <pivot:PivotViewerNumericProperty              Id="YearPublished"
Options="CanFilter" DisplayName="YearPublished" Binding="{Binding Year}" />
            </pivot:PivotViewer.PivotProperties>

        <pivot:PivotViewer.ItemTemplates>

        <pivot:PivotViewerItemTemplate>
                        <Border Width="300" Height="100" BorderBrush="#FF081134"
BorderThickness="2" CornerRadius="4" >
                            <Border.Background>
                                <LinearGradientBrush EndPoint="0.5,1"
StartPoint="0.5,0">
                                        <GradientStop Color="#FF8284EA" Offset="0"/>
                                        <GradientStop Color="White" Offset="1"/>
                                </LinearGradientBrush>
                            </Border.Background>
                            <StackPanel Margin="2" >
                                <TextBlock Text="{Binding Title}" FontSize="24"
FontFamily="Garamond" FontWeight="Bold"/>
                                <TextBlock Text="{Binding Authors}" FontStyle="Italic"
FontWeight="Bold"/>
                                <TextBlock Text="{Binding Genre}"/>
                                <TextBlock Text="{Binding Isbn}"/>
                                <StackPanel Orientation="Horizontal" >
        <TextBlock                              Text="Publisher:" FontWeight="Bold"/>
        <TextBlock                              Text="{Binding Publisher}"/>
        <TextBlock                              Text="  Year Published:"
FontWeight="Bold"/>
        <TextBlock                              Text="{Binding YearPublished}"/>
                                </StackPanel>
                            </StackPanel>
                        </Border>
        </pivot:PivotViewerItemTemplate>
        </pivot:PivotViewer.ItemTemplates>
            </pivot:PivotViewer>
    </Grid>
</UserControl>
```

The XAML in the example binds to a SampleDataSource that I've created, which
you need to change to point to your own data. The PivotViewerItemTemplate
defines how each item is displayed in the Pivot control, and the
PivotProperties defines which properties in the data are used for things such
as filtering.

3. Press F5 to run the application, which will display as shown in Figure 13-7. Once the control is displayed, you will be able to change the sort order, filter data, and even the view (see Figure 13-8).

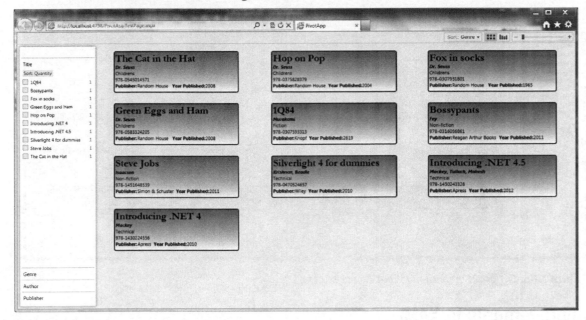

Figure 13-7. PivotViewer control

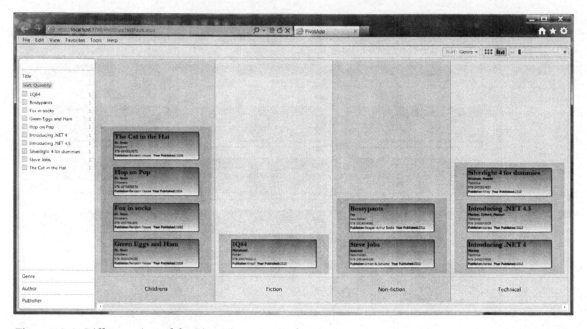

Figure 13-8. *Different view of the PivotViewer control*

Improvements to XAML

With each new version of Silverlight, there is always something new in the language. Silverlight 5 is no different, and there are a number of changes in the markup language. This version includes the addition of implicit data templates, changes to style bindings, introduction of relative source binding, and markup extensions in XAML. One of my favorite features is the ability to set breakpoints in XAML from within Visual Studio, and debug through it. These changes are covered in the following sections.

Implicit Data Templates

In Silverlight, you can specify data templates for controls such as ListBox. This allows you to specify how each item in the list box will be displayed on screen. To see how this works, let's take an example of a simple Book class defined as follows:

```
public class Book
{
    public string Isbn { get; set; }
    public string Title { get; set; }
    public string Authors { get; set; }
    public int Pages { get; set; }
}
```

To display this in a nice way, you would do something like this in XAML, which would result in a nice display of each item as shown in Figure 13-9:

```xml
<ListBox x:Name="BooksListbox" Height="400" Margin="10 10 10 10">
    <ListBox.ItemTemplate>
        <DataTemplate>
            <StackPanel>
                <TextBlock Text="{Binding Title}" FontSize="16" />
                <TextBlock Text="{Binding Authors}" FontSize="12" />
                <StackPanel Orientation="Horizontal">
                    <TextBlock Text="ISBN:" FontSize="9" FontStyle="Italic"/>
                    <TextBlock Text="{Binding Isbn}" FontSize="9" FontStyle="Italic"/>
                </StackPanel>
            </StackPanel>
        </DataTemplate>
    </ListBox.ItemTemplate>
</ListBox>
```

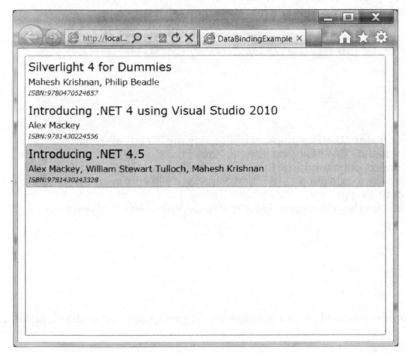

Figure 13-9. ListBox databound to Book objects

If the data template is to be used over and over again, it makes more sense to create a separate template and bind to the template using its name. For instance, if the name of the template is BookTemplate and it is defined in your Application resource file, then you can bind the template name as shown in the following XAML snippet:

```xml
<ListBox x:Name="BooksListbox" Height="400" Margin="10 10 10 10"
        ItemTemplate="{Binding Mode=OneWay, Source={StaticResource BookTemplate}}" >
</ListBox>
```

But, wouldn't it be cool if we could just specify the list box to use a certain template depending on its type, rather than specifying a data template name? That is what the new implicit data template feature allows you to do. To enable implicit data template binding, you need to remove the key x:Key="BookTemplate" and add a property called DataType and set it to the name of the class you intend to use as shown in the following XAML snippet in your Application resources:

```
<Application xmlns="http://schemas.microsoft.com/winfx/2006/xaml/presentation"
             xmlns:x="http://schemas.microsoft.com/winfx/2006/xaml"
             x:Class="DataBindingExample.App"
             xmlns:my="clr-namespace:DataBindingExample"
             >
    <Application.Resources>
        <DataTemplate DataType="my:Book">
            <StackPanel>
                <TextBlock Text="{Binding Title}" FontSize="16" />
                <TextBlock Text="{Binding Authors}" FontSize="12" />
                <StackPanel Orientation="Horizontal">
                    <TextBlock Text="ISBN:" FontSize="9" FontStyle="Italic"/>
                    <TextBlock Text="{Binding Isbn}" FontSize="9" FontStyle="Italic"/>
                </StackPanel>
            </StackPanel>
        </DataTemplate>
    </Application.Resources>
</Application>
```

You can then remove the ItemTemplate binding property while using the list box and allow the list box to automatically use the data template depending on its type. One of the nice features about implicit data type binding is that it also supports polymorphism. In other words, if you use items that have classes derived from Book and they have a data template defined, Silverlight will automatically pick the right template depending on the derived type.

To see this in action, let's create another class called EBook that derives from Book, defined as the following:

```
public class EBook : Book
{
    public string Format { get; set; }
    public int Size { get; set; }
}
```

You need to modify your App.xaml to specify a data template for the new EBook class as shown in the XAML snippet:

```
<DataTemplate DataType="my:EBook">
        <StackPanel>
            <TextBlock Text="{Binding Title}" FontSize="16" />
            <TextBlock Text="{Binding Authors}" FontSize="12" />
            <StackPanel Orientation="Horizontal">
                <TextBlock Text="ISBN:" FontSize="9" FontStyle="Italic"/>
                <TextBlock Text="{Binding Isbn}" FontSize="9" FontStyle="Italic"/>
            </StackPanel>
            <StackPanel Orientation="Horizontal">
                <TextBlock Text="Format:" FontSize="9" FontStyle="Italic"/>
                <TextBlock Text="{Binding Format}" FontSize="9" FontStyle="Italic"/>
```

```
            </StackPanel>
            <StackPanel Orientation="Horizontal">
                <TextBlock Text="Filesize:" FontSize="9" FontStyle="Italic"/>
                <TextBlock Text="{Binding Size, StringFormat='\{0:d\} bytes'}"
FontSize="9" FontStyle="Italic"/>
            </StackPanel>
        </StackPanel>
    </DataTemplate>
```

Now, depending on the data type of the item in your ItemSource, Silverlight will automatically choose the right template, as shown in Figure 13-10.

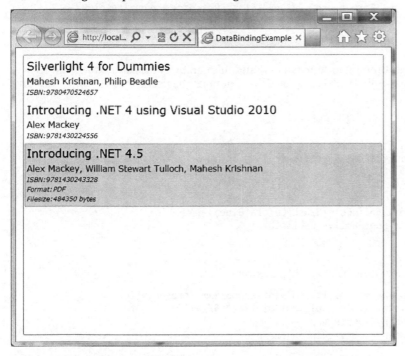

Figure 13-10. ListBox implicitly bound to Book (and EBook) objects

Style Binding

Prior to Silverlight 5, when creating a style for a control, you would have to set static values to properties as shown in the following code snippet:

```
<Style TargetType="TextBlock">
    <Style.Setters>
        <Setter Property="FontSize" Value="40" />
        <Setter Property="FontFamily" Value="Gabriola" />
        <Setter Property="Foreground" Value="Blue" />
    </Style.Setters>
</Style>
```

This would set the font size to 40, font family to Gabriola, and the foreground color of all text boxes to blue. Databinding support was very limited, and you could bind the setter property to a static resource. For instance, if you had declared a resource in App.xaml called FavouriteColor, you could access the static resource as shown in the following XAML snippet:

```xml
<Application.Resources>
    <SolidColorBrush x:Key="FavouriteColor" Color="Blue" />
    …
    <Style TargetType="TextBlock">
        <Style.Setters>
            …
            <Setter Property="Foreground" Value="{StaticResource FavouriteColor}" />
        </Style.Setters>
    </Style>
    …
```

Silverlight 5 lets you do proper binding to setter values, and this can be demonstrated with an example. Consider you have a class called UserPreference that contains the user's favorite color and font as shown in the following code:

```csharp
public class UserPreference
{
    public SolidColorBrush FavouriteColor { get; set; }
    public FontFamily FavouriteFont { get; set; }

    public UserPreference()
    {
        FavouriteColor = new SolidColorBrush(Colors.Blue);
        FavouriteFont = new FontFamily("Gabriola");
    }
}
```

Now, you can bind to this object directly in your App.xaml:

```xml
<Application xmlns="http://schemas.microsoft.com/winfx/2006/xaml/presentation"
             xmlns:x="http://schemas.microsoft.com/winfx/2006/xaml"
             x:Class="StyleBindingExample.App"
             xmlns:my="clr-namespace:StyleBindingExample"
             >
    <Application.Resources>
        <my:UserPreference x:Key="preference" />

        <Style TargetType="TextBlock">
            <Style.Setters>
                <Setter Property="FontSize" Value="40" />
                <Setter Property="FontFamily" Value="{Binding FavouriteFont,
Source={StaticResource preference}}" />
                <Setter Property="Foreground" Value="{Binding FavouriteColor,
Source={StaticResource preference}}" />
            </Style.Setters>
        </Style>
    </Application.Resources>
</Application>
```

Relative Source Binding to Ancestors

Relative source binding allows you to create bindings to properties in its parent (or any one of its ancestors). This is particularly useful for something like a data template in a list box, for instance. But it can also be demonstrated with the following simple XAML snippet:

```
<StackPanel Tag="Top Level">
    <StackPanel Tag="Next Level">
        <StackPanel Tag="Lowest Level">
            <TextBlock Text="{Binding Path=Tag, RelativeSource={RelativeSource
AncestorLevel=1, AncestorType=StackPanel}}"></TextBlock>
            <TextBlock Text="{Binding Path=Tag, RelativeSource={RelativeSource
AncestorLevel=2, AncestorType=StackPanel}}"></TextBlock>
            <TextBlock Text="{Binding Path=Tag, RelativeSource={RelativeSource
AncestorLevel=3, AncestorType=StackPanel}}"></TextBlock>
        </StackPanel>
    </StackPanel>
</StackPanel>
```

In this example, I've set the Tag property on the StackPanel at the three different levels to different values. The TextBlock binds the Text property to a RelativeSource property specifying at what ancestor level it needs to find the control and also what type of control it needs to bind to. Silverlight will display a stack panel, with three TextBlock controls showing the values in the order Lowest Level, Next Level, and Top Level.

Markup Extensions in XAML

Custom markup extensions have been around in WPF and have now been introduced to Silverlight 5. In previous releases of Silverlight, you probably used markup extensions that were already built into Silverlight, but never realized you were using them. Some of the commonly used ones include {Binding} and {StaticResource}. As the name implies, it extends the standard XAML syntax.

Creating and using a custom markup extension is a lot more intuitive when reading the XAML as shown in the following example. The XAML uses a custom markup extension called TruncationExtension that truncates the length of string to just 12 characters as follows:

```
<StackPanel x:Name="LayoutRoot" Background="White">
    <TextBlock Text="{my:TruncationExtension Text=Mahesh Krishnan, Length=12}"  />
    <TextBlock Text="{my:TruncationExtension Text=Alex Mackey, Length=12}" />
    <TextBlock Text="{my:TruncationExtension Text=William Tulloch, Length=12}" />
</StackPanel>
```

To create your own markup extension, you either need to derive from the MarkupExtension class or implement IMarkupExtension<T>. The code for the class TruncationExtension, which we have used in this example, is shown below:

```
public class TruncationExtension : IMarkupExtension<string>
{
    public string Text { get; set; }
    public int Length { get; set; }

    public string ProvideValue(IServiceProvider serviceProvider)
    {
        return (Text.Length > Length) ?
```

```
        string.Format("{0}...", Text.Substring(0, Length-3)) :
        Text;
}
```

The XAML Debugging Experience

One of the new features of Silverlight 5 is the ability to set breakpoints in XAML and inspect values. This is particularly helpful when you use databinding. As with setting a breakpoint in code, click the margin of the line at which you want to set a breakpoint. When the application is run, the debugger will break in the line as shown in Figure 13-11.

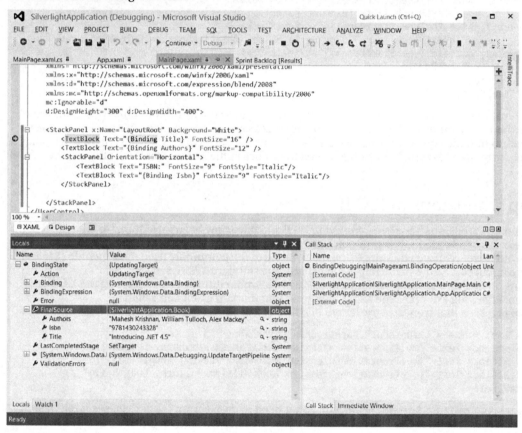

Figure 13-11. Breakpoints and Locals window in XAML

Notice that the Locals window is showing the BindingState, which in turn shows the kind of action being performed (UpdatingTarget, in this case), and FinalSource, which shows the value of fields that are being data bound.

Changes to Graphics

One of the big changes introduced in Silverlight 5 is the ability to add 3D graphics to your application. In addition, there are some changes made to improve the performance of animations. These two changes are covered in this section.

3D in Silverlight

Silverlight 5 now supports 3D graphics that will come in handy if you are creating games, graphs, and charts or modeling objects. To code 3D graphics in Silverlight, you need to learn XNA, which is out of the scope of this book. You also need to install DirectX SDK and XNA Game Studio on to your workstation. The Solar Wind 3D application found at `http://code.msdn.microsoft.com/Solar-Wind-3D-Sample-4cb56170` is a good 3D graphics sample application shipped by Microsoft.

■ **Note** GPU Accelerator must be turned on in the plug-in in order to run 3D. You also need to get user confirmation to run the graphics or run the application in elevated trust mode.

Independent Animations

Typically, animations run on the UI thread. This is not necessarily bad, but when you have CPU-intensive work also running on the same thread, your animation can become jerky. One way to fix the problem is to move the CPU-intensive work to a background thread. Another way to solve this is to use independent animations. Independent animations, which have been introduced with Silverlight 5, allow you to run animations in a separate thread. This thread is called a composition thread. Silverlight will automatically promote your animation to use this thread if you enable hardware acceleration for the plug-in and set the `BitmapCache` property on the element you are animating.

■ **Caution** If you use certain types of unsupported drawing features, Silverlight will not use independent animations. Pixel shader is an example of an unsupported drawing feature.

Changes to Trusted Applications

With Silverlight 5, you can now create top-level windows for trusted applications running Out-of-Browser. In addition, you also have unrestricted access to the file system and can make calls to unmanaged code present in DLLs. These changes are covered in this section.

Multiple-Window Support

While running your application in Out-of-Browser, or OOB, mode, you can now create additional top-level windows. These windows are instances of the newly introduced Window class and need to be created in code.

Creating Multiple Windows

To see how this works, follow these steps:

1. Choose File ➤ New ➤ Project… from the menu or press Ctrl+Shift+N. This will bring up the New Project dialog box. Choose Silverlight from the left-side options and select Silverlight Application from the list to create a new Silverlight project. In this sample, I have used WindowDemo as the project name.

2. The newly created solution will contain two projects—WindowDemo and WindowDemo.Web. Select the WindowDemo project from the Solution Explorer and press Alt + Enter to open up the Properties window.

3. Turn on the Enable running application out of the browser check box and then press the Out-of-Browser Settings… button to bring up the Out-of-Browser Settings dialog box. Turn on the Require elevated trust check box when running out of the browser check box and then press OK.

4. Open MainPage.xaml page by double-clicking it from the Solution Explorer.

5. Add a button to the page from the toolbox and from the properties panel, add a button-click event handler by double-clicking the Click event, and add code as shown in the following snippet:

```
private void Button_Click_1(object sender, RoutedEventArgs e)
{
    var window = new Window
    {
        Height = 300,
        Width = 400,
        Title = "Hello World Window"
    };

    window.Show();
}
```

6. Now press F5 to run the program and press the button in the screen to display the hello world window.

Adding Content to the Window

An empty window without any content is meaningless except in a demo. So, let's see how we can add content to this window:

1. Right-click the Silverlight project from the Solution Explorer and select Add ➤ New Item. When the Add New Item dialog box opens up, select a Silverlight User Control from the list box and press OK.

2. Update the content of the newly created control by dragging and dropping controls or editing its XAML directly.

3. Update the code that creates the new window to specify the content as shown in the following code snippet:

```
var window = new Window
{
    Height = 300,
    Width = 400,
    Title = "Hello World Window",
    Content = new SilverlightControl1()
};
```

Unrestricted File System Access

With Silverlight 4, there were restrictions on where you could read or write files. These restrictions have now been removed in Silverlight 5. The only caveat, of course, is that you run the application in Full Trust mode. Once in that mode, you can create directories, and read or write files anywhere in the file system. This simple code snippet is an example of creating a HelloWorld.txt file in the temp directory:

```
private void WriteToFile()
{
    var fileName = @"C:\temp\HelloWorld.txt";
    using (var fs = File.CreateText(fileName))
    {
        fs.WriteLine("Hello World!");
    }
}
```

Calling Native Code from Silverlight

With Silverlight code, you can now call unmanaged native code from within a fully trusted Silverlight application. This has massive implications as you can do fairly low-level stuff such as interfacing with your bar code reader or call any function from a DLL that event talks to drivers installed on your machine.

■ **Caution** Calling native code only works on machines running on the Windows operating system. If you are running Silverlight on a Mac, for instance, this feature will not work.

Calling native code in Silverlight is done in a similar way as to how it is done in the rest of .NET—using P/Invoke or Platform Invoke. The following code snippet shows how it is used with a simple

MessageBeep function that is found in User32.dll. As with regular .NET, the attribute DllImport is used in front of the extern function to declare it. Once it is declared, it can be used like any normal function:

```
[DllImport("User32.dll")]
private static extern bool MessageBeep(uint type);

private void Button_Click (object sender, RoutedEventArgs e)
{
    MessageBeep(0);
}
```

■ **Tip** The site http://pinvoke.net contains all the DllImport definitions of all the native Windows DLLs. It is a great site to look for any specific methods you may want to use in your Silverlight application. Just copy and paste the definitions from the site onto your own class and use them.

Performance Improvements

Last but not least, Silverlight 5 has also made significant performance improvements in a number of areas. The main ones include the following:

- Improved XAML parse times

- Performance improvements around network latency

- Performance improvements around laying out text blocks.

- 64-bit browser support

- Hardware accelerated rendering when running in IE 9 Windowless mode

You do not need to make any changes to your code to make use of these improvements. They are just built into Silverlight 5.

Conclusion

The emergence of HTML5 in the last two years has seriously challenged platforms such as Silverlight, which probably does not have a long-term future; however, it is still being widely used due to the ease with which you can create Rich Internet Applications. It will be a number of years before it is eventually replaced with another technology. But until such time, new features and improvements continue to happen in Silverlight. In Silverlight 5, a number of improvements have been made to Text, to XAML, to graphics support, and in the area of writing trusted applications. These changes have been covered in depth in this chapter

■ ■ ■

CHAPTER 14

Windows 8 Applications

From a .NET developer's point of view, one of the most significant releases in 2012 is Visual Studio 2012. But from Microsoft's point of view, the most significant release would have to be that of Windows 8. Applications specifically written for Windows 8 bring a big paradigm shift not only in how users experience applications, but also in how developers write them. This chapter talks about how you can get started creating these new styles of applications using Visual Studio 2012.

Windows 8 Apps

Windows has been the predominant operating system used in PCs for a long time. Microsoft originally thought that they could put this OS onto other devices such as PDAs, mobile phones, and other handheld devices and the same success would follow. In fact, I used to think that some of the older smart phones, which ran a modified version of the Windows operating system for the phone, were really cool—they even ran applications such as Excel on them!

I, like several other users, didn't know any better until the iPhone was launched. The iPhone provided a user experience that incorporated touch, fluid animation, and sensors such as a gyro, accelerometer, proximity sensors, and GPS in such a way that it left its competitors far behind. When the iPhone, and later the Android smart phones, started dominating the market, Microsoft took notice. Microsoft went back to the drawing board and came up with a brand-new design and OS to run on its smart phones. This new design had the following design principles:

- **Typography:** The designers believed that type is beautiful and well-placed type can lead to more content. They believed that apart from being visually pleasing, type can also be functional.

- **Motion:** The designers believed that motion is a very key part of bringing an application to life—so transitions and animations are very important in a UI design.

- **Content, not chrome:** Running the phone on a small form factor meant that the emphasis had to be on the content—the information the user needs and cares about—more than the chrome, which includes all the UI elements such as toolbars and menus that surround it.

- **Honesty:** The phone delivers digital content, and the designers believed that the design should be authentically digital (in other words, not pretend to be something else or use metaphors in design to signify that it isn't digital).

Although the Windows Phone 7, which uses the new design for its apps, is still a distant third behind Android and iPhones in terms of market share in the smart-phone segment, Microsoft saw the potential of new-style apps. The success of iPad and Android tablet devices also opened up a fast growing market segment that Microsoft could just not ignore—touch-based devices.

To counter these threats, Microsoft has come up with a strategy to create and run new-style applications on the next version of its operating system—Windows 8. Windows 8 will run on both tablets and desktops, and it brings a shift in the way that applications are developed, how they are installed, and how users interact with these applications.

The principles behind the new design, which Microsoft now refers to as Modern UI (see sidebar), extend what was originally designed for the phone into Windows 8 and are listed as follows:

- **Show pride in craftsmanship**: Make sure UI designers and developers focus on the smallest of things in the application and are pixel perfect in every way.

- **Be fast and fluid**: Be extremely responsive to user interaction and use things such as touch and animation to create a compelling user experience.

- **Be authentically digital**: Embrace the fact that application runs in a digital medium and create applications accordingly.

- **Do more with less**: Focus more on the content, remove clutter, and ensure that the user does not have any distractions while working with the application.

- **Win as one**: Seamlessly combine with other applications as well as the devices present in the system to work as one.

These applications will be sold via the Windows Store, and they are also referred to as Windows Store apps.

MODERN UI, WINDOWS 8 APPS, WINDOWS STORE APPS

As you read through this book and other material that is available in the public domain (including documentation from Microsoft), you will come across applications written for Windows 8 being referred to as Windows 8 apps or Windows Store apps. You will also see the term Modern UI being used.

Classic Apps

So, what happens to all the existing applications that have been written in .NET? Does all this new Windows 8/Modern UI stuff mean we have to throw them away? Not at all. That would make all the previous chapters in this book redundant, wouldn't it?

You can still write applications for .NET, and they will continue to run on Windows 8. There are some apps that will be really well suited for the Modern UI principles, some that may require quite a few changes, and some that may just not be suitable. For example, running Visual Studio as a Windows Store app may not work at all. But there are several line-of-business apps that may fit really well with the Modern UI's design principles.

The non-Windows 8 apps—the ones that will continue to run in .NET or Silverlight—will coexist with the newer style of apps. Some people call them *legacy apps*, but I prefer the term *classic apps*.

■ **Note** The Windows 8 operating system will run on a wide range of hardware and form factors including tablets running on ARM processors. The version of Windows 8 running on tablets with ARM processors is called Windows RT, and it will have restrictions on the applications it can run. Apart from certain applications such as Microsoft Word and Excel, it can only run apps purchased through the Windows Store.

Windows 8 Apps—Fundamentals

Writing Windows 8 applications is quite different to the way you've been writing applications so far. Apart from certain guidelines on how the user interface should look like, it has quite a few things that should be taken into consideration—like running applications full screen, how long-running operations should be async, how applications communicate with each other, and so on. This section gives you an introduction to these concepts.

Writing Code in Windows: A Brief History

When Windows first came out several years ago, developers used to write code in C. The Windows SDK, which the applications accessed, was available in DLLs that were shipped with Windows. People then moved on to writing applications using other languages such as C++, but the underlying SDK still remained the same. Although additions and changes were made to this SDK with newer versions of the operating system, fundamentally it stayed the same. When .NET came about, people had a choice of using several languages such as C# and VB.NET to write applications in order to run on Windows, but the .NET runtime itself ran on Windows and used the Windows SDK.

Code written to run directly on the Windows SDK using a language such as C++ is referred to as *native code*, and code written to run on the .NET Common Language Runtime (CLR) is referred to as *managed code*. .NET provided a nice layer of abstraction over the Windows SDK, and it also provided features such as garbage collection and the ability to program in modern programming languages.

If you want to continue writing code using .NET for Windows, it is still possible in Windows 8. In addition, a new Windows runtime, or WinRT, has been introduced that lets you write Windows 8 applications using code that looks like .NET code but runs directly on the WinRT. On the surface, WinRT looks like a subset of .NET, but it really isn't. Even though it contains a lot of classes that .NET developers are familiar with and use the same .NET languages to code, it contains a whole range of changes and a new programming paradigm that developers will have to learn. In addition, one of the key inclusions is the ability to code in HTML5 and JavaScript.

Let's look at part of this paradigm shift that I talk about in the subsequent sections.

Embrace the Modern UI Guidelines

At the beginning of this chapter, I spoke briefly about the Modern UI design guidelines. The Modern UI, or the UX, is markedly different from any other designs you may have encountered in the past. Touch is now a first-class citizen, and your application needs to ensure that it works well with touch gestures. You need to ensure that the touch targets are large enough to be "fat-finger" friendly.

In addition, your applications have to be fast and fluent with animations and transitions. Modal message boxes and dialog boxes are passé in the Modern UI. So, you need to figure out how you to get around that. You also need to think about how users navigate from one screen to another.

Windows Store apps are fully immersive apps—what this means is that they run full screen and as mentioned earlier, we need to think "content not chrome." In other words, we need to figure out how we provide the equivalent of toolbars and menus to users.

■ **Tip** Microsoft has provided a rich set of resources on the Modern UX design principles. You can find these resources at `http://msdn.microsoft.com/library/windows/apps/hh779072`.

Install through Windows Store

When users want to install your Windows 8 application, they install it through the Windows Store. So, as a developer, you no longer need to create an installer or worry about how you provide newer versions of your applications to your users. Instead, you package and submit your application to the Windows Store where people can either buy it or install it for free.

If you already own a smart phone and download applications to it this way, you are already familiar with this paradigm.

When a newer version of your application is available, Windows Update notifies your users of the newer version and they may choose to update the application. When they no longer need your application, they just remove it and Windows will take care of all the cleanups.

■ **Note** If you are a developer, you can install an unpackaged app to the OS without having to go through the Windows Store.

Everything Is Async (Well, Almost)

Windows has had multi-threading support from its very early days, but updating the UI could only be done through one thread—this thread, which is referred to as the UI thread, is responsible for processing user actions such as mouse moves and also updating the various screen elements. If you use this thread to perform a long-running operation, it makes the operating system unresponsive.

One of the main tenets of Windows 8 is to make applications fast and fluid. Having an unresponsive UI because of a long-running task on the UI thread would defeat this. So, the designers of Windows 8 decided that in the Modern UI, all calls that take up time to execute will have to be asynchronous. If a method has the potential to take more than 50ms to complete, it will have to be an asynchronous call.

So, if you make a call to the operating system to read a file or make a call to another server across the network, it will have to be async. As it turns out, about 10–15% of calls in WinRT had to be made asynchronous in order to keep the UI thread responsive. As you learned in earlier chapters, the introduction of await-async in C# makes this easier.

Everything Is Restricted (Well, Kinda)

All along, when you've written applications, you've been able to access file system resources such as the document or picture library, devices such as webcams, or even use the network rather freely. In

Windows Store apps, you only have restricted access. Before you start panicking, let me clarify that this is not as bad as it sounds.

When you write your application, you need to create a manifest file where you request access to these "capabilities." When you submit your application to the Windows Store, Microsoft will check to make sure that the capabilities you have requested are in line with what the application supposedly does. Customers can also look at the capabilities the application uses before they decide to install it. Some of the capabilities that Windows 8 apps support include the following:

- Documents, music, pictures, and video libraries

- Microphone and webcams

- Text messaging

- Removable storage

- Location

- Proximity

- Internet, public, and private networks

- Certificate store

Your Application Runs Forever (Well, At Least It Appears To)

When you want to close an application now, all you have to do is hit the *x* at the top of your window or press File ➤ Exit from the menu. In a fully immersive application in Windows 8, you generally don't see these options. So, your application seemingly runs forever—well, at least as long as the system allows it to. When there are too many applications running and the system runs out of resources, the operating system may decide to close Modern UI applications that are not currently active (but running in the background).

▓ **Tip** You can close an application in Windows 8 if you really want to although most people would not bother. Just hit Alt+F4. If that doesn't work, touch the top of your application (or click on the top of the application with your mouse when your cursor changes to a hand). Then when the size of the screen changes, drag it to the bottom of the screen and drop it.

When the user decides to start a Windows 8 application again, it has to start off from where the user left it originally. This means that you, as a developer, should have saved the state of the application including the documents and the screen it was in before the application was closed by Windows— maybe even the cursor position. This brings with it challenges and new ways of thinking on how and when to save all this information.

RIP, SAVE BUTTON

Most applications that you use on a day-to-day basis like Word, Excel, or if you are a developer, Visual Studio, all have a Save button in the tool bar—and the data the user has typed into the document doesn't get saved until the user presses this button.

This Save button is usually represented in the toolbar as a three-and-half-inch floppy disk—something that isn't even used anymore. This relic from the past is an indication that the Save button has seen its use-by date. Under the new paradigm, the Save button doesn't exist. Applications automatically save what the users have typed, and if the users don't want it to be saved, they just undo their operations. I know, it sounds quite extreme, but welcome to the new world of thinking.

Applications Running in the Background Aren't Really Running …

Like any modern OS, you can run multiple applications at once in Windows 8. These applications can also have multiple threads and do different things simultaneously. However, users interact with only one application at a time, and Windows 8 applications run full screen (there are exceptions to this rule, but for the most part, they do run full screen), which means that there can only be one active application. When your application is active, it means all the other Windows 8 apps are not active. There are three states in which an application can be in: *Not running*, *running*, and *suspended*.

As soon as you start or switch to another application, that app moves into the running state and pushes the previously running application into a suspended state. As the system starts to run out of resources, a suspended application is shut down and it moves to a Not running state.

When an application is in the running state, the system gives it all the attention it needs. The application is therefore very responsive and fast. As soon as the application moves in to a suspended state, it does not get any attention from the OS—not even a single CPU cycle. *Does that mean you can't run anything in the background?* Not exactly. There are some ways to get around this problem, which we will look at later.

Interfacing with Other Windows 8 Apps

Windows 8 also allows Windows 8 Store apps to communicate with other Windows 8 Store apps. *But how do you communicate and what do you communicate?* This is specified by a mechanism known as *contracts*. Your application can share its content with another application by providing a source contract that other applications can use, or your application can provide a target contract and use the content from another application that provides the source to you.

Like capabilities, these contracts are also specified in the manifest file. Some common contracts available in Windows 8 apps are the following:

- **Search contract:** Allows users to search your application

- **Share contract:** Allows users to share content of your application with other apps

- **Play to contract:** Allows users to play digital media in your application

Enough Talk

Now that you've gotten an overview of Windows 8 applications and what they do, let's see what the screens look like.

Figure 14-1 shows the Start screen with the Windows 8 applications present in the machine. This is the kind of screen that will show up as soon as you log in to Windows 8. If you are familiar with the Windows Phone user interface, you will see an immediate parallel with the way the screen is presented with tiles. The tiles on the screen are "live tiles." In other words, they will automatically update themselves when new content for the tile arrives.

Figure 14-1. The Start screen

To scroll to the right or left of the screen, you use your finger to flick the screen left or right. If your computer does not support touch, you can still use the scrollbar at the bottom of the screen to scroll to the left or right to look at other applications. To launch an application from the start screen, all you need to do is tap the tile (or click with your mouse).

Figure 14-2 shows a typical Windows 8 app—the weather app running. There are a few things you will notice about the application straight away:

- It is a fully immersive application. That is, it runs full screen.

- It has no chrome. In other words, there are no window frames or menus to clutter the screen.

- As you click on arrows icons on the screen, you see fluid animation when things show up or disappear.

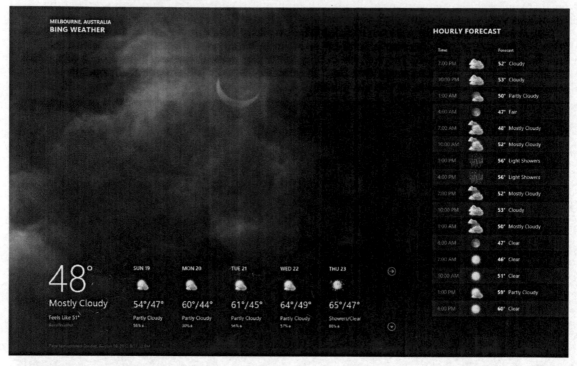

Figure 14-2. A typical Windows 8 app

If you are running the same weather app that you have on screen, you must be wondering how you can change the city for which you want the weather information displayed. After all, there are no menus or buttons to do that. This is where the application bar, or AppBar, comes into play. Right-click the mouse and you will see the AppBar appear on the screen, as shown in Figure 14-3. You can also get the AppBar by swiping your finger up from the bottom of the screen.

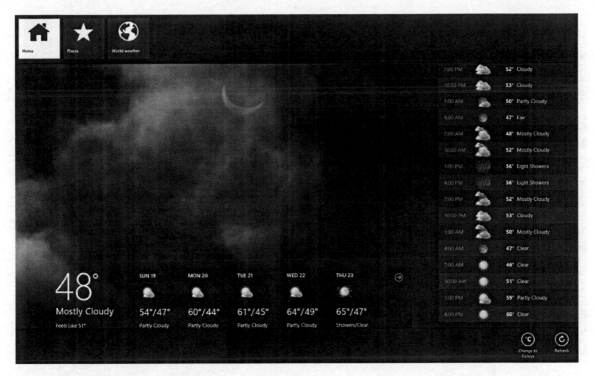

Figure 14-3. The AppBar in action

Depending on the type of application and what you are currently doing in the application, you may have the AppBar appear both at the top and bottom. This gives you application-specific options. In this case, there are options to look at world weather, remove the city for which the weather is being displayed, and so on.

One of the key features of Windows 8 apps is the ability to share information with other applications. Let's assume you are reading a news article in one of the Windows 8 applications and you want to share this on Facebook, Twitter, or even through your mail. You can do this by invoking what are known as *Charms* and selecting the Share option from it. You can invoke Charms at any time while your application is running by swiping the right-hand side of the tablet with your finger or just by moving your mouse to the right bottom corner of the screen. Figure 14-4 shows Charms in action.

Figure 14-4. Charms in action

You can use Charms to search for specific things in your application, share your application data with others, go back to the Home or Start screen, use devices to print, or use settings to change application-related settings.

Figure 14-5 shows the Share options available for the USAToday application—in this case, just mail.

Figure 14-5. Sharing application data with others

Sometimes you may want to see what is happening in one application (say, your mail client) while continuing to use another (such as your browser). In these scenarios, Windows 8 allows your Modern UI apps to be snapped to one side, while the other application is still active. Figure 14-6 shows one such example: the weather application is snapped to the side while the main application where you are reading the news occupies the major portion of your screen. You can write your application to be smart enough to show a different view to the user when it is snapped to the side as the screen real estate available to you is limited.

Figure 14-6. Application snapped to the side

Figure 14-7 shows the roles reversed where the USAToday application is snapped while the Bing Weather app takes center stage. You will notice that the image in the USAToday app is much smaller and the text is formatted differently.

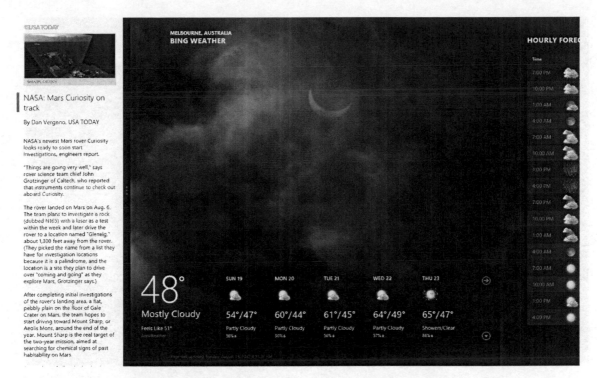

Figure 14-7. Application snapped to the side

To switch between applications in Windows 8, you simply press Alt+Tab as you used to. You can also press Windows+Tab to bring the Application-switching panel on the side as shown in Figure 14-8. This panel can be useful to see what applications are running before you switch to them.

Figure 14-8. Application-switching panel

Creating Your First Windows 8 Store App

There are two main ways in which you can create Windows 8 Store apps::

- **Using XAML and a language such as C#, VB.NET, or C++:** In this case, the view or the UI is created using XAML. If you have written applications using WPF or Silverlight, you will already be familiar with XAML. The code behind file for XAML, where all the logic lies, is written in a language such as C#, C++, or VB.NET. In the examples used in this chapter, we stick to just XAML and C#.

- **Using HMTL5, CSS, and JavaScript:** In this case, the view or UI is written using HTML and CSS. The code that runs the application is written in JavaScript. Developers who currently write applications for the web may find writing applications using HTML5 and JavaScript for Windows 8 applications a lot easier.

■ **Note** The choice of using XAML or HTML to write the application does not affect the way the application looks or behaves. But as WinRT is written in C++, using C++ along with XAML may give you the best results in terms of performance.

Your First Windows Store App Using XAML/C#

To write your first Windows Store application in C#, follow these steps:

1. Select File ➤ New ➤ Project from the menu to bring up the New Project dialog box. Select the Windows Store template listed under Visual C# on the left panel to reveal a set of Windows Store app projects you can create, as shown in Figure 14-9.

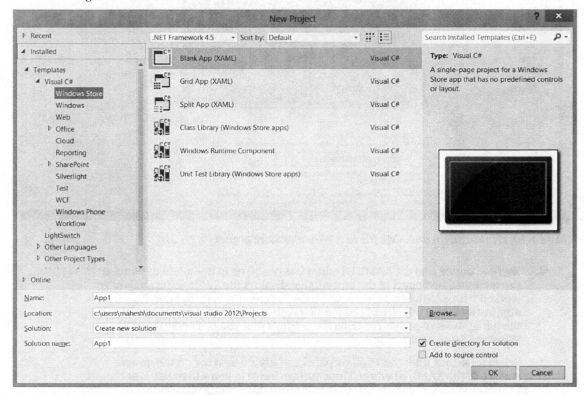

Figure 14-9. Create project dialog box for a Windows Store app

2. Select the Blank Application option from the list of available projects, type in a name for the project, and press OK. This will create a Windows Store project with two XAML files called App.xaml and MainPage.xaml. In addition, you will also have additional files and folders that have been automatically generated for you.

3. Open the MainPage.xaml file in Visual Studio by double-clicking it. It will open the XAML file in the XAML designer and the screen will look similar to Figure 14-10.

333

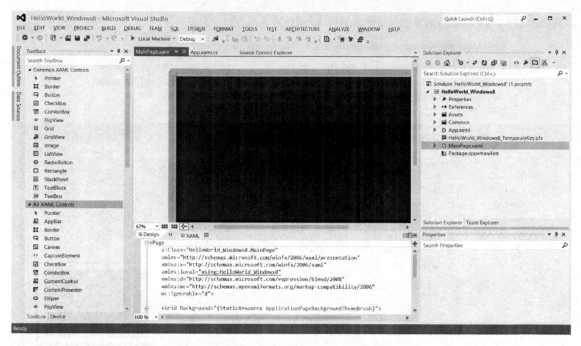

Figure 14-10. Working with an XAML file in a Windows Store project

4. You will notice that the XAML UI editor has two parts to it— a design panel at the top and a text panel at the bottom that displays the XAML as text. If you've worked with XAML before in Visual Studio for creating WPF or Silverlight applications, you will already be familiar with it. A toolbox panel is available on the left of the screen that contains the controls that you can add to your Windows Store application.

5. Select a TextBox from the Toolbox panel and draw a TextBox on the design surface of the XAML UI editor. Once you've drawn it, you will notice that the Properties panel shows the properties for the added text box, as shown in Figure 14-11. If the Properties panel is not visible, press Alt+Enter.

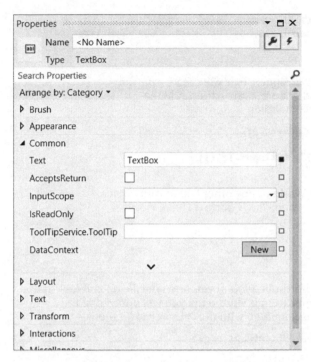

Figure 14-11. Properties panel

6. Set the name for the text box to txtInput in the Properties panel. This is needed to access the control from the code behind file.

7. Add a button and a text box to the MainPage.xaml file as well and set the name of the TextBlock to txtOutput.

8. Increase the size of the fonts of the added controls so they look nice and big, set the button Content property to Say Hello, and clear the Text properties of the TextBox and TextBlock. Once you've done all that, the XAML for the file should look like the following snippet:

```
<Page
    x:Class="HelloWorld_Windows8.MainPage"
    xmlns="http://schemas.microsoft.com/winfx/2006/xaml/presentation"
    xmlns:x="http://schemas.microsoft.com/winfx/2006/xaml"
    xmlns:local="using:HelloWorld_Windows8"
    xmlns:d="http://schemas.microsoft.com/expression/blend/2008"
    xmlns:mc="http://schemas.openxmlformats.org/markup-compatibility/2006"
    mc:Ignorable="d">
    <Grid Background="{StaticResource ApplicationPageBackgroundThemeBrush}">
        <TextBox x:Name="txtInput" HorizontalAlignment="Left" Height="66" Margin="50,42,0,0"
TextWrapping="Wrap" VerticalAlignment="Top" Width="414" FontSize="48"/>
        <Button Content="Say Hello" HorizontalAlignment="Left" Height="66" Margin="469,42,0,0"
VerticalAlignment="Top" Width="275" FontSize="36"/>
```

```
        <TextBlock x:Name="txtOutput" HorizontalAlignment="Left" Height="151"
Margin="50,113,0,0" TextWrapping="Wrap" VerticalAlignment="Top" Width="694" FontSize="48"/>
    </Grid>
</Page>
```

9. Double-click the button from the XAML designer. This will create a button click handler in the code behind file and open it in the editor. Add the following line (shown in bold) to the even handler:

```
private void Button_Click_1(object sender, RoutedEventArgs e)
{
    txtOutput.Text = string.Format("Hello, {0}", txtInput.Text);
}
```

10. Press F5 to run the application. Type in World or any other text of your choice into the text box, hit the Say Hello button and watch the text Hello, World appear.

The App.xaml and App.xaml.cs Files

The App.xaml.cs file contains the entry point into the application. If you open the file up and look at the OnLaunched method, which gets called when the application is started up, you will notice that the MainPage class is created here. Following is the code generated with the OnLaunched method:

```
protected override void OnLaunched(LaunchActivatedEventArgs args)
{
    if (args.PreviousExecutionState == ApplicationExecutionState.Terminated)
    {
        //TODO: Load state from previously suspended application
    }

    // Create a Frame to act navigation context and navigate to the first page
    var rootFrame = new Frame();
    rootFrame.Navigate(typeof(MainPage));
    // Place the frame in the current Window and ensure that it is active
Window.Current.Content = rootFrame; Window.Current.Activate();
}
```

The App.xaml file contains resource dictionaries that hold styles and templates common to the whole application. If you open the file, you will see that it includes one resource dictionary called Common/StandardStypes.xaml. This file contains standard styles of the resources that you can use in your Windows Store app. The markup in App.xaml file follows:

```
<Application
    x:Class="HelloWorld_Windows8.App"
    xmlns="http://schemas.microsoft.com/winfx/2006/xaml/presentation"
    xmlns:x="http://schemas.microsoft.com/winfx/2006/xaml"
    xmlns:local="using:HelloWorld_Windows8">
    <Application.Resources>
        <ResourceDictionary>
            <ResourceDictionary.MergedDictionaries>
```

```
            <!--
                Styles that define common aspects of the platform look and feel
                Required by Visual Studio project and item templates
            -->
            <ResourceDictionary Source="Common/StandardStyles.xaml"/>
        </ResourceDictionary.MergedDictionaries>
    </ResourceDictionary>
    </Application.Resources>
</Application>
```

Assets and Common Folder

If you open up the Solution Explorer to look at the auto-generated files and folders, you will notice two folders—one called Assets and the other called Common (see Figure 14-12).

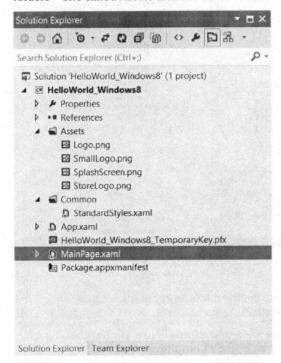

Figure 14-12. Solution Explorer showing folders created by default—Assets and Common

The Assets folder contains images that are used for the logo, the splash screen (when the application is starting up), and the image to be used when the application is published to the Windows Store.

The Common folder, according to the documentation, contains classes and XAML styles that simplify application development. You would have seen that the StandardStyles.xaml file is used as a resource dictionary in the previous section. New files get added in this folder when you add new items to the project. For instance, if you add a Basic Page from the Add New Item dialog box, a bunch of files get added under this folder.

337

The Manifest File

You saw in the previous section that the Assets folder contains images that can be used for logos within the application. *But how does Windows know which image to use and for what?* This is where the application manifest file comes into play.

If you double-click the `Package.appxmanifest` file from the Solution Explorer, it will open the manifest file within Visual Studio. The manifest file opened in Visual Studio is shown in Figure 14-13 and contains four tabs—Application UI, Capabilities, Declaration, and Packaging.

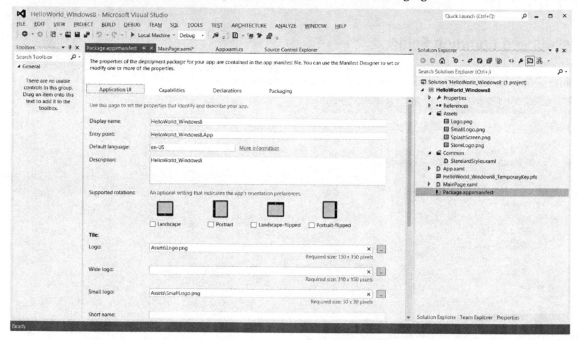

Figure 14-13. The manifest file of a Windows Store app

- **Application UI:** This tab contains the options to set the name, entry point, images for logos, supported initial rotations, and so forth.

- **Capabilities:** This contains the capabilities that the application will use. Options include items such as use of document library, webcam, microphone, removable storage, the Internet, and so on.

- **Declarations:** This tab contains declarations for the applications. Declarations are used to specify features such as whether this application will be a share target, whether it can provide search, and so forth.

- **Packaging:** This tab is used to set properties that will be used to package the application before it is deployed to Windows Store.

Controls in Windows Store Apps

If you are already familiar with Silverlight or WPF, you will feel right at home with the controls in Windows 8. You will find that most of the controls that you've been using in WPF or Silverlight are also present in Windows 8. Table 14-1 lists some of the popular controls.

Table 14-1. Common controls in Windows Store apps

Control	Description
AppBar	Container for holding buttons and other UI components for the application bar
Border	Control for drawing a border around another control
Button	Button control that can be pressed
Canvas	A container where controls can be explicitly positioned
CheckBox	Control that allows user to have a checked and unchecked state, in addition to an indeterminate state
ComboBox	Control that combines a drop-down list box and a read-only text box
Ellipse	A control for drawing an ellipse
FlipView	Used to display items one at a time, but having a flip behavior for navigating through a list of `FlipViewItems`
Frame	A content control that supports navigation
Frame	A content control that supports navigation
Grid	A container that holds controls in rows and columns
HyperlinkButton	A hyperlink that can be clicked to perform an action—like a button
Image	Control that displays an image
ListView	Displays a list of data items
Popup	Container to display its contents as a popup
ProgressRing	Control that displays a spinning ring, which is used to indicate an action in progress

Control	Description
RadioButton	A button that is used to make a selection—radio buttons are mutually exclusive. In other words, if another button in the same group is pressed, then the currently checked button is unchecked.
Rectangle	A control that draws a simple rectangle
RichEditBox	A text box that supports rich text content such as fonts, images, and hyperlinks
RichTextBlock	A TextBlock that supports rich text content
ScrollBar	Used for scrolling
ScrollViewer	Container that includes items that can be scrolled
SemanticZoom	A control that has a zoomed-in version and zoomed-out version of itself
Slider	A control that contains a thumb that can be used to represent a certain value and can also be used interactively to change the value
StackPanel	A container that stacks its controllers either vertically or horizontally
TextBlock	A control that is used to display readonly text
TextBox	A control that is used to capture user input

Laying Out Controls

There are a whole bunch of containers, such as Grid, StackPanel, WrapGrid, and ScrollViewer, that can be used to lay out your controls. The most commonly used container is Grid, which is the default container when you create pages in a Windows Store app from Visual Studio.

The usage of a Grid control is very similar to its counterpart in WPF and Silverlight. You initialize a set of Column and Grid definitions in XAML and add controls to individual cells of the grid. The following is a sample XAML snippet for a Grid control:

```
<Grid Background="{StaticResource ApplicationPageBackgroundThemeBrush}">
    <Grid.ColumnDefinitions>
        <ColumnDefinition Width="121*"/>
        <ColumnDefinition Width="562*"/>
    </Grid.ColumnDefinitions>
    <Grid.RowDefinitions>
        <RowDefinition Height="50*"/>
        <RowDefinition Height="60*"/>
        <RowDefinition Height="500*"/>
    </Grid.RowDefinitions>
    <Button Content="Button 1"  />
    <Button Content="Button 2" Grid.Column="1"/>
```

```
        <Button Content="Button 3" Grid.Column="1"  Grid.Row="1" />
    </Grid>
```

A StackPanel is another container that is very simple to use. All you need to do is add controls to it, and it automatically places them either vertically or horizontally based on the Orientation property. The following is a sample XAML snippet for a StackPanel:

```
<StackPanel  Orientation="Horizontal">
    <Button Content="Button 1"  />
    <Button Content="Button 2" />
    <Button Content="Button 3" />
</StackPanel>
```

You will notice that the XAML for these controls are exactly the same as the ones used for Silverlight or WPF. Other containers such as Canvas or ScrollViewer also work the same.

A Look at Some Windows 8 App Specific Controls

Controls for Windows 8 apps, such as Button, TextBox, and ListBox, work exactly like their WPF and Silverlight counterparts. In addition to these controls, there are some new controls that have been added to help with the Modern UI style. Let's look at a few of them.

The AppBar

Earlier in this chapter, we saw how the AppBar is used in Windows Store applications (Figure 14-3). To add an AppBar to your application, all you need to do is drag and drop the AppBar control from the toolbox on to your page and configure its properties.

The buttons in the AppBar use a special style called AppBarButtonStyle that is defined in the StandardStyles.xaml file that gets auto-generated for you when you create the file in Visual Studio. The font used in the AppBar buttons is Segoe UI Symbols. This font provides symbols that allow you to display Windows 8 style icons in these buttons. In the following markup, the AppBar is placed at the bottom of the page and contains four buttons in a horizontal StackPanel—one each for the different symbols in a deck of playing cards, as shown in Figure 14-14. This AppBar will automatically show up when the user presses the right button when the application is running (or do the right swipe action in the case of a tablet).

```
<Page
    x:Class="Win8Controls.MainPage"
    xmlns="http://schemas.microsoft.com/winfx/2006/xaml/presentation"
    xmlns:x="http://schemas.microsoft.com/winfx/2006/xaml"
    xmlns:local="using:Win8Controls"
    xmlns:d="http://schemas.microsoft.com/expression/blend/2008"
    xmlns:mc="http://schemas.openxmlformats.org/markup-compatibility/2006"
    mc:Ignorable= "d">
    <Page.BottomAppBar>
        <AppBar HorizontalContentAlignment= "Stretch" Height= "88"
VerticalContentAlignment= "Stretch" >
            <StackPanel Grid.Column= "1" Orientation= "Horizontal">
                <Button Content= "&#x2661;" Style= "{StaticResource AppBarButtonStyle}"
AutomationProperties.Name= "Heart" />
```

```
                    <Button Content= "&#x2662;" Style= "{StaticResource AppBarButtonStyle}"
AutomationProperties.Name= "Diamond"/>
                    <Button Content= "&#x2664;" Style= "{StaticResource AppBarButtonStyle}"
AutomationProperties.Name= "Spade"/>
                    <Button Content= "&#x2667;" Style= "{StaticResource AppBarButtonStyle}"
AutomationProperties.Name= "Clover"/>
            </StackPanel>
        </AppBar>
    </Page.BottomAppBar>
...
</Page>
```

■ **Tip** To find out what the symbols in Sego UI Symbol font look like and to use them in your application, you can use the Insert Symbol dialog box from Microsoft Word. Just browse through the symbols present, choose a symbol, insert it into Word, and then cut and paste it into your application. Although you can paste the symbol directly into the Content of a button, the preferred approach is to paste the hexadecimal value as in the previous snippet.

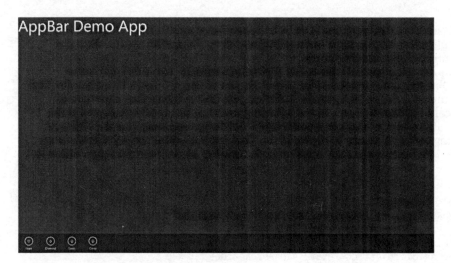

Figure 14-14. Sample app with an AppBar

In addition to the style AppBarButtonStyle in StandardStyles.xaml, there are a few other styles for commonly used button types. These styles are, however, commented out, as you may not require all of them. To use them in your own markup, uncomment these styles from StandardStyles.xaml and simply use them in your own code. For example, to display buttons with Yes, No, or Edit in the AppBar, you need to find the styles YesAppBarButtonStyle, NoAppBarButtonStyle, and EditAppBarButtonStyle in StandardStyles.xaml and uncomment them. You can then simply specify the style:

```
        <AppBar HorizontalContentAlignment="Stretch" Height="88"
VerticalContentAlignment="Stretch" >
            <StackPanel Grid.Column="1" Orientation="Horizontal">
                <Button Style="{StaticResource YesAppBarButtonStyle}" />
                <Button Style="{StaticResource NoAppBarButtonStyle}" />
                <Button Style="{StaticResource EditAppBarButtonStyle}" />
            </StackPanel>
        </AppBar>
```

You can explore all the pre-defined button styles by looking in the StandardStyles.xaml file

The FlipView

When you have a list of items that need to be displayed one at a time, such as a series of images, then the FlipView control can be used. Figure 14-15 shows an example of a FlipView in action. You will be able to flip between the images in the example by just swiping your finger across or clicking the arrows that appear on the sides.

A very simple example of a FlipView control is shown in the following markup:

```
<StackPanel Background="{StaticResource ApplicationPageBackgroundThemeBrush}">
    <TextBlock Margin="30" Style="{StaticResource HeaderTextStyle}" Text="FlipView
Example" />
    <FlipView Margin="30">
        <FlipViewItem>
            <Image Source="Images/Image1.JPG" />
        </FlipViewItem>
        <FlipViewItem>
            <Image Source="Images/Image2.JPG" />
        </FlipViewItem>
        <FlipViewItem>
            <Image Source="Images/Image3.JPG" />
        </FlipViewItem>
    </FlipView>
</StackPanel>
```

Figure 14-15. A FlipView example

As seen in the markup, `FlipView` is merely a collection of `FlipViewItem` objects. Each `FlipViewItem` can contain other controls in them, but like a list box, you can also specify an `ItemTemplate` that defines the databinding and the view of individual fields:

```
<FlipView ItemsSource="{Binding Source={StaticResource mySource}}">
    <FlipView.ItemTemplate>
        <DataTemplate>
            <StackPanel Margin="20">
                <TextBlock Text="{Binding Title}" FontSize="32" />
                <Image Source="{Binding Image}" />
            </StackPanel>
        </DataTemplate>
    </FlipView.ItemTemplate>
</FlipView>
```

CarouselPanel

The `CarouselPanel` helps you to scroll through a list of items using simple finger gestures. When you reach the end of the list, the carousel automatically starts from the beginning. You can also use the mouse scrollview and scrollbar to scroll, but this control comes in very handy with finger swipes. A very simple XAML implementation that allows you to scroll through a small set of images is shown in the following code snippet:

```
<ListBox Width="300" Height="700"  HorizontalAlignment="Left"  >
    <ListBoxItem>
        <Image Source= »Images/Image1.JPG » />
    </ListBoxItem>
    <ListBoxItem>
        <Image Source= »Images/Image2.JPG » />
    </ListBoxItem>
    <ListBoxItem>
```

```
            <Image Source= »Images/Image3.JPG » />
        </ListBoxItem>
        <ListBox.ItemsPanel>
            <ItemsPanelTemplate >
                <CarouselPanel />
            </ItemsPanelTemplate>
        </ListBox.ItemsPanel>
    </ListBox>
```

The resulting image will look like Figure 14-16. You will notice how as you scroll past the last item in the list, the first item starts appearing again.

Figure 14-16. CarouselPanel starting to display the first item as it scrolls past the last item

---

■ **Note** The CarouselPanel can only be used with an ItemsControl.

SemanticZoom

SemanticZoom is used to display and navigate through a large set of data. Like the other controls we've discussed in this section, the SemanticZoom control is also heavily optimized for touch gestures. It allows you to tap, swipe, pinch, and stretch with your fingers to navigate through large amounts of data.

The SemanticZoom control has two zoom modes:

- Zoomed-in mode where you can look at items in a fine-grained way

- Zoomed-out mode where you can look at items in a coarse-grained way, usually by some kind of grouping

To see how this works, drag and drop the SemanticZoom control on to an empty page. The markup that gets generated for you looks like the following:

```
<SemanticZoom>
    <SemanticZoom.ZoomedInView>
        <GridView/>
    </SemanticZoom.ZoomedInView>
    <SemanticZoom.ZoomedOutView>
        <ListView/>
    </SemanticZoom.ZoomedOutView>
</SemanticZoom>
```

As you can see, there is a ZoomedInView and a ZoomedOutView element in the generated markup. Inside these markups, you will find empty GridView and ListView controls. You need to replace these empty views with the right markup to get the SemanticZoom to work.

Figure 14-17 shows a zoomed-in view, and Figure 14-18 shows a zoomed-out view of a simple book collection. The book collection is grouped by genre, and as you can see from the figure, when the SemanticZoom is zoomed out, only the genre is shown, and when it is zoomed in, it shows details of all the books under each genre.

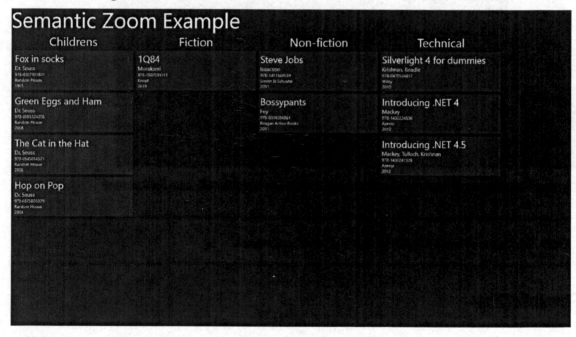

Figure 14-17. Zoomed-in view in a SemanticZoom control

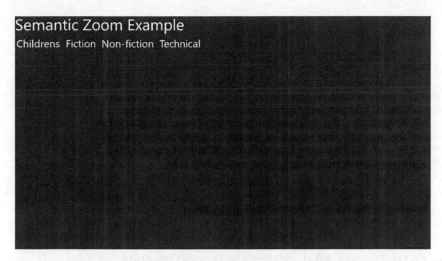

Figure 14-18. Zoomed-out view in a SemanticZoom control

In order for this example to work, follow these steps:

1. From Visual Studio, select File ➤ New ➤ Project… to bring up the New Project dialog box. Select the Windows Store style template on the left panel in the dialog box and then select Blank Application from the project template list. Change the name of the application to SemanticZoom.

2. Open the MainPage.xaml file and add a resource section by adding the following markup to the file:

```
<Page
    x:Class="SemanticZoom.MainPage"
    xmlns="http://schemas.microsoft.com/winfx/2006/xaml/presentation"
    xmlns:x="http://schemas.microsoft.com/winfx/2006/xaml"
    xmlns:local="using:SemanticZoom"
    xmlns:d="http://schemas.microsoft.com/expression/blend/2008"
    xmlns:mc="http://schemas.openxmlformats.org/markup-compatibility/2006"
    mc:Ignorable= "d">
    <Page.Resources>
        <CollectionViewSource x:Name="BookCollection" IsSourceGrouped="True"
ItemsPath="Items"/>
        <DataTemplate x:Key="BookTemplate">
            <Border Background="{StaticResource ListViewItemPlaceholderBackgroundThemeBrush
}">
                <StackPanel Margin="5" HorizontalAlignment="Left" Width="400">
                    <TextBlock Text="{Binding Title}" FontSize="32"  />
                    <TextBlock Text="{Binding Authors}" FontSize="18"/>
                    <TextBlock Text="{Binding Isbn}" FontSize="14"/>
                    <TextBlock Text="{Binding Publisher}" FontSize="14"/>
                    <TextBlock Text="{Binding YearPublished}" FontSize="14"/>
                </StackPanel>
```

```
        </Border>
      </DataTemplate>
    </Page.Resources>
...
</Page>
```

This markup creates a static resource called BookCollection, to which we are going to add a list of books. The property IsSourceGrouped is set to true to indicate that we will be grouping the list, and the property ItemsPath is used to identify the name of the property that contains the list of items in that group. In addition, we've also added a data template called BookTemplate to display an object with the properties Title, Authors, Isbn, Publisher, and YearPublished.

3. Replace the Grid present in the file with the following markup:

```
...
</Page.Resources>
  <StackPanel Background="{StaticResource ApplicationPageBackgroundThemeBrush }">
      <TextBlock Text="Semantic Zoom Example" FontSize="72"/>
      <SemanticZoom HorizontalAlignment="Left" >
          <SemanticZoom.ZoomedInView>
              <GridView  x:Name="ZoomIn" Height="700" SelectionMode="None"
                         ItemsSource="{Binding Source={StaticResource BookCollection}}"
                         ItemTemplate="{StaticResource BookTemplate}"
                         VerticalAlignment="Center">
                  <GridView.GroupStyle>
                      <GroupStyle>
                          <GroupStyle.HeaderTemplate>
                              <DataTemplate>
                                  <StackPanel HorizontalAlignment="Center">
                                      <TextBlock Text="{Binding Genre}" FontSize="40"
HorizontalAlignment="Center"/>
                                  </StackPanel>
                              </DataTemplate>
                          </GroupStyle.HeaderTemplate>
                      </GroupStyle>
                  </GridView.GroupStyle>
              </GridView>
          </SemanticZoom.ZoomedInView>
          <SemanticZoom.ZoomedOutView>
              <ListView x:Name="ZoomOut" Height="700" SelectionMode="None"
VerticalAlignment="Center" >
                  <ListView.ItemTemplate>
                      <DataTemplate>
                          <TextBlock Text="{Binding Group.Genre}" FontSize="48" />
                      </DataTemplate>
                  </ListView.ItemTemplate>
                  <ListView.ItemsPanel>
                      <ItemsPanelTemplate>
                          <StackPanel Orientation="Horizontal" />
```

```
                </ItemsPanelTemplate>
            </ListView.ItemsPanel>
        </ListView>
      </SemanticZoom.ZoomedOutView>
    </SemanticZoom>
  </StackPanel>
</Page>
```

This markup adds two controls to the page—a TextBlock to hold the title of the application and a SemanticZoom control. The SemanticZoom's ZoomedInView contains a GridView control that is databound to the BookCollection object we added as a static resource in Step 2. The SematicZoom's ZoomedOutView contains a list panel that just displays the different genres.

4. Open the file MainPage.xaml.cs and add a method called InitData as shown:

```
private void InitData()
{
    var data = new[]
    {
        new { Title="Silverlight 4 for dummies", Isbn="978-0470524657 " , Publisher="Wiley",
Authors="Krishnan, Beadle" , YearPublished="2010" , Genre="Technical" },
        new { Title="Introducing .NET 4", Isbn="978-1430224556" , Publisher="Apress",
Authors="Mackey" , YearPublished="2010" , Genre="Technical" },
        new { Title="Introducing .NET 4.5", Isbn="978-1430243328" , Publisher="Apress",
Authors="Mackey, Tulloch, Krishnan" , YearPublished="2012" , Genre="Technical" },
        new { Title="Fox in socks", Isbn="978-0307931801" , Publisher="Random House ",
Authors="Dr. Seuss" , YearPublished="1965" , Genre="Childrens" },
        new { Title="Green Eggs and Ham ", Isbn="978-0583324205 " , Publisher="Random House
", Authors="Dr. Seuss" , YearPublished="2008" , Genre="Childrens" },
        new { Title="The Cat in the Hat", Isbn="978-0545014571 " , Publisher="Random House ",
Authors="Dr. Seuss" , YearPublished="2008" , Genre="Childrens" },
        new { Title="Hop on Pop", Isbn="978-0375828379 " , Publisher="Random House",
Authors="Dr. Seuss" , YearPublished="2004" , Genre="Childrens" },
        new { Title="Steve Jobs", Isbn="978-1451648539 " , Publisher="Simon & Schuster",
Authors="Isaacson" , YearPublished="2011" , Genre="Non-fiction" },
        new { Title="Bossypants", Isbn="978-0316056861" , Publisher="Reagan Arthur Books",
Authors="Fey" , YearPublished="2011" , Genre="Non-fiction" },
        new { Title="1Q84", Isbn="978-0307593313" , Publisher="Knopf", Authors="Murakami" ,
YearPublished="2619" , Genre="Fiction" },
    };

    var query = from item in data
                orderby item.Genre
                group item by item.Genre into g
                select new { Genre = g.Key, Items = g };

    BookCollection.Source = query.ToList();
    ZoomOut.ItemsSource = BookCollection.View.CollectionGroups;

}
```

This code creates a sample data for a collection of books, and we've also got a LINQ query that groups the data based on their genre. In addition, the source of the BookCollection object declared in the resources is set and the ZoomOut ListView control's ItemsSource is set.

5. From the constructor of the page, call InitData to initialize the data:

```
public MainPage()
{
    this.InitializeComponent();
    InitData();
}
```

6. Now press F5 to run the application. The application will open up in the zoomed-in view. If you use your scroll wheel, while pressing down the Control button (zoom out) or just pinching the display with your fingers, the zoomed-out view will be visible.

7. To zoom in again, you can either click on the genre grouping or stretch the screen with your fingers.

Sharing Data with Other Applications

One of the nice things about Windows Store apps is the ability to share information from your application with others. To see how this works, follow these steps:

1. Create a new Windows Store blank app project. You can give it any name you want, but I've chosen the name ShareSource.

2. Open MainPage.xaml file and replace the content with the following XAML:

```
<Page
    x:Class="ShareSource.MainPage"
    IsTabStop="false"
    xmlns="http://schemas.microsoft.com/winfx/2006/xaml/presentation"
    xmlns:x="http://schemas.microsoft.com/winfx/2006/xaml"
    xmlns:local="using:ShareSource"
    xmlns:d="http://schemas.microsoft.com/expression/blend/2008"
    xmlns:mc="http://schemas.openxmlformats.org/markup-compatibility/2006"
    mc:Ignorable="d">

    <StackPanel Background="{StaticResource ApplicationPageBackgroundThemeBrush}">
        <TextBlock Text="Sharing Text Application" Style="{StaticResource HeaderTextStyle}" />
        <TextBox x:Name="txtShare" Margin="40" AcceptsReturn="True" Height="300" FontSize="24"
/>
    </StackPanel>
</Page>
```

This adds two controls to the display, one TextBlock for the title of the application, and one TextBox that will hold the contents of the text that needs to be shared with other applications.

3. Open the `MainPage.xaml.cs` file and modify the `OnNavigatedTo` method as shown in the following code snippet:

```
protected override void OnNavigatedTo(NavigationEventArgs e)
{
        DataTransferManager.GetForCurrentView().DataRequested +=
_dataTransferManager_DataRequested;
}
```

This adds an event handler for the current view when data is requested.

4. Now, add an event handler method that sends the text data from the text box by setting properties in the DataRequestedEventArgs parameter that is passed to the event as shown in the following code snippet:

```
void _dataTransferManager_DataRequested(DataTransferManager sender, DataRequestedEventArgs
args)
{
    var textToShare = txtShare.Text;
    var requestData = args.Request.Data;

    requestData.Properties.Title = "Sharing text for textbox";
    requestData.Properties.Description = textToShare;
    if (!String.IsNullOrEmpty(textToShare))
    {
        requestData.SetText(textToShare);
    }
    else
    {
        args.Request.FailWithDisplayText("Textbox is empty");
    }
}
```

The DataPackage object called requestData contains methods such as SetText, SetUri, and SetBitmap that are used to pass data from the screen on to other applications that can accept such data.

5. Now press F5 to run the application. If you invoke the Share charm without typing anything into the text box, you will see the message "Textbox is empty" as shown in Figure 14-19.

Figure 14-19. Message from the application when there is nothing to share

If you entered any text into the text box, the Share panel will show all the applications that can consume the text content. In this case, there is only one application—Mail, as shown in Figure 14-20.

Figure 14-20. Sharing text from the text box

Picking Data from Other Applications

In the previous section, you saw how your application can be ShareSource, but typically, you want to create applications that can also be a ShareTarget. In other words, you want applications that consume data from other applications. To create a simple application that consumes text data (which is an inverse of the previous example), follow these steps:

1. Create a new Windows Store blank app project. You can give it any name you want, but I've chosen the name ShareTargetApp.

2. Right-click the project from the Solution Explorer and choose Add ➤ New Item…

3. In the Add New Item dialog box, select Share Target Contract, change the name of the file to ShareTargetPage.xaml, and press OK.

4. You will be prompted with a message box to add certain dependencies into the project automatically. Press Yes to add the files automatically. This will add files to the common folder, create a ShareTargetPage.xaml file, make modifications to the application manifest file, and also changes to the App.xaml.cs file.

5. Press F5 to run the application. You will notice that all you get is an empty screen. This is because you haven't made any changes to the MainPage.xaml file, and as we want to keep this example simple, this is totally fine. Press

Alt+F4 to close the application. We really want to invoke this application from another application that wants to share data with it.

6. Now, run the ShareSource example that we created in the previous section, type something in to the text box, and invoke the Share Charm. You will notice that the ShareTargetApp will also be shown in the list of apps with which you can share data, as shown in Figure 14-21.

Figure 14-21. Sharing data with our Share Target

7. Choose the ShareTargetApp from the Charms menu. This will display a panel for sharing data with the ShareTargetApp, as shown in Figure 14-22.

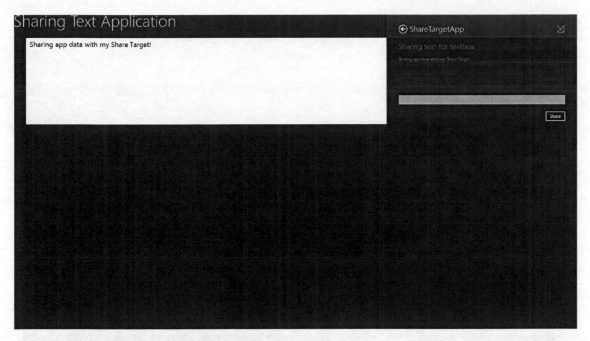

Figure 14-22. Sharing data with ShareTargetApp

8. You can type some additional comments in the field shown and press Share to start sharing the data with the ShareTargetApp.

The Magic That Binds It All Together

I am sure the first question that comes to your mind is *How does the ShareSource application know that it can share information with the ShareTargetApp?* The answer to that lies in the application manifest file. When you added the Share Target Contract item to the project, Visual Studio automatically updated the application manifest file to specify which data formats can be shared with this application. To manually set this, open the Package.appxmanifest file from the Solution Explorer by double-clicking it. Open the Declarations tab, which should look like Figure 14-23.

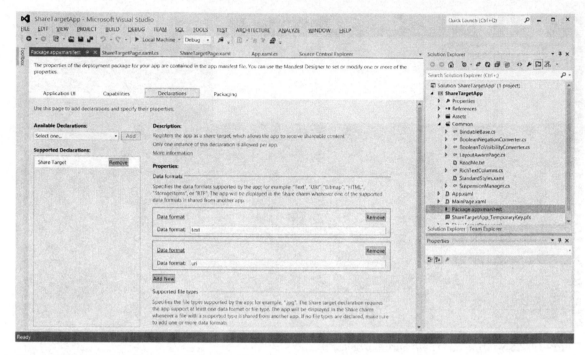

Figure 14-23. Declarations tab in the manifest file

The Share Target declaration is used by Windows 8 apps to specify that it can act as a share target, and the Data Formats Properties section allows you to specify what data formats you can use within your application. In this example, it supports both text and URI. You can also add file types that this application can support by adding them in the Supported file types section.

Invoking the Share Target UI

In the previous example, the file that Visual Studio code generated to display the user interface when invoked as a share target from another application is ShareTargetPage.xaml. You can change this file to suit your application needs, but a very simple way of extending it is to replace the to-do comments in the XAML that was generated:

```
<common:LayoutAwarePage
    x:Name="pageRoot"
    x:Class="ShareTargetApp.ShareTargetPage"
    DataContext="{Binding DefaultViewModel, RelativeSource={RelativeSource Self}}"
    IsTabStop="false"
    xmlns="http://schemas.microsoft.com/winfx/2006/xaml/presentation"
    xmlns:x="http://schemas.microsoft.com/winfx/2006/xaml"
    xmlns:local="using:ShareTargetApp"
    xmlns:common="using:ShareTargetApp.Common"
    xmlns:d="http://schemas.microsoft.com/expression/blend/2008"
    xmlns:mc="http://schemas.openxmlformats.org/markup-compatibility/2006"
```

```xml
    mc:Ignorable="d"
    d:ExtensionType="ShareTarget">

<Page.Resources>
    <common:BooleanToVisibilityConverter x:Key="BooleanToVisibilityConverter"/>
    <common:BooleanNegationConverter x:Key="BooleanNegationConverter"/>
</Page.Resources>

<!--
    This grid acts as a root panel for the page that defines three rows:
    * Row 0 contains the standard share target header.
    * Row 1 contains a TextBox for adding a comment.
    * Row 2 contains the standard share target footer.
-->
<Grid Style="{StaticResource LayoutRootStyle}">
    <Grid Margin="40,20,40,60">
        <Grid.RowDefinitions>
            <RowDefinition Height="180"/>
            <RowDefinition Height="Auto"/>
            <RowDefinition Height="*"/>
        </Grid.RowDefinitions>
        <Grid.ColumnDefinitions>
            <ColumnDefinition Width="Auto"/>
            <ColumnDefinition Width="*"/>
        </Grid.ColumnDefinitions>
        <!-- The standard share target header displays metadata about the shared item -->
        <Image
            Source="{Binding Image}"
            Stretch="Uniform"
            Visibility="{Binding ShowImage, Converter={StaticResource
BooleanToVisibilityConverter}}"
            VerticalAlignment="Top"
            MinWidth="80"
            MinHeight="80"
            MaxWidth="240"
            MaxHeight="160"
            Margin="0,0,20,0"/>
        <StackPanel Grid.Column="1">
            <TextBlock
                Text="{Binding Title}"
                Margin="0,-10,0,20"
                TextWrapping="NoWrap"
                Foreground="{StaticResource ApplicationSecondaryForegroundThemeBrush}"
                Style="{StaticResource SubheaderTextStyle}"/>
            <TextBlock
                Text="{Binding Description}"
                MaxHeight="60"
                Foreground="{StaticResource ApplicationSecondaryForegroundThemeBrush}"
                Style="{StaticResource BodyTextStyle}"/>
        </StackPanel>
        <Grid Grid.Row="1" Grid.ColumnSpan="2">
            <!-- TODO: Add application scenario-specific sharing UI -->
```

```
            </Grid>
            <TextBox
                Grid.Row="1"
                Grid.ColumnSpan="2"
                Margin="0,0,0,27"
                Text="{Binding Comment}"
                Visibility="{Binding SupportsComment, Converter={StaticResource
BooleanToVisibilityConverter}}"
                IsEnabled="{Binding Sharing, Converter={StaticResource
BooleanNegationConverter}}"/>
            <!-- Standard share target footer -->
            <Grid Grid.Row="2" Grid.ColumnSpan="2">
                <ProgressRing
                    IsActive="{Binding Sharing}"
                    MinWidth="20"
                    MinHeight="20"
                    HorizontalAlignment="Left"
                    VerticalAlignment="Top"
                    Margin="0,5,0,0"/>
                <TextBlock
                    Text="Sharing&#x2026;"
                    Visibility="{Binding Sharing, Converter={StaticResource
BooleanToVisibilityConverter}}"
                    HorizontalAlignment="Left"
                    Margin="25,0,0,0"
                    Style="{StaticResource ItemTextStyle}"/>
                <Button
                    AutomationProperties.AutomationId="ShareButton"
                    AutomationProperties.Name="Share"
                    TabIndex="1"
                    Content="Share"
                    IsEnabled="{Binding Sharing, Converter={StaticResource
BooleanNegationConverter}}"
                    HorizontalAlignment="Right"
                    VerticalAlignment="Top"
                    Margin="0,-5,-3,0"
                    Click="ShareButton_Click"/>
            </Grid>
        </Grid>
    </Grid>
</common:LayoutAwarePage>
```

In the code behind of this file, you need to replace the to-do section in comments to perform whatever action you want to do when data is shared with your application:

```
private void ShareButton_Click(object sender, RoutedEventArgs e)
{
    this.DefaultViewModel["Sharing"] = true;
    this._shareOperation.ReportStarted();

    // TODO: Perform work appropriate to your sharing scenario using
    //       this._shareOperation.Data, typically with additional information captured
```

```
//         through custom user interface elements added to this page such as
//         this.DefaultViewModel["Comment"]

    this._shareOperation.ReportCompleted();
}
```

In addition to this file, Visual Studio also makes some modifications to App.xaml.cs, so that it calls the Activate method on the ShareTargetPage class when the share target is invoked:

```
protected override void OnShareTargetActivated
(Windows.ApplicationModel.Activation.ShareTargetActivatedEventArgs args)
{
    var shareTargetPage = new ShareTargetApp.ShareTargetPage();
    shareTargetPage.Activate(args);
}
```

Handling the Life Cycle of a Windows Store App

A Windows Store application, as mentioned in an earlier section, runs only when it is the active application. When another application is started, the currently running application is suspended, and the other application becomes the active application. When you switch back to the suspended application, it becomes the active one, and any other application that was running becomes suspended. When the operating system needs more resources, it terminates a suspended application and it moves to a terminated state. There are also other states the application can be in, as explained in Table 14-2.

Table 14-2. Application states in a Windows Store app

State	Remarks
NotRunning	This basically means the application is not running. This is the state the application is after it has been installed from the Windows Store, terminated (or even crashed!) when the application is running, or after a reboot or re-login.
Running	This means the application is running. An application can be invoked either by clicking on a tile or switched back to it after it is suspended.
Suspended	When the user switches over to another application, the current app goes into a suspended state. It can also occur when Windows enters a low-power state. When the application is in a suspended state, it continues to remain in memory.
Terminated	When an application is closed after being in a suspended state, it is terminated. This typically happens when the system needs resources to run other applications.
ClosedByUser	This occurs due to a user-initiated close when the application is running—it is triggered either by a Close gesture or pressing Alt+F4.

When an application is run, you need to check in your startup script what the previous state was and perform some actions accordingly. In particular, you should check if your application was terminated. If it was, then you need to restore the application's previous session state and continue from where the user left off. This could mean switching the user to the right screen and restoring the fields and scroll position to exactly the same state as they were when the user switched away from the application.

So, where do you store session data and how do you do it? The answer to the first question is simple—in local storage. The answer to the second question is a little bit more complicated, but you do it using the SuspensionManager. The SuspensionManager is a class that gets automatically generated when you add a Basic Page to your project (by right-clicking the project in Solution Explorer and choosing Add ➤ New Item). The Basic Page template also generates a class called LayoutAwarePage, which has virtual methods called LoadState and SaveState that you override in your derived classes. The page that the Basic Page template generates is also derived from LayoutAwarePage.

The SuspensionManager class has a method called RegisterFrame, which allows the navigation history of the frame to be saved and restored by the session manager. The SuspensionManager also has methods called SaveAsync and RestoreAsync that take care of saving and retrieving the session data using local storage.

■ **Tip** While debugging your application from Visual Studio, the Windows Store application doesn't really get suspended. *So, how can you test it?* The answer is simple—Visual Studio has a toolbar called Debug Location. The toolbar contains options to Suspend, Resume, and Suspend and shutdown. This can be used to put the application in the state you desire.

To see how this all falls together, follow this example:

1.   Create a new blank app project. You can give it any name you want, but I've chosen the name LifeCycleSampleApp.

2.   Right-click the project from Solution Explorer and choose Add ➤ New Item… When the Add New Item dialog box appears, select the Basic Page template from the list, change the name of the file to BasicPage.xaml, and press OK. You will be prompted whether you want to add missing files automatically. Press Yes. This will not only add the BasicPage.xaml file to your project, but also add a whole heap of files such as SuspensionManager.cs and LayoutAwarePage.cs

3.   Open the App.xaml.cs file and add the following line to the top of the file:

```
using LifeCycleSampleApp.Common;
```

This ensures that we can use the SuspensionManager class in the App.xaml.cs file.

4.   Change the method OnLaunched to be async and also call the RestoreAsync method present in the SuspensionManager manager as shown in the following code snippet:

```
protected override async void OnLaunched(LaunchActivatedEventArgs args)
{
    // Do not repeat app initialization when already running, just ensure that
    // the window is active
    if (args.PreviousExecutionState == ApplicationExecutionState.Running)
    {
```

```
        Window.Current.Activate();
        return;
    }

    if (args.PreviousExecutionState == ApplicationExecutionState.Terminated)
    {
        //TODO: Load state from previously suspended application
        await SuspensionManager.RestoreAsync();
    }

    // Create a Frame to act navigation context and navigate to the first page
    var rootFrame = new Frame();
    if (!rootFrame.Navigate(typeof(MainPage)))
    {
        throw new Exception("Failed to create initial page");
    }

    // Place the frame in the current Window and ensure that it is active
    Window.Current.Content = rootFrame;
    Window.Current.Activate();
}
```

5. Before the application restores the state, it needs to be saved. To do that, modify the OnSuspending method to call the SaveAsync method present in the SuspensionManager as shown:

```
private async void OnSuspending(object sender, SuspendingEventArgs e)
{
    var deferral = e.SuspendingOperation.GetDeferral();
    //TODO: Save application state and stop any background activity
    await SuspensionManager.SaveAsync();
    deferral.Complete();
}
```

6. The code generated App.xaml.cs file navigates to the MainPage.xaml at startup. You can either change the MainPage class to derive from the LayoutAwarePage base class or change the App.xaml.cs file to load the BasicPage class you created. For this example, use the latter. In addition, you also need to register the frame with the SuspensionManager. Replace the OnLaunched method as shown to allow for these changes:

```
protected async override void OnLaunched(LaunchActivatedEventArgs args)
{
    // Do not repeat app initialization when already running, just ensure that
    // the window is active
    if (args.PreviousExecutionState == ApplicationExecutionState.Running)
    {
        Window.Current.Activate();
        return;
    }
    // Create a Frame to act navigation context and navigate to the first page
    var rootFrame = new Frame();
```

```
    SuspensionManager.RegisterFrame(rootFrame, "rootFrame");
    if (args.PreviousExecutionState == ApplicationExecutionState.Terminated)
    {
        //TODO: Load state from previously suspended application
        await SuspensionManager.RestoreAsync();
    }

    if (!rootFrame.Navigate(typeof(BasicPage)))
    {
        throw new Exception("Failed to create initial page");
    }

    // Place the frame in the current Window and ensure that it is active
    Window.Current.Content = rootFrame;
    Window.Current.Activate();
}
```

7. Open the BasicPage.xaml file and add a TextBox to it as shown in the following markup:

```
<Grid Style="{StaticResource LayoutRootStyle}">
….
<TextBlock x:Name="pageTitle" Grid.Column="1" Text="{StaticResource AppName}"
Style="{StaticResource PageHeaderTextStyle}"/>
        </Grid>
        <TextBox x:Name="MyTextBox" HorizontalAlignment="Left" VerticalAlignment="Top"
Height="150" Margin="20" Grid.Row="1" TextWrapping="Wrap" Width="500" />
....
```

This TextBox is used as an example to show how the data can be persisted.

8. Open the BasicPage.xaml.cs file and add two overridden methods called LoadState and SaveState as shown in the following code snippet:

```
protected override void LoadState(Object navigationParameter, Dictionary<String, Object>
pageState)
{
    if (pageState != null && pageState.ContainsKey("TextBoxValue"))
    {
        MyTextBox.Text = pageState["TextBoxValue"] as string;
    }
}
protected override void SaveState(Dictionary<String, Object> pageState)
{
    pageState["TextBoxValue"] = MyTextBox.Text;
}
```

These methods will automatically save the state and restore the state as needed.

■ **Tip** Microsoft has provided guidelines on how Windows 8 style apps should behave during suspend and resume. It can be found at http://msdn.microsoft.com/en-US/library/windows/apps/hh465088.

Running in the Background

As you saw in the previous section, when an application is suspended, it does not receive any CPU cycles to do work. What this means is that the application that is currently running gets the user's undivided attention. There will be no lag or delay in the user interface because an application running in the background is chewing up resources or valuable CPU cycles. *Does that mean you cannot run anything in the background?* Well, kind of, but there are ways to get around this. Windows 8 has a concept of a background task that you can use to run code that doesn't have any user interaction. To use a background task, you need to implement the IBackgroundTask interface as shown:

```
using Windows.ApplicationModel.Background;
namespace BackgroundTaskApp
{
    class BackgroundTask : IBackgroundTask
    {
        public void Run(IBackgroundTaskInstance taskInstance)
        {
            //Do background operation here
        }
    }
}
```

This background task's Run method will be called by the operating system when a certain event, such as a certain time or network becoming available, is triggered. To get it to work, the application needs to do the following things:

- Register the triggers on which the application's background tasks need to be called—this is done using the application manifest file.

- Register the class that needs to be called when the trigger is reached. This is done in code.

Hooking Up a Background Task to an Application

To hook up a background task to an application, follow these steps:

1. Either create a new Windows Store application or use an existing application on which you want to add a background task.

2. From the Solution Explorer, right-click the solution file and choose Add ➤ New Project. In the Add New Project dialog box, choose the Class Library (Windows Store apps) template and call the name of the project BackgroundTasks.

3. Select the Tasks project from the Solution Explorer and press Alt+Enter. This opens up the Properties tab for the project. Change the output type to WinMD. WinMD stands for *Windows Metadata file*.

4. In the Tasks project, add a new class called BackgroundTask and make it implement the IBackgroundTask interface as shown in the following snippet:

```
using System.Diagnostics;
using Windows.ApplicationModel.Background;

namespace BackgroundTasks
{
    public sealed class BackgroundTask : IBackgroundTask
    {
        public void Run(IBackgroundTaskInstance taskInstance)
        {
            Debug.WriteLine("Starting {0}...", taskInstance.Task.Name);
            //Add your actual background task code here
            Debug.WriteLine("Finished {0}...", taskInstance.Task.Name );
        }

    }
}
```

5. To register the application so that background tasks can be called, open the application manifest file by double-clicking the Package.appxmanifest file for the Windows Store project from the Solution Explorer. Then go to the Declarations tab and from the Available Declarations drop-down list, choose Background Tasks and press Add. This will display a bunch of options as shown in Figure 14-24.

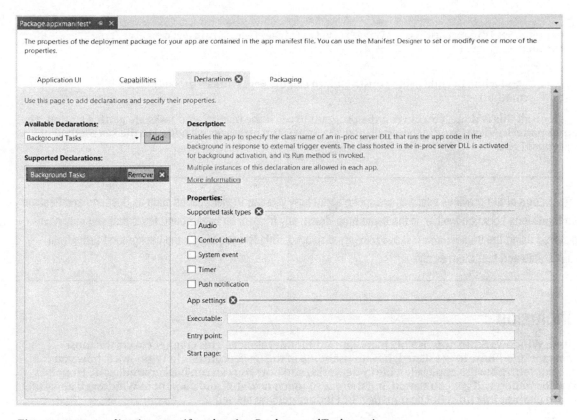

Figure 14-24. Application manifest showing BackgroundTasks options

6. In the manifest file, select the task System event for this example. In the Entry point field, you need to fill in the name of the class that implements the IBackgroundTask interface, which in this case will be BackgroundTasks.BackgroundTask.

7. Right-click the References from the Solution Explorer for the Windows Store project and choose Add References.... In the Reference Manager dialog box, choose the BackgroundTasks project and press OK.

8. To register what kind of System event to process, open the App.cs file in the Windows Store project and add a method called RegisterBackgroundTask, as shown:

```
private void RegisterBackgroundTask()
{
    var builder = new BackgroundTaskBuilder
                        {
                            Name = "My Background Task",
                            TaskEntryPoint = "BackgroundTasks.BackgroundTask"
                        };
```

```
    builder.SetTrigger(new SystemTrigger(SystemTriggerType.ServicingComplete, true));
    builder.Register();
}
```

    9.   Add a line of code in the constructor to call the `RegisterBackgroundTask` method.

Once all this is done, you can run the program to see if the background tasks are getting started. The Output panel in Visual Studio should display the Start/Stop messages we added in the `Run` method of `BackgroundTask`.

■ **Tip** In one of the previous sections, we spoke about how you can trigger actions such as Suspend and Resume from the Debug Location toolbar. In the same drop-down, any triggers for background tasks that you may have registered using the `BackgroundTaskBuilder` are displayed. This lets you trigger the background tasks from Visual Studio and test them easily.

Conclusion

Writing Windows Store apps is a big paradigm shift for developers. This chapter covers the most important bits—how to get started, how to use some of the newer controls in Windows 8, how you can share content, how the application life cycle works, and how you can run background tasks. Hopefully, this information will get you started, but there is so much new stuff and content in Windows 8 apps, that a single chapter just does not do it justice. But it does get you started …

■ **Note** We only covered XAML/C# in this chapter. A lot of web developers may end up choosing HTML/JS to do Windows 8 programming. Apress has a book called *Pro Windows 8 Development with HTML5 and JavaScript*, written by Adam Freeman, which talks about how you can build Windows 8 apps with HTML5 and JavaScript.

■ ■ ■

NuGet Introduction

NuGet is a Microsoft technology that makes it very easy to include, update, and distribute stand-alone libraries within your application. NuGet was first released a few years ago as an extension to Visual Studio 2010.

With Visual Studio 2012, NuGet is included out of the box and used extensively. For example, NuGet is used to retrieve the latest version of many project types' dependencies when projects are first created. NuGet is an excellent dependency management tool for your projects and can even include packages at build time.

NuGet Package Manager

There are a couple of ways to install NuGet packages. Probably the easiest method is using the graphical Package Manager. The package manager can be accessed in two ways. The first is from the main menu (Tools ➤ Library Package Manager ➤ Manage NuGet Packages for solution):

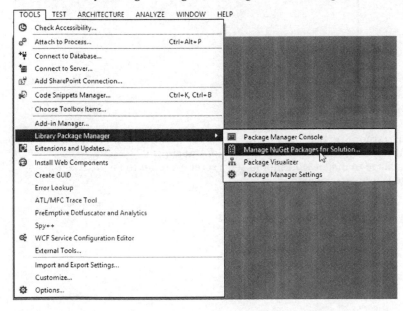

Figure A-1. Accessing NuGet from Tools menu

The second is by right-clicking on the project or solution in Solution Explorer and selecting the Manage NuGet packages option from the context menu:

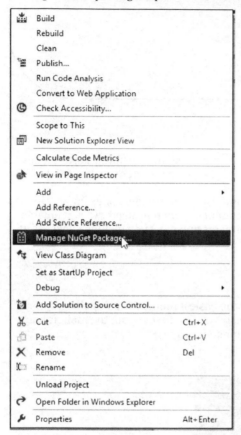

	Build
	Rebuild
	Clean
	Publish...
	Run Code Analysis
	Convert to Web Application
	Check Accessibility...
	Scope to This
	New Solution Explorer View
	Calculate Code Metrics
	View in Page Inspector
	Add ▶
	Add Reference...
	Add Service Reference...
	Manage NuGet Packages...
	View Class Diagram
	Set as StartUp Project
	Debug ▶
	Add Solution to Source Control...
	Cut Ctrl+X
	Paste Ctrl+V
	Remove Del
	Rename
	Unload Project
	Open Folder in Windows Explorer
	Properties Alt+Enter

Figure A-2. Accessing NuGet from Tools menu

It doesn't really matter which method you use, but I prefer to use the Solution Explorer method. There is also a more powerful command line interface that we will look at shortly.

Once you have opened the package manager, you should see a screen similar to Figure A-3 that allows you to install, uninstall, and update packages.

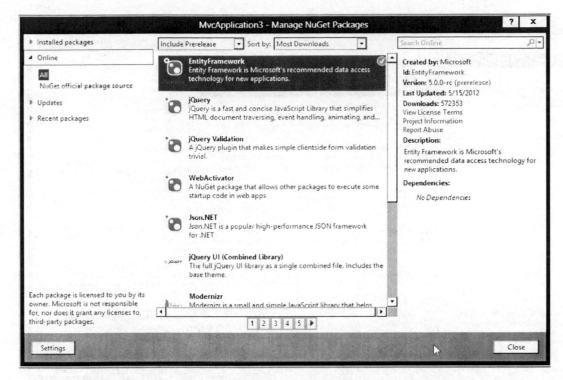

Figure A-3. Accessing NuGet package manager

Notice how the NuGet package manager has a number of tabs to allow you to review installed packages, available updates, and any recently applied packages.

The other interesting option is that if you click the Settings button, you can configure additional package sources—this might be useful in enterprises or high-security environments where you want to review and control available packages as you can put these all on a network share.

Let's install the NUnit test framework from Package Manager. Select the online tab and then in the search box search for NUnit. Packages will be filtered to match those containing this term as shown in Figure A-4.

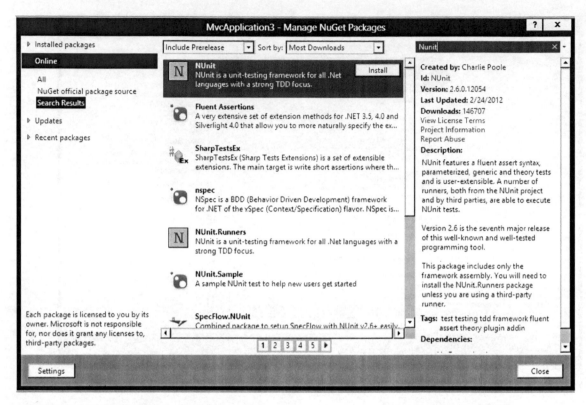

Figure A-4. NUnit packages

To install the NUnit package, click the install button and NUnit will be installed—easy, eh? If you examine your solution, you will find NUnit assembly is now referenced and a new file called packages.config has been created that just contains information about the packages installed.

If you want to remove a package, simply go to the package manager console and click the Uninstall button and it will be uninstalled (see Figure A-5).

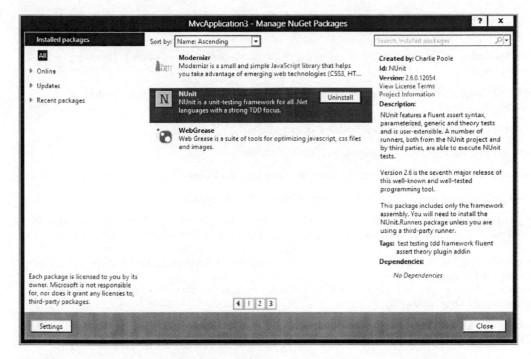

Figure A-5. Uninstall option for NUnit package

Another option for installing packages is with the NuGet command line utility.

NuGet Command Line

The NuGet command line uses Powershell (v2) with some NuGet specific extensions (called cmdlets in Powershell world). It's much more powerful than the package manager window and is used when you create your very own packages.

Let's use the command line to install the xunit framework.

To bring up the NuGet command line console, go to Tools ➤ Library Package Manager ➤ Package Manager Console and you should see a screen similar to Figure A-6.

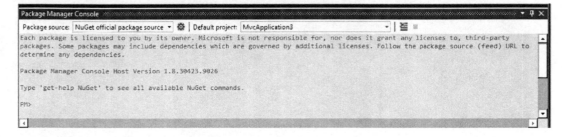

Figure A-6. Package Manager console

There are a number of different NuGet command line commands. The following list contains some of the more commonly used commands:

- `get-package -ListAvailable` (retrieves list of available packages—warning: there are a few!)

- `get-package -ListAvailable -Filter NUnit` (returns packages with NUnit in title or description)

- `install-package nunit` (installs NUnit package)

- `uninstall-package nunit` (uninstalls NUnit package)

- `get-package -updates` (gets any updates for installed packages within solution)

- `update-package nunit` (updates NUnit package to latest version)

When you install a package, it will be installed in the default project and any dependent references will also be installed. You can configure where NuGet packages are installed with the `-projectName` option.

It can be useful to get information about how to use a command. To do this, simply type get-help before the command name.

For example, get-help `install-package` will show other options for this command and you should see an output similar to the following:

```
Install-Package [-Id] <string> [-IgnoreDependencies] [-ProjectName <string>] [[-Version]
<string>] [[-Source] <string>] [-IncludePrerelease] [<CommonParameters>]
```

Creating Your Own Packages

Creating your own NuGet packages is very easy. There are again two main ways to accomplish this. By far, the easiest method is using the NuGet Package explorer tool, which can be installed from http://docs.nuget.org/docs/creating-packages/using-a-gui-to-build-packages. (If you would rather do this via the command line, which is more powerful, please refer to http://docs.nuget.org/docs/creating-packages/creating-and-publishing-a-package.)

Once you have installed the NuGet package explorer, you should see a screen similar to Figure A-7.

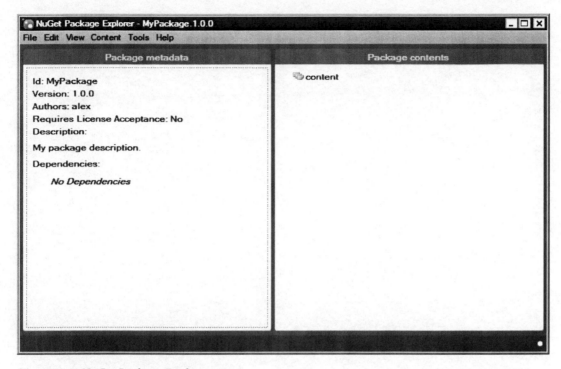

Figure A-7. NuGet Package Explorer

From this screen, you can specify your package contents by right-clicking on the right pane and selecting a context menu option. You can modify the descriptive properties of your package by selecting Edit ➤ Edit Package Meta data. Once you have created your package, simply select Save from the File menu. You can then install it by doubling-clicking on the Nupkg file or adding it to a local NuGet repository.

If you want to distribute your NuGet packages via Microsoft's repository, you must first register for an account at http://nuget.org/account/Register. This will give you an API key that you can then use when you publish your packages (under the File ➤ Publish menu).

In summary, NuGet makes it very easy to distribute and update packages within your application. You may wish to consider creating a NuGet package for commonly used libraries within your team or to distribute dependencies internally.

Index

■ X, Y, Z